What pec

American Turning Point

This is a book full of brilliant ideas for change that could form the basis of addressing some of the big challenges for the United States in this turbulent century: the political, socio-economic, and judicial divisions in the nation in particular. It offers detailed ideas which are practical and thought-provoking. Highly recommended for every citizen who cares about the trajectory of America!

Admiral James Stavridis, United States Navy (Ret.), 14th Chair of the Board of Trustees of the Rockefeller Foundation, former Supreme Allied Commander of NATO and the former Dean of The Fletcher School of Law and Diplomacy at Tufts University

The precipitous decline in bipartisanship and non-partisanship upsets the delicate balance in the USA of critical ideas and institutions such as democracy, freedom, capitalism, innovation, and free enterprise; thereby threatening to choke the engine of the entire US GDP. Bob Viney has sounded the right alarms and offered viable solutions based on wisdom free from blind emotionalism.

Ed Rigaud was Vice President, Food & Beverage Products, and Vice President, Government Relations in North America, for Procter & Gamble, and the first Executive Director of the National Underground Railroad Freedom Center in Cincinnati, becoming President and CEO in 2000. He founded and serves as CEO of Enova Premier, LLC, a leading Tier-1 supplier of tire and wheel assemblies to the automotive industry. Ed has served on the Boards of the national Institute of Museum and Library Services, the Federal Reserve Bank of Cleveland, Xavier University in Cincinnati, Xavier University of Louisiana,

Children's Hospital of Cincinnati, the Ohio Board of Regents, the Cincinnati Zoo, and the Northern Kentucky Chamber Board. Ed Rigaud holds a masters degree in biochemistry from the University of Cincinnati, and six honorary doctorates.

Bob Viney has done an exceptional job of identifying the many obstacles that inhibit the ability of our democracy to function as it should and has proposed significant changes that are needed. Hopefully, our concerned citizens and elected leaders will be influenced to work toward the goals he has emphasized.

William V. Muse is President Emeritus of the National Issues Forums Institute and Senior Associate of the Kettering Foundation; former President of the University of Akron and Auburn University, and Chancellor of East Carolina University; former Vice-Chancellor at Texas A&M and former Dean of the business schools at Appalachian State University, the University of Nebraska at Omaha, and Texas A&M University.

Bob Viney's *American Turning Point: Repairing and Restoring our Constitutional Republic* delivers a passionate, deeply informed and researched examination of the root causes of the nation's polarization and its failure to better meet the needs of all the people. He offers concrete options and proposals on how to address these root causes. While few readers will agree with all of his proposals, even fewer will fail to agree that he has bravely and boldly identified concrete, positive changes in how we govern ourselves.

John E. Pepper, Jr., served as CEO and Chairman of the Procter & Gamble Company during his 40-year career at the company. Following retirement, he served as Vice President of Finance and Administration at his alma mater, Yale University, and as Chairman of the Board of the Walt Disney Company. He also served as the senior fellow of the Yale Corporation. He is a founding board member and former CEO of the National

Underground Railroad Freedom Center and co-founder of the Cincinnati Youth Collaborative.

Bob Viney signals a crisp, clear chord that rings loud and crystal clear. His *American Turning Point* is prescient with the sound of truth. It is a welcome reflection for our country soon reaching (in the next 20 years) the monumental turning point when white Caucasian America will no longer be the majority. This book centers our repurposing on the values behind our remarkable republic's growth from 1776 to 2021 and boldly calls for improvements that must be considered to take us safely into the future. This is gifted, caring insight for a country in need of repurposing and hope.

Tim Love served as Vice-Chairman of Omnicom Group, a leading global advertising and marketing services company during a 42-year career in the advertising industry, and retired in 2013 as CEO of the Asia Pacific, India, Middle East and Africa regions. He is currently Chairman of the Board of Advisors of BoomAgers, a marketing communications agency focused on the 50+ year-old generation. His book, *The Book That Gets Better with Age*, has won six literary awards in the category of "health & aging."

Tim was a founding member and first chairman of the advertising industry's Multicultural Advertising Internship program in 1972 and a co-founder of Business for Diplomatic Action (BDA) which focused on improving global business cooperation. He has been a TEDx speaker and had numerous articles published with his insights on branding, globalization and cultural understanding: "Think Like the Sun: The Secret to Global Brand-Building," "Our Language Impediment," "Self-Regulation in a New Media World," and a white paper for the US Department of State following 9/11: "Walk the Talk: What Corporations Can Do about Rising Anti-Americanism."

Following retirement, Tim taught a "Branding and

Communication" course at Oxford's Saïd Business School, and has lectured at the Lee Kuan Yew School of Public Policy in Singapore, Harvard University, Yale School of Management, Columbia University, the University of Illinois, Miami University in Ohio, Northeastern, Savannah College of Art and Design, Mudra Institute of Communications in India and Ave Maria University. He served on the faculty of the US Marketing Communications College, a pro-bono initiative at the Foreign Service Institute of the US State Department, and has been appointed to the Business Advisory for Guangzhou (China's historic business portal, formerly Canton), China.

Bob Viney in his book, *American Turning Point: Repairing and Restoring our Constitutional Republic,* provides the 60 +% of the population in the middle of the political spectrum critical themes to drive discussion on the future direction of our country's federal governance. He lays out the causal issues driving today's polarization limiting the effective governing of the country. Critical policy areas are identified where the demonstrated real needs and interests of the 60% demand effective governing solutions. His proposals addressing these challenges appear daunting, if not radical. Yet he provides the reader provocative game-changing options on how we can choose to shape our government.

John Leikhim serves on the Board of Advisors to Hyperquake, a multi-solution network to give clients holistic brand-building and business-building support to drive growth, and as an Advisory Board Member for Clarkson University's Honors Program. He is a retired Procter & Gamble Research & Development executive.

Researching and recommending possible solutions to the current challenges which are creating major divisions throughout the USA is a most unique mission for Bob Viney as author of this book. As citizens recognize the unifying strength of deliberative discussion and turning words into action for the greater good, this compelling commentary is a must-read to serve as guidelines toward creating a more perfect union and rebuilding our democracy for current and future generations.

Michele Black Abrams, past member of the National Association of Community Leadership Directors and former Program Director of Leadership Middletown; started Community Leadership programs in Hamilton and West Chester-Liberty; graduate of Leadership Ohio 2001 and Leadership Warren County 2011; chairman of Think Regional Southwest Ohio Leadership Summit; host of the local cable television series, Feelin' Good, sponsored by Warren County Community Services; recipient of the AARP Andrus Award for Outstanding Community Service for the state of Ohio in 2019; current chairman of the Curriculum and Public Relations Committee for Miami University's Institute for Learning in Retirement program at the Voice of America Learning Center.

American Turning Point

Repairing and Restoring Our
Constitutional Republic
Becoming One Indivisible Nation in the
Era of Divisiveness

American Turning Point

Repairing and Restoring Our
Constitutional Republic
Becoming One Indivisible Nation in the
Era of Divisiveness

Robert Viney

CHANGEMAKERS
BOOKS

Winchester, UK
Washington, USA

JOHN HUNT PUBLISHING

First published by Changemakers Books, 2022
Changemakers Books is an imprint of John Hunt Publishing Ltd., No. 3 East Street,
Alresford, Hampshire SO24 9EE, UK
office@jhpbooks.com
www.johnhuntpublishing.com
www.changemakers-books.com

For distributor details and how to order please visit the 'Ordering' section on our website.

ISBN: 978 1 78904 953 4
978 1 78904 954 1 (ebook)
Library of Congress Control Number: 2021942975

A CIP catalogue record for this book is available from the British Library.

Design: Stuart Davies

UK: Printed and bound by CPI Group (UK) Ltd, Croydon, CR0 4YY
Printed in North America by CPI GPS partners

We operate a distinctive and ethical publishing philosophy in all areas of our business, from our global network of authors to production and worldwide distribution.

Contents

Service to the nation with sacrifice and accountability are the cornerstones of our country's strength and unity. This book is dedicated to those American citizens, past, present and future, who have taken the oath of office to serve their country and have made sacrifices in their personal lives to put service to the country, the teams of other citizens with whom they have served, and the organizations in which they have served, above themselves.

This book is also dedicated to those citizens who have enrolled in the many lifelong learning classes at three local universities in which I have presented this material and who, through their interest, their questions and their expressions of value in the content, have provided the encouragement for me to proceed with this book.

I would not have been exposed to those lifelong learning opportunities without the encouragement and sponsorship of my partner, Michele Abrams, who has been a participant, a presenter and a volunteer member of the program administration for Miami University's Institute for Learning in Retirement. She also endured many days and evenings alone while I worked on writing and editing this book.

I would also like to thank my sons, Michael and Christopher, for their input on the earliest drafts, and for my brother, William, and my sister, Cheryl, who not only read the first draft but also provided pages of comments. And I am indebted to my friends and former colleagues who provided the endorsements that are included in this book and are posted on the websites. These endorsements will play a critical role in enabling the important actions which will follow the publication and release of this book.

Finally, this book is dedicated primarily to those who will hopefully read it and choose to become involved in the follow-up activity to move these suggested changes and solutions forward. These are the citizens who will realize the greatest benefit in their lives, if we and they are successful in implementing the changes that will "Repair and Restore Our Constitutional Republic." I hope that will include you.

About the Author

Before you begin reading the details of my personal concerns with the state of our country, our Constitutional Republic, and the potential solutions to the divisiveness and lack of effective solutions in how we are governed today, which drove me to write this book, it would probably be appropriate to introduce myself and the circumstances that led to the writing of this book.

I'm a private citizen living in Mason, Ohio, just north of Cincinnati. In the past decade before I focused full-time on this issue, I owned a small business—a business and executive coaching practice. I worked with small to mid-sized business owners and executives to help them set and achieve higher goals and outcomes. I have also served as an adjunct professor at the University of Cincinnati, teaching courses in Organizational Leadership, Business Ethics and Team Building since 2013, until the COVID-19 pandemic in 2020.

Growing up, I went to public schools in several states, as my father was a Naval Academy graduate and a career naval submarine officer. I entered the US Naval Academy two weeks after I graduated from high school, and took the oath of office to "support and defend the Constitution" and our country for the first time when I was 17½. I graduated from the Naval Academy "with merit," equivalent to "cum laude," and served in nuclear fast-attack submarines. I made several special-operations patrols during the Cold War and Vietnam War in the summer of 1972.

After six years on active duty, I left the Navy and worked in the private sector for 30 years, holding senior marketing and executive leadership roles in both Fortune 100 public companies and private mid-sized and startup companies. While working for a major global company, I had the great privilege of living, working and traveling overseas, and experiencing and learning about other cultures, their histories, and their governmental and societal systems. In another role at that company and continuing into a new role with another company, I gained the experience of working on a public policy issue—reducing solid waste—collaborating with industry associations, national and state governments, and public interest groups to implement effective solutions during 1989–93.

About seven years ago I began working with a local non-profit group focused on economic development, job growth and quality-of-life improvements across 15 counties in southwest Ohio. Last year, I started working on the Leadership Council with a local entrepreneurial company building the hydrogen-refueling technology needed to facilitate the transition to a sustainable, renewable, zero carbon-emission energy economy. I developed a concern with the political partisanship and divisiveness that led to ineffective public policies during 2013–14 and the nature of the debates in 2015–16 that led to the presidential election in 2016. I developed a course for adult lifelong learning programs at three local universities to share these concerns and present alternatives to partisan governing. The very positive response from about 200 students during 2016–2018 led to the writing of the book as a way to introduce the ideas to a much broader audience.

I see myself more as a citizen of the United States, rather than identifying with any single state or region of the country, or as a member of any political party. I've lived in many states and a couple of countries outside the USA, have been registered as a member of both major parties (at different times), and have voted for members of both political parties in my life. I am essentially a non-aligned Independent voter today, as I do not support either political party. I do contribute to, support and vote for individual candidates based on how I evaluate their policies at election time, regardless of their party.

Like many US voters today, I am anxious for real change

2

in our country—more than just a change in the party, or in the personality or demographics of the President. Those are not meaningful changes. I am interested in supporting those candidates of either party, of any personality or demographic group, who speak to working with respect and humility to develop innovative, non-partisan solutions to address the beliefs, needs and concerns of most Americans. I do not support candidates from either party who seek to enforce their partisan beliefs, needs and concerns on other Americans, without respect or regard for those who have different needs and concerns than their own.

But the focus today on governing to their partisan base, and excluding or ignoring the needs, the concerns and the ideas of the other party, by the elected representatives of both parties when in the majority, is not the most dangerous aspect of our current politics. The loyalty to party and party leaders in too many of our elected representatives has exceeded loyalty to their oaths of office to the Constitution, to serving the country overall, and to honoring the rule of law; and this represents a growing danger to our representative Constitutional Republic. This is leading too many of our elected leaders to focus on governing by one party to its minority base, versus serving the needs of our overall citizenry, regardless of which party they belong to; and leading too many of our fellow citizens to demonize citizens of the other party as "unAmerican," merely as a result of which candidate they voted for in an election.

When we understand the kinds of societies that are governed by one party, where loyalty to party and party leaders is the only loyalty that matters, we can understand the danger that rampant partisanship represents. Those single-party societies and governments are not the kinds of societies or governments that honor the rule of law over loyalty to a leader, nor do they honor the rights and liberties of individual citizens.

I am afraid the kind of meaningful change we need today is

going to come only from the citizenry, not from our political leaders. Our leaders simply receive too many personal benefits from the existing system, and are unlikely to favor the major changes to this system suggested in this book. Many citizens may also be unwilling to accept these changes because they are fearful of the unknown outcomes that would result. I sincerely hope that the discussions in this book will help alleviate most of these concerns. It will take a committed, large majority of citizens who value these changes, for these proposals to take effect.

Finally, a caveat. I'm not educated or trained as a lawyer and have never served as a legislator. In this book, all references to and inferences drawn from the principles and values expressed in the Declaration of Independence and our Constitution are based on my personal "lay" view of the concepts therein. Suggestions on policy approaches to national issues recommended in this book are similarly based on a lay citizen's view of how to craft more effective laws, and make effective changes to the Constitution. But while our Constitution was drafted by some lawyers, many of the contributors were also just lay citizens. So, while the language proposed herein as changes to legal documents may not be precisely "right," I hope the ideas and directions proposed herein will be found to have great merit by a majority of my fellow citizens.

Preface

I wrote this book because, like many citizens, I am concerned that our national government, particularly our Congress, has lost its intended focus on serving the nation, by developing truly national policies that reflect the needs and concerns of most Americans as its first priority. But I am equally concerned about the increasing divisiveness in our citizenry. This is of course reflected in the intolerance and disregard of the political points of view of other citizens who have a different life experience and circumstance than ourselves. But it has also been expressed in despicable rhetoric and even violence among citizens, and between citizens and leaders, directed towards those with whom they disagree.

The content of this book comes principally from a course I created from research during 2015–16 and taught to over 200 students in the adult lifelong learning programs at the University of Cincinnati, the University of Dayton and Miami University during 2016–2018. The classes were taught in six different regional campus locations in five different counties in southwest Ohio. Three of these four counties are suburban/rural areas that in most elections choose Republican candidates. The other county is an urban/suburban area that often elects Democrat candidates.

The response from this group of students with a fairly diverse political orientation was very positive. Comments I received from students often mentioned learning things they had not known and feeling hopeful that we as citizens could change today's partisan political environment. As a result of these responses, I decided to share the content with a broader audience through a book, with the goal of building public support for the solution provided in the book. This solution involves approving six new Amendments to the Constitution as a package which I call "The

Bill of Public Service and Accountability." These Amendments would essentially establish new, constitutionally required "Citizen Rules" to define how "We the People" prefer to be governed in our Constitutional Republic, in which our elected officials would put serving the country over their own careers, or the interests of their party or their major donors.

One of the key factors causing our current problems is that the rules for how Congress operates, for how we are governed, as currently established under the Constitution, are made by the congressional members themselves in each House. Over the years, these process rules have become focused to a very large extent on serving the interests of the members themselves rather than on serving the interests of the country overall. One of the key elements of the solution, then, is to define new rules for how Congress operates that the citizens themselves will have an opportunity to approve.

The title of this book, *American Turning Point: Repairing and Restoring Our Constitutional Republic*, reflects my concern that: (1) we are on a path that will put our country's democracy and our economic and national security at risk; (2) we cannot count on our elected leaders to lead change to a system that so well benefits them individually; and (3) there is no single party or ideology that will succeed in uniting our wonderfully diverse country. Unless we agree as a country that "We the People" need to unite to change our political system, I fear that we will be the first generation to pass on a weaker democracy and economy and a less secure country to our grandchildren than our grandparents passed on to us. What we decide as citizens in the next few years may well determine the future nature of our society, the quality of the Constitutional Republic we all treasure, and the security of our country, for generations to come.

It seems that partisan ideologies and the concerns of private donors, political special-interest groups, and political party affiliations now rank higher among the priorities of most of our elected representatives than do the interests of most Americans and the country overall. Our political leaders in both major parties seem to be more concerned about raising funds for their next election than in working together to solve key problems and develop effective policies to govern the nation as a whole.

The political leaders of both parties, when they hold the majority in Congress, campaign and govern as partisans, promising benefits and making policies that appeal exclusively to their donors, party activists and base voters. When our elected leaders from both parties govern primarily to their own party's base, they are by default ignoring the needs, interests and concerns of those citizens who didn't vote for them. Since most elections are decided in the range of 52%–48%, or as much as 60%–40% in the rare "landslide," this means that the governing party typically ignores as much as 40%–48% of those citizens they are supposed to represent.

Does this approach seem like the kind of "representative democracy" our Founding Fathers envisioned for this new experiment in self-government? Does this seem like a system that is likely to lead to greater unity as a society and strength as a nation in the future?

Without, hopefully, employing exaggeration, let me add a thought on the role of rampant party loyalty in societies in history, and whether there's anything we might take away from such societies. Let's briefly consider Germany, Communist Russia and China. Germany was a democracy in the 1920s. But after the Nazi party was elected to the majority behind the party leader, Adolf Hitler, loyalty to the Nazi party and its leader rose above loyalty to the country and overwhelmed the rights of citizens in the minority. Loyalty to the Communist party in Russia and China, and loyalty to the Communist party leader, has from the beginning of Communist rule become the same as loyalty to the nation. In these societies, the concerns of the minority party, and the views and rights of a large number of citizens, ceased to exist, and the societies ceased to be free societies.

One of the core principles of our Founders in establishing this experiment in self-government of the people, by the people, and for the people, was that America would be a country where the loyalty of our leaders and our citizens was to the Constitution and the rule of law, not to any single political party or political leader. But at the current level of partisanship in our country, we see both parties, to an increasing extent, treating the other party and their supporters as the "enemy" of their party and elected leaders, and most tragically, as the enemies of the country. Equally as damaging to our country is the fact that partisanship is also creeping into the historically non-partisan elements of our democracy; this includes some of the professionals in our government departments, such as state, defense, intelligence, justice, and law enforcement, and most concerningly, the judicial branch, including the federal judges and the Justices of the Supreme Court.

Another area where our leaders seem to have lost focus is the principle of the "separation of powers" to guard against the allocation of powers leading to corrupt behaviors. That principle is the oversight of the powers granted to one branch by other branches, or in other words, our system of "checks and balances." Thus, while the power to legislate is invested in the Congress, the President must agree with and can veto any legislation passed by Congress. The Supreme Court has the power to review all legislation and can declare legislation to be unconstitutional. And Congress through its oversight role has the power to review and question the executive branch regarding the implementation of legislation and other executive actions authorized under the Constitution.

It is critical for the strength of the Constitutional Republic handed down to us from our Founders that the congressional powers of oversight that are key to the strength of the system of checks and balances also be strong. If we are not able to reverse these trends and restore loyalty to country over loyalty to a party or to an individual leader, might we be in danger of continuing to move along the spectrum toward the kinds of societies in Germany, China and Russia described above? If that possibility is not enough to encourage most citizens to reconsider too strong a loyalty to a party and the demonization of the "other" party and their supporters, then I very much fear that we will over time edge dangerously closer to those types of societies, almost without realizing it. That may be the slipperiest slope of all slippery slopes.

Many leaders and experts have accurately described the problems of our divided country, of our broken congressional system, and of our divisive governing approach made dysfunctional by rampant partisanship. But no one has yet suggested a real set of concrete, practical actions that could be enacted to effect the changes that would overcome these problems. This book, like others, will seek to describe the problems, but it will also describe a set of desired changes that could overcome these problems, and then most importantly, suggest specific actions that can lead to implementing the changes and improvements we need. This will hopefully begin a broad, ideally national discussion on potential actions, which will lead to the enactment of real changes in the actions of our elected and appointed leaders, and in our country's citizens and voters.

When our 535 Senators and Congressional Representatives do not act as national leaders by truly serving the national interest first, and our citizens fear and reject the points of view of those who differ from themselves, can we really consider that we are living up to the Pledge of Allegiance we teach our children, and that is recited at the opening of every session of the Senate and House: that we are "one nation...indivisible"?

Since each of the major parties represents no more than 35%–40% of registered voters, it is really not national leadership to develop policies reflecting the narrow interests of only one party and its base. Nor is it national leadership to seek to divide the country based on disrespecting and even demonizing those who have different beliefs, needs and concerns than ourselves.

To have policies that reflect being "One Indivisible Nation," we need leaders of both parties to come to national leadership roles with a spirit of respecting each other's beliefs, needs and concerns. In governing, we need our leaders to be committed to developing policies that accommodate the needs and concerns of their own and the other party, so that the policies work for *most* Americans, not just their party or region, or the special interests and donors who supported their election.

We are a wonderfully diverse nation, and demographic trends clearly indicate that we will become increasingly diverse in the future. This is a concern for many people who fear we may lose elements of our national culture, but increasing diversity is truly a source of our national strength, of our creativity and innovation. It is in fact a source of competitive advantage for the USA in the global marketplace of ideas, and yes, of commerce. The diverse life experiences of our citizens that enrich our country in so many ways also lead to the diversity in the beliefs, needs, fears and concerns of different voter groups.

Our national leaders need to respond to and embrace their responsibility to accommodate diversity within our national policies and bring people together. Those goals cannot be achieved by one party and one party's ideology alone. These goals can only be achieved by respecting and incorporating the needs and concerns of both parties in developing policies to govern the nation. Unfortunately, the approach taken today seems to be to ignore any points of view other than our own— and to govern with points of view that are far too often based purely on ideologies that have no or too little basis in fact, and sometimes are espoused even when facts disprove the effectiveness of favored ideological approaches.

In my own life experience, I've seen that there is no single party or ideology that by itself consistently develops the most effective policies for the country overall. Therefore, does it seem reasonable to believe that one party or partisan ideology alone is likely to ever unite the country? When in the majority and in control of the political agenda, both parties consistently work to serve their own interests at the expense of the country and of the other party. As a result, over the past 18 national elections since the end of World War II, we've chosen to be "led" by the policies and priorities of one party for eight years, followed by eight years of the policies and priorities of the other party, with the exception of three elections.

Neither party when "in power" seems capable of or even interested in working with the other to develop policies that respect the priorities of both parties and thus the country as a whole. And as a result, they focus exclusively on their own needs and ignore the needs of the other half of the country, and the pendulum shifts against them eventually. In response, the minority party, most often excluded from policy development, adopts the position of opposing all initiatives of the majority party, essentially rooting for their failure. And so it has gone, for most of the past 70 years.

This is the inevitable outcome of a "win-lose" competition between the parties—of the politics of "or" rather than "and" thinking. If our political leaders were to choose to collaborate on "win-win" policies that reflect the needs of both parties, we would have leaders in the minority party who would root for the success of policies enacted with the majority party, instead of cheering for their failure in order to create advantage for themselves in the next election. Obviously, that success and failure impacts our economic and national security, and to have obstruction to policies treated mostly as fodder for the next election weakens our country.

One other aspect of the competitive, combative nature of the divisiveness in our politics today is our lack of ability to base discussions of policy options on a single set of facts or agree to a common set of truths. The rise of "alternative" facts, misinformation, and conspiracy theories with no basis in fact has been both meteoric and destructive to collaborative policy development and bipartisan governing. This issue has been largely dealt with successfully in business and commercial speech, and a similar approach might now be essential with regard to political speech and campaign messages distributed via all media and social media vehicles and channels.

Let's expect our leaders to work together honestly to *govern* the country, not to constantly cater solely to their individual party's bases. They should be focused on working together to improve or change policies that aren't working as intended or as needed, without the constant fault-finding and finger-pointing, and seeking to make a future campaign issue out of every learning outcome. And as the electorate, we need to vote for leaders who have the humility, empathy and patriotism to respect the needs and concerns of others, and stop electing people who are arrogant enough to believe that their beliefs are the *only* right way to govern, and who demonize those who have different beliefs than their own.

I have seen "win-win" policies work in business to generate the highest level of effectiveness in organizations and the most favorable outcomes, in circumstances where the opposing points of view exist in an "interdependent" reality—such as in a large business with multiple profit centers. Those companies with strong "silos" of people who refuse to work together for the benefit of their common customers eventually lose to more innovative companies with an outward focus. Does anyone doubt that our country is one such interdependent reality, where the success, security and freedoms of any group of citizens depend on the success, security and freedoms of *all* citizens? Or doubt that that principle is what is enshrined in the last sentence of the Declaration of Independence?

We need to lose the blindness and self-interest that leads too many of us to believe that those of us in cities don't need to accommodate the needs of people in rural areas, and vice versa; that older citizens don't need to accommodate the needs of younger citizens, and vice versa; that white citizens don't need to accommodate the needs of citizens of color, and vice versa; that wealthy citizens don't need to accommodate the needs of poorer citizens, and vice versa; or that safely employed citizens don't need to accommodate the needs of the unemployed or under-employed citizens, and vice versa.

Today, the two major parties most often present voters with an "or" choice between two very distinct policy options developed separately. Most often, these are false choices, based on partisan positions designed to divide the country rather than unite the country. The best solution for the country overall is most often an "and" choice involving elements from both policy options.

We need to adopt that mindset of "and" thinking, not "or" thinking, when it comes to developing policy solutions to address the real needs in the country. Otherwise, how can we honestly say the Pledge of Allegiance with integrity—that we are or strive to be "one nation...indivisible"? Said another way, can we honestly say we love our country and yet ignore or despise nearly half our fellow citizens?

Finally, while I do view myself primarily as a practical person focused more on outcomes than on processes, I recognize that the proposed changes and the actions to enact them suggested within these pages have never been done in our history. No change to the Constitution has ever been made as proposed in this book. However, my "lay citizen" reading of the Constitution indicates that there's nothing proposed herein that violates or is expressly prohibited by the Constitution. But I also recognize that what is proposed here is not specifically prescribed in the Constitution either. I'm sure there will be a serious challenge to these proposals by those in power today, who stand to lose significant benefits from the existing system. Thus, it will be up to us, the citizens, to decide if these are the changes we want to see made in our governing processes, and to get involved to make it happen.

Albert Einstein defined insanity as "doing the same things over and over again in the same way and expecting a different result." Don't we seem to be living in an insane reality today, politically? The flip side of this core truth is: "If we want to achieve a result we've never had, we have to be willing to do things we've never done." Let's be willing to take actions we've never taken before, to stop the insanity in our political and governing processes and change the country we all love for the betterment of all of us, but especially for our future generations.

Introduction

In America today, our national government system has lost its intended purpose to govern by enacting truly national policies that reflect the needs and concerns of most Americans as its first priority. We now have a political process where the government is focused primarily on elections and campaigning actions in two-year intervals, rather than "doing the right things" to govern the overall country effectively for the long term. In place of working together to serve the country overall, our leaders seem to place donor and special interests, partisan interests and their own career self-interests far above constituent and national interests. Loyalty to party, fellow party members and party leaders seems greater than loyalty to the country overall and to the oath of office that all elected leaders take.

There is also an increasing divide in our citizenry, reflected in the intolerance and disregard of the points of view, needs and concerns of other citizens who have a different life experience and circumstance than ourselves. Today, it seems ideologies that favor a particular party or special-interest group are the currency valued by too many leaders and citizens, rather than looking to facts, history, or an objective analysis of data and trends to help guide collaborative policy development that would best serve the country overall. In place of the values of working together to serve the country, we have arrogance and selfishness displayed by too many of our elected leaders.

We seem to be on a path that will put our country's democracy, and our economic and national security, at risk. We cannot sustain a strong America if we allow ourselves to be a divided country, constantly at war with ourselves, punctuated by a major combative election every two years. Many people can see and even enumerate the problems we face today, but there seem to be few, if any, voices speaking about a real solution.

Many citizens feel powerless to make a difference even if they wanted to do so. And our political leaders in both parties, who benefit greatly from the status quo, seem to have no interest in making the sacrifices that are required to lead real change.

What action or actions can we take that would truly change the system and our current course? This book will seek to describe a possible solution, by changing the focus of Congress and our elected leaders to one of true public and national service; putting the public's and the country's interests first, and minimizing the impact of rampant partisanship, donor influence and the career self-interest of our elected leaders. This solution will not be based on any ideology other than the ideology of "what works," and what actions seem to follow from objective analysis of data, facts and relevant history.

Elected politicians in Washington will not lead this change; it will need to be a citizen-led movement that enacts these changes. But for us as citizens to lead this change, we'll need to agree across the country that "We the People" need to change ourselves first, and then unite to change our political system. And if we, the citizens, are not willing to change ourselves, how can we expect our elected leaders to be other than a reflection of our own unwillingness to change?

Will we as citizens choose to accept the status quo or will we seek to "repair and restore" our Constitutional Republic by leading the changes to our system of government to one that respects and accommodates our differences in a collaborative, "win-win" legislative process, regardless of which party is in the majority? The answer will determine the future nature of our democracy, our society, and the security of our country.

In this book, we will explore the following questions as we work toward identifying a proposed solution for a better government:

- What are the current problems we need to change? How

do they manifest themselves in the governing process, and in our results?

- What are the real root causes of the problems, the core actions that result in the dysfunctional governing system that exists today?
- What potential actions might enable us to overcome those causes? We'll look at some specific issues and the "new solution" that might emerge from a new non-partisan, fact-based, "win-win" approach to governing.
- What would the ideal operation of Congress look like, in order to generate better results from Congress that are *not* based on political ideology from either side of the political spectrum?
- And finally, what can we do as individual citizens to help implement the new solution and help make the changes we'd like to see become reality?

There is a quote from President John F. Kennedy that is not quite as well known as the line from his inaugural address urging us to ask what we can do for our country. This quote speaks to the "office" of citizen and its critical role in the success of our democracy:

For, in a democracy, every citizen, regardless of his interest in politics, "holds office"; every one of us is in a position of responsibility; and, in the final analysis, the kind of government we get depends upon how we fulfill those responsibilities. We, the people, are the boss, and we will get the kind of political leadership, be it good or bad, that we demand and deserve.

I think President Kennedy was saying that just as a company would flounder if the boss did not hold the employees responsible for their performance, so will our country flounder if the citizens do not hold their elected representatives responsible for their performance.

The Constitution is not overly prescriptive with regard to congressional "rules" for how our leaders should execute their duties in governing the country. Our Constitution is primarily a "structural" document. That is, it defines *what* the structure of the government would be and the division of powers between the branches of government. The rules for *how* to govern were left to the members of Congress; they were empowered to define the details of *how* government should operate. Article 1, Section 5 of the Constitution states simply that: "Each House may determine the rules of its proceedings." However, we have to ask whether, today, this trust in Congress to make its own rules has been and is still good for our country.

The Founders fully anticipated that some leaders would eventually exhibit "bad" behavior in office and either break the law or violate the public trust by abusing the power of their offices. That is one of the reasons for the checks and balances in our Constitution that are designed to ensure that no one branch of government could become too powerful by acting independently of the other branches, and for the powers of impeachment.

The Founders also had a belief that citizens would not tolerate "bad" behavior by their representatives. The primary remedy that was planned for in the Constitution was voting out the representatives of the people who fail to serve the people first. But 230 years ago, it would have been impossible for the Founders to predict how the self-interest of a professional legislative class, the influence of donors and their huge contributions over legislators and our electoral processes, or the rise of rampant partisanship and majority party control, would impact what was designed to be a representative democratic process among our legislators.

There is an axiom in business that if you put average

people in a great system, you will get great results. But if you put great people in a poor system, you'll get poor results. If the organizational system is not designed to get the results you want, it is unlikely that even great people will be able to generate great results. The system people operate within very much determines the results the people can achieve.

Does it seem today that over the past 50 years or so, the rules defined by Congress for *how* Congress operates have been established more to benefit the interests of the incumbent members of Congress rather than to benefit the interests of the country and its citizens overall?

If the answer is yes, then perhaps it is time for the citizens to define the rules for *how* Congress should operate, in order that Congress would operate to benefit the interests of the country and citizens overall. After all, do not the members of Congress work for the citizens? Aren't "We the People" supposed to be the true "bosses" in this relationship? Shouldn't "We the People" be the ones defining the rules for how Congress governs us?

It's time "We the People" stopped tolerating unsatisfactory performance by self-focused leaders working in a flawed operational system. The structure of Congress as defined in the Constitution is just as viable and worthy of our awe and support as ever. However, the rules congressional members have defined for themselves today are, in important ways, not viable for an effectively functioning representative government. Perhaps it is now time for "Citizen Rules" to be enacted—the rules that define how "We the People" want our leaders to exercise the powers and responsibilities we have delegated to them in the Constitution.

The direction of our country is truly in our collective hands as citizens. This book will ideally and hopefully provide the *what* and the *how* to change our country's current political path. Are we the generation that will decide to change these trends? If not us, who? If not now, when?

Americans don't fear much in the world, but today we are acting out of fear of the changes in our national demographics that increased diversity in the country is bringing. While we've always been a nation of immigrants and struggled to accept each new "wave" into the American identity, we've never been faced with the degrees of diversity in race, creed and culture that the newest immigrants are bringing with them. At the same time, the rise of women and ethnic minorities into positions of leadership in all aspects of our society seems to be exacerbating the sense of loss of national identity for many; an identity which has historically been based on a male, Caucasian leadership experience.

This is the great challenge our country faces today. Will we succeed in maintaining the values and principles of our Founders and our Founding Documents in the face of the challenges of greater diversity and societal change? This generation needs to provide the leaders and to be the foot soldiers in meeting this challenge. It is perhaps a greater challenge to our existence as a country than the external threats of Fascism in World War II or Communism in the Cold War, because today's threats, these challenges we face today, are *internal* threats, not external threats. But the fate and future of our country and the world is no less at stake on the outcome, on whether we choose to rise to meet the challenge together, as our Founders did, and as the Greatest Generation did before us; or whether we choose to allow the current environment in our country to continue.

What are the changes in how our government leaders operate that would result in a greater tendency to work together for the benefit of the country? Consider the suggested changes listed below:

- Restore commitment to core values — service to country, community and each other.
  - These values have been largely preserved by our

20

military and many public service organizations in our communities. We don't have military units that are divided by party, race, sex, religious belief, or sexual orientation. Soldiers, sailors and airmen and their support teams focus on their mission, to serve and protect the country and their comrades. Don't we still have the strongest and most effective fighting force in the world despite the increased diversity in our citizens?

∘ Should our citizens and political leaders be held to less than these standards? If they don't meet this standard, are they worthy of the citizens who volunteer to make sacrifices and serve our country and the Constitution?

• Understand, respect and accommodate differences in the needs and concerns of citizens who think and believe differently than ourselves, and have a different life experience than we do.

• Govern to support and accommodate the needs and concerns of *all* citizens, not just those in the base of the winning candidate or party.

• Ensure full transparency and accountability to the public in the development and implementation of all legislative and executive activities by both Congress and the Administration.

• Strengthen the congressional oversight role for executive implementation of legislation and actions within their constitutionally designated powers.

• Ensure that both parties work together to develop "win-win" policies, instead of the win-lose or winner-takes-all competition for power that exists between the parties today.

• Focus on policies to benefit the national interest, not partisan, donor or special interest.

• Elect leaders who serve rather than seek to be served—

or to derive special benefits for themselves from their positions—and who embrace a high standard of ethical behavior.

- Elect citizen legislators with a similar degree of commitment to the country to that shown by our citizen soldiers:
  - ° Embrace core principles of serving the country over self; service mindset, not privilege;
  - ° Act with transparency and integrity in actions (such as, remove gerrymandering of districts; eliminate special-interest issues in governing; etc.);
  - ° Follow the Constitution; represent the needs of all citizens, not just the member's base; show accountability for the results achieved in how the people's money is spent;
  - ° Lead by example in terms of ethics and character for those in public service positions.

What are the causes of the problems with the failure of the many members of Congress and the Administrations to serve the nation, and put the interests of the country overall above the interests of their party? Why are we experiencing rampant partisanship, dysfunctional governing, a lack of holding other members accountable in their own party, and the accelerated growth in the deficit, all resulting in a decade of low approval ratings from the public and a general sense that voting will not make a difference?

This book identifies three main causes for these issues today: (1) putting personal career interests first, including a focus on raising money and being re-elected above all other considerations; (2) loyalty to party and to party leaders, as party loyalty leads to the party support for re-election, favored committee assignment, and the absence of a primary election challenge from within the party; and (3) putting the interests of special-interest donors above those of the overall electorate in a district or state, or in the country overall.

These powerful and compelling influences are not likely to dissipate on their own, nor are today's leaders who benefit from them likely to initiate changes to eliminate or minimize them. It is up to "We the People," the average citizens of the United States, to collectively act as the owners, as the "bosses" of our government, and to change the rules that congressional members have determined for themselves with regard to how they govern and how government operates. To effect this change, we need to develop and implement "Citizen Rules" for how "We the People" want to be governed.

What would a set of "Citizen Rules" look like that would result in our elected leaders exhibiting the behaviors identified above? Listed below are suggested key topics for new "Citizen Rules" to be defined and incorporated in the Constitution, to ensure that our elected leaders would likely fulfill the goals above.

Specific changes to improve how we are governed — to be discussed and detailed in separate chapters:

1. Setting term limits, compensation, and health and retirement benefits for members of Congress and senior Administration officials
2. Defining new rules for the legislative processes to limit partisanship; confirming primacy of "Citizen Rules" in the Constitution over procedural rules enacted by members of Congress
3. Defining timing requirements for Senate votes on treaties and presidential appointments; limiting the duration of acting presidential appointments; limiting absolute presidential reprieves and pardons
4. Strengthening congressional oversight of executive

implementation; strengthening the independence of Inspectors General and key executive departments in the Administration

5. Defining rules for the budgeting, taxing and spending processes: balance, timing, accountability, transparency, and effectiveness

6. Prohibiting Congress members from paid lobbying roles after serving in Congress or the Administration

7. Prohibiting laws exempting Congress from laws enacted on citizens

8. Changing the allocation and certification of Electoral College votes in presidential elections

9. Limiting the terms of Supreme Court justices and federal court judges

10. Ensuring fair and equitable access to registration and voting for all citizens, and elections free from fraud

11. Defining rules for campaign financing—donation limits and disclosure requirements

12. Defining rules for truthful messaging and timing of campaign advertising

13. Providing an independent council to oversee voting-district alignments after census

14. Defining rules for ethical behaviors and financial conflict of interest, and for handling non-salary personal income for President, Vice President, and all senior elected and appointed officials

15. Defining a non-partisan judicial process for impeachment and actions considered as impeachable offenses

16. Establishing a program of required national service for all citizens between the ages of 18 and 29

The following is a brief overview of the content provided in each chapter in the book. Each chapter contains a detailed discussion of the subject topics.

Chapter 1: The Challenge to Being "One Nation" in the Era of Partisanship

- The importance of *inter*dependence to our independence and strength as a country
- The danger of party and partisanship to our representative democratic republic
- The value of diversity to our culture of creativity and innovation
- The difference in winner-takes-all and win-win approaches to governing
- The importance of economic community to our country's long-term economic and national security

Chapter 2: Questions to Frame the Changes We Might Want to Consider

- Process for developing solutions to complex but under-performing organizations:
  - First, looking at where the desired outcomes are not being realized;
  - Next, identifying the barriers and root causes of the unrealized outcomes;
  - Then, defining and exploring solutions to overcome the barriers and address the key root causes of the unrealized outcomes;
  - Finally, developing an action plan to implement the solution with specific measures to determine if the solution actions are working.
- Asking 13 questions to gauge the reader's current mindset, each with two optional responses for the reader to choose and rate his or her interest in changing how Congress operates:
  - Option (a): Readers who are comfortable with the

partisan divisions in government and comfortable with the operating rules congressional members have made for themselves;

- Option (b): Readers who are troubled with the partisan divisions in government and open to major changes, to new "Citizen Rules," in how Congress operates.

Chapter 3: What Are the Current Problems with Congress Today and Their Root Causes That We Might Want to Address?

- Introduce the concept of "Citizen Rules."
- Walk through the four-step process for developing solutions to complex but under-performing organizations:
  - Discuss 11 of the most serious desired outcomes that are not being realized in how Congress operates today;
  - Discuss three root causes of unrealized outcomes;
  - Identify and discuss seven solutions to overcome the barriers and address the root causes of unrealized outcomes;
  - Define an action plan with 16 elements to implement the solutions—the "Citizen Rules."

Chapter 4: Looking at the Details of the Changes

- Discuss the details of each of the 16 specific "Citizen Rules" changes to how Congress operates.
  - Review the risks and benefits of each of the proposed changes.

Chapter 5: Background and Details of Key "Win-Win" Policies

This chapter discusses several key policy solution approaches that, while not included in the Amendments to the Constitution, detail the innovative policy solutions that could be possible in a new governing environment—an environment that starts with establishing agreement on the goals of major policies that would address major national needs before seeking to define the policy details, and where the parties collaborate in developing the actions to implement the policy goals, instead of putting personal, partisan and donor interests above the country's interests.

The policy topics that are included in the discussions in this chapter include the following:

- Pro-growth economic policy—commercial profitability, middle-class incomes
- Budget, deficit, and tax policies
- Accountability, tracking and reporting of public program results with integrity
- Healthcare access, affordability and cost reduction
- Investments in energy and transportation infrastructure
- Investments in a skilled and educated workforce
- Religious practices and non-discrimination—LGBTQ rights
- Mass shootings, gun control, gun owner rights
- Immigration reform, integration of permanent residents, acceptance of temporary workers, borders, and internal treatment of illegal non-citizens
- Protecting the fairness and security of elections

These topics are grouped into discussions of potential "win-win" policy approaches that might represent the kinds of solutions that address the needs of most of the country. Many of the policy discussions identify both the benefits and risks of key aspects of the solution as objectively as possible.

- Policy 1—Economy: economic growth policy, middle-class income growth, narrowing the income gap, job growth, reducing the deficit

- Goal 1: Develop economic policies to reach specific growth goals
- Goal 2: Develop tax and spending plans to achieve specific increases in overall middle-class incomes and reduce wealth and income gaps
- Goal 3: Include both short-term annual and long-term deficit management and debt reduction plans
  - Questions, facts and history on taxes, budgets, economic growth and deficits
  - New idea: policy to simultaneously achieve economic growth, middle-class income growth, job growth, narrowing income gap, reducing the deficit
  - Growth policy—approach to taxes, spending, economic growth and deficits

- Policy 2—Improve healthcare access and affordability for all Americans
  - Goal 1: Deliver specific improvements in healthcare outcomes across the country
  - Goal 2: Deliver specific improvements in access to affordable healthcare services for all citizens
    - Questions about healthcare policy approaches
    - Suggestions for new healthcare policy approaches
    - Discussion of pros and cons

- Policy 3—Investing in energy and transportation infrastructures
  - Goal 1: Repair and maintain the existing infrastructures to a B+ Grade
  - Goal 2: Develop and fund an innovative infrastructure approach for the twenty-first century
    - Transition energy economy to zero carbon, limiting air and water pollution
    - New transportation approaches beyond more

highway lanes

- ► New energy approaches for 24/7/365 reliability of renewable sources and enhanced security from outside cyberattacks
- Policy 4—Investing in a skilled and educated workforce
  - ○ Goal 1: Invest in growing the number of technically skilled workers
  - ○ Goal 2: Invest in reducing student loan debt for university and technical skills training programs
- Policy 5—Comprehensive immigration and border security
  - ○ Goal 1: Reduce illegal immigrants and drug flows into the United States from all sources
  - ○ Goal 2: Set reasonable levels of legal entries for all categories of immigrants, including seasonal workers, family members of immigrants, and asylum seekers
  - ○ Goal 3: Address the existing population of undocumented immigrants via a new Two-Tier Visa Entry and Residency Status Policy
  - ○ Goal 4: Enforce the laws against illegal entry and overstaying of visas
- Policy 6—Gun safety, mass shootings and gun rights
  - ○ Goal 1: Reduce the number of mass shooting events
  - ○ Goal 2: Reduce the number of deaths and injuries when mass shooting events occur
  - ○ Goal 3: Reduce the number of gun deaths in crime and gang activities
- Policy 7—Ensure and protect voting integrity and voting rights
  - ○ Goal 1: Provide oversight for congressional district alignments to prevent gerrymandering
  - ○ Goal 2: Establish requirements for truthful campaign and issue messaging
  - ○ Goal 3: Ensure the security and accuracy of voting

records
- ◦ Goal 4: Ensure fair and convenient access to voting processes for all citizens in all states
- • Policy 8—Religious practices and non-discrimination
  - ◦ Goal: Resolve conflict in religious practice rights and non-discrimination in public commerce

Chapter 6: Summary and Details of the Specific Amendments to Be Proposed

- • Overview of proposed Bill of Public Service and Accountability
  - ◦ Summary and scope of each of the six Amendments that implement the "Citizen Rules"
  - ◦ Details of each Amendment and contributions to desired changes
  - ◦ Discuss the pros and cons of each Amendment

Chapter 7: How Do These Changes to the Constitution Get Enacted?

- • Overview of options to enact changes
- • Proposed process and detailed discussion of actions

Chapter 8: What Can We Do as Individual Citizens to Help Make the Changes We'd Like to See Become Reality?

- • How can citizens support changes in Congress by our actions and choices?
  - ◦ Changing the citizen mindset—your role
  - ◦ Why should you be involved and support the changes?

Appendix

- Part 1: Full text of the proposed Amendments
- Part 2: Relationship to other government improvement initiatives
  - ◦ End Citizens United
  - ◦ Balanced Budget Amendment
  - ◦ Repeal of the Electoral College

Now, on to the details!

Chapter 1

The Challenge to Being "One Nation" in the Era of Partisanship

The approval ratings for Congress have been at historically low levels among Americans for the better part of the last decade. The approval ratings reached high levels, between 45% and 55%, in the late 1990s to early 2000s, when the Republican Congress, led by Speaker Gingrich, worked together with the Democrat Clinton Administration to balance the budget. But when the war in the Middle East began in 2001, approval ratings fell to levels between 30% and 40%. And since the financial crisis of 2008, the approval ratings have been consistently in the 10%–20% range. These declines have come during the majority control of Congress and/or the Administration by both parties, first one and then the other. They have also come at a time when the partisan divides in both our political leadership and our citizenry have risen to historically high levels. And it's unlikely that the partisanship evident in two impeachment trials in just 13 months is going to result in any increase in that rating.

Without favoring either party or any political ideology, this book will seek to identify what the principal problems are with a Congress that has consistently earned such low approval ratings in the minds of the nation's citizens. We will then explore what changes might be made to minimize or eliminate those problems, and how those changes might be enacted. But in considering changes to the operation of our government, many of which would require some changes to the Constitution itself, it seems wise to review the core principles and values enshrined in our Constitution by our Framers that should guide any consideration of change.

America is fundamentally, of course, about self-governance

by citizens. To be effective, this requires citizens to be committed to serving the country and to care about the lives of fellow citizens. This also requires leaders, once elected, to govern as leaders of the country overall and not just of those voters in their base. In the civil non-secular governing of ourselves in our country, our leaders do not pledge allegiance to a monarch, a dictator, a military leader, a religious leader or any single person or party over the nation and the Constitution. Preserving our Constitutional Republic demands citizen involvement, and commitment to the values of our Founding Documents. Effective representative government requires the same of our elected leaders. In America, no one, not even the Congress or the President, is above the law.

America is also of course about political equality and equal justice for all citizens. Our Forefathers fled Europe to seek the freedom to practice their religions without persecution or discrimination. With profound wisdom, they sought to simultaneously safeguard the right to practice any and all religions, and to separate religion from government. In most countries in Europe in those times, religious beliefs and laws were an integral part of civil law. In every country where religious beliefs and laws are integrated into civil law, discrimination and/or oppression of those with different religious beliefs or ethnic backgrounds also always exists. That was an outcome our Forefathers wisely sought to eliminate in our new government.

But in addition, our Forefathers also fled societies with rigid "class" barriers in civil law and society based on birthright. This resulted in what the Declaration of Independence refers to as the "tyranny" of the monarchs and the ruling elite in England. Our Founders wanted no such special distinction for an "elite" class in America, no matter the source of that "elitism"; they sought to establish a just society that offered every citizen the freedom and liberty for each to pursue their own ideals of happiness.

The writings of many of our Founders during the period of

deliberations on the new Constitution indicate that the concept of the "citizen legislator" was considered by many delegates as the ideal model for the new government. In his book *The Liberty Amendments*, Mark R. Levin writes that Thomas Jefferson addressed this issue in a letter to James Madison, stating his concern that there was no provision in the draft Constitution of mandatory rotation among officials in Congress or for term limits: "The concept of representation at the time was not one of 'professional' or lifetime 'public service,' but citizen participation and part-time service," writes Levin. He also states that: "The nation's Founders believed in the concept of 'citizen/servant' — someone who had a life and a career in the private sector, but who offered his experience and talents to public service for a limited time, and then returned to private life."

James Madison's *Notes on Debates*, excerpted in Levin's book, describes Benjamin Franklin's uniquely interesting perspective on the issue of citizen legislators and term limits. Levin quotes Franklin as stating at the Constitutional Convention on July 26, 1787, that:

In free governments the rulers are the servants and the people are their superiors and sovereigns. For the former therefore to return among the latter was not to *degrade* them but to *promote* them. And it would be imposing an unreasonable burden on them, to keep them always in a state of servitude, and not allow them to become again one of the masters.

The values and principles handed down to us by our Founders are not limited to life, liberty and the pursuit of happiness, to the equality of all people, or to the concept of government by the consent of the governed. They include a commitment to protect these values, values worth defending with our lives; not only for ourselves but for others as well. Backed by the selfless actions of generations of Americans before us, those principles have been established as the basis for a nation unique in the history of the world. Sustaining these values is the responsibility of each generation to ensure that future generations of Americans will be able to enjoy the same freedoms, quality of life and opportunity as ourselves.

Commitment to these values often involves some period or degree of personal sacrifice, of service to others, and of commitment to country above self, as the price of the liberty we all enjoy. These values are enshrined in the final sentence at the end of the Declaration of Independence, written before we were even a country, when the signers confirmed the central truth that providing and sustaining our *independence* depends on the strength of our *interdependence*:

> And for the support of this Declaration, with a firm reliance on the protection of divine Providence, we mutually pledge to each other our Lives, our Fortunes and our sacred Honor.

Through the ideals and values expressed in our Declaration of Independence, the Founders not only laid the foundation for the greatest country the world has ever known; they also embedded in succeeding generations the courage to face risk and endure sacrifices in seeking a better future for themselves and their country.

The importance of interdependence to the core of the idea that is America was further confirmed in the change from the Articles of Confederation, enacted as our first government structure after the American Revolution, to the Constitution we have today. In that first (and so far only) Constitutional Convention, representatives from every one of the original 13 states came together with the purpose of forming "a more perfect union" under a new central, national government, replacing the primary focus on individual state governments that existed under the Articles of Confederation. That purpose, recorded in the Preamble to the new Constitution, confirmed that the future of America would be based on the union, the interdependence, of the several states:

We the People of the United States, in order to form a more perfect Union, establish justice, insure domestic tranquility, provide for the common defence, promote the general welfare, and secure the blessings of liberty to ourselves and our posterity, do ordain and establish this Constitution for the United States of America.

This Preamble essentially defined the purpose of the Constitution and the government it established. All of the Articles and Amendments that follow the Preamble are designed to support the purposes, the goals, expressed in the Preamble: "a more perfect Union...a just society...domestic tranquility... the common defence...the general welfare, and...the blessings of liberty." Are not, then, the liberties in the Bill of Rights not a purpose of the Constitution, but a means to support and achieve the purposes expressed in the Preamble?

The phrase *E Pluribus Unum* is the essence of America's uniqueness in the world: "From many, one." Today, there are many other democracies and republics among the countries of the world. But it is America's ability to be both highly diverse culturally and socially, and united politically and in the values to which we pledge allegiance, that has been the source of the unique strengths in our national spirit, our communities and our economy that have enabled us to be the major, and sometimes sole, source of power and influence for good in the world.

Yet today, we are experiencing the rise of a new challenge to these principles and values in America: the rise of partisanship. While political parties are nearly as old as America, the current domestic influence of partisanship is not what our Founders intended. In fact, it is something that deeply worried our first two Presidents over 200 years ago, as they could see even then the emergence of partisanship, and its potentially dangerous influences. During the period of ratification of the new Constitution by the states, which took place between September of 1787 and May of 1790, John Adams, who would become our first Vice President and second President, wrote the following in October of 1789:

> There is nothing which I dread so much as a division of the republic into two great parties, each arranged under its leader, and concerting measures in opposition to each other. This, in my humble apprehension, is to be dreaded as the greatest political evil under our Constitution.

Our first President, George Washington, echoed this sentiment in his farewell address. After having served as President for two terms, and then setting the example for both the concept of "citizen servant" and the peaceful transfer of power from one sitting President to another, Washington cautioned the nation about the risk of partisanship in September of 1796:

> However [political parties] may now and then answer popular ends, they are likely in the course of time and things, to become potent engines, by which cunning, ambitious, and unprincipled men will be enabled to subvert the power of the people and to usurp for themselves the reins of government, destroying afterwards the very engines which have lifted them to unjust dominion.

Do these cautionary statements by our first two Presidents seem to accurately reflect the current nature of our politics? Given these statements by two of our more notable Founding Fathers, one might wonder why the Constitution did not prescribe in more detail how Congress should operate in order to minimize the impact of partisanship.

I believe the explanation lies in the sequence of the very real "experiments" that were necessary in working towards our first Constitution and government. Following the victory in the Revolutionary War over England, the first governing document, the Articles of Confederation, established a weak central government and left most power with the states. There was a Congress of state representatives, but there was no national or central executive or judicial function. After nearly eight years, that governing model was found to result in a weak country not able to unite for the common good.

When the country's leaders met to begin the work of defining a new government model for the United States, they drafted a Preamble to clearly state the purpose that this new Constitution must fulfill: "In order to form a more perfect Union...," as mentioned earlier. Our Founders knew that America needed to establish a union of the states that would be "more perfect" than what existed under the Articles of Confederation.

Thus, a convention of the states was called in 1787 to draft a new governing document to strengthen the central government with certain powers granted to it over all states. But, as the first move toward defining a stronger central authority, the Founders were probably reluctant to prescribe too many details of how this authority would operate. So the Constitution focused primarily on defining the structure of the new government, the separation of powers between the branches, and the principle of checks and balances on the powers of each branch by the others, that would define the new government.

The Founders left the task of prescribing the operating details largely to the members of the Congress itself. Our Founders believed that should the elected members fail to represent the interests and will of the governed, then the citizens would simply vote them out of office and replace them. Unfortunately, their remarkable wisdom and insight did not enable them to perceive how the impact of money, gerrymandering of districts, and the partisanship interests of career politicians, as opposed to citizen legislators, would undermine and weaken the influence of citizens in our elections.

Our Forefathers lived their lives constantly facing the risks of unknown change. From the first settlers arriving in the new world; to those who bravely took up arms against England, the most powerful military in the world at that time; to those who settled the unknown wilderness west of the original colonies; our Forefathers readily and courageously faced life-threatening dangers to realize the opportunities of a better life. As our inheritance, Americans do not fear much in the world, and fear of change is *not* something we have inherited from our Founders or from our predecessors in the Greatest Generation.

But today many of our citizens are acting out of fear of the changes in our national identity that are brought about by increased ethnic and racial diversity in the country. While we've always been a nation of immigrants, we have also struggled at times to accept each new "wave" of immigrants into the American identity without discrimination and exploitation— including the struggle of accepting former slaves as equal citizens. However, it is undeniable that each new generation of immigrants, and the descendants of former slaves, have proven to add significant strength to both our economy, our culture and our society over time.

To be sure, we've never been faced with the degree of diversity in race, ethnicity, creed and culture that the newest immigrants represent today. The rise of women and ethnic minorities into positions of leadership in all aspects of our society seems to be exacerbating, for some of our citizens, the sense of loss of a national identity, which has historically been based on a male, Caucasian, European, Christian leadership

39

experience. Today, many citizens seem to fear that continuing legal immigration, which has always been a key element of American society and strength, will change the cultural identity of America and undermine our core strengths. Also at the core of this opposition, today as in past generations, is the fear that this new wave of legal immigration will adversely impact existing Americans economically and socially in their communities.

But our diversity has always been a unique element of our country in the world, and a major part of our core strength. The national identity of America is not based on the characteristics of race, creed or the country of origin of our citizens, though we may have started with a narrow range of differences in these elements in our initial population. What makes our Founding Documents unique and enduring is that they define a national identity based on a belief in the universal ideals of the right to life, liberty and the pursuit of happiness, in a government that derives its power from the consent of the governed, and in a society that guarantees freedom, justice and equal opportunity for all. Further, these documents embraced those citizens with religious beliefs and countries of origin different than the majority of our Forefathers.

The personal values of our greatest military heroes, the nearest models of those national values to our Founders, are those demonstrated by the recipients of our Congressional Medal of Honor. These heroes have defined those core values as courage; integrity; patriotism; citizenship; commitment; and personal sacrifice for others. It is the humility and personal sacrifice of putting the interests of the country, the community, your fellow citizens, and your fellow soldiers, above your own that is the true unique essence of millions of American heroes throughout our history. But those values are being undermined by partisanship, self-interest, and the hubris of both leaders and citizens believing in the absolute right of their own rigid ideologies, and the resulting intolerance of other ideologies.

Partisanship is driving greater divisions in our leaders and in our citizenry than we have experienced in over 150 years, since the time of the Civil War. It is being used to divide our country by demonizing those in the other party, for the basis of winning elections and securing and holding political power. What has followed have been periods of one-party partisan governing, where only the needs and concerns of the majority party's base and donors are the key aspects driving major policy directions in legislation.

In the past several decades of national elections, the differences between the candidates of the major parties have rarely been as large as 60%–40%. Most often the differences are between 55%–45% and 51%–49%. Yet the rules that our leaders have defined for the operation of Congress, and the focus of most Administrations, have given total control over the legislative process to the majority party, even if it only reflects a 1% advantage in the vote or one seat in the House and Senate. This has meant that the needs and concerns of the nearly 45%–49% of citizens who are in the electoral minority are totally ignored and too often rejected by the majority in making national policy. As a result, the minority party doesn't play the role of advocating for minority interests in national legislation, but in constantly opposing the majority party's legislative proposals.

In the recent past, policies influencing major elements of society have been enacted only by the majority party under similar periods of one-party governing by both parties. This trend toward one-party governing does not represent the values and principles of the Constitutional Republic that is America, and it is proving to be destructive of America's strength from unity. It is far from what the Founders intended in crafting the remarkable document that our Constitution represents.

How can we come to this conclusion? Perhaps because the word "party" does not appear anywhere in the Constitution; it was obviously not a core element of how our Founders

41

envisioned this first grand experiment in self-governance. Based on the statements by our first two Presidents we quoted earlier, this was probably not an accidental oversight.

To be sure, the liberty and freedoms enshrined in our Constitution were intended to provide for a "competition of ideas" within the concept of self-governance. But our Founders intended a civil debate of competing ideas, guided by true respect for differences, reflecting the pledge of interdependence in the Declaration of Independence, and leading to the accommodation of differences. They did not intend for a majority of just 51%–55% to result in having 100% of the power, or to "tyrannize" the minority by excluding the ideas, needs and concerns of 45%–49% of the citizenry. Nor did they intend for the minority to play just an oppositional or obstructionist role resulting in a dysfunctional government nearly incapable of governing effectively.

The key principle of our Constitutional Republic is that elected officials serve the country overall after the election, and seek to understand and address the needs and concerns of all citizens, not just those citizens in their base, or those who voted for them.

Elections should and do have consequences, but our self-governance was not intended to be a winner-takes-all blood sport between the parties and partisan members for their own self-interest. One party governing can never unite a country which cherishes the diversity of ideas, beliefs, and thought, and values the spirit of interdependence of its citizens.

You may recall a famous quote from President Abraham Lincoln during his campaign for a Senate seat from Illinois in 1858, when, in discussing the division of the country on the issue of slavery, he quoted the Bible in stating: "A house divided against itself cannot stand." The full quote from the Bible has some interesting and relevant details. Quoting the reaction of Jesus to being accused that his healing powers came from the

Devil, not from God, the apostle Matthew in the New Testament wrote: "Every kingdom divided against itself is brought to desolation; and every city or house divided against itself shall not stand" (Matthew 12:25). Could that be the fate America might suffer if we do not eliminate the level of divisiveness we are experiencing today?

The best approach I know to achieving collaboration and uniting in agreed action between different points of view, within a single group or organization, is the principle of the "win-win" solution that Stephen Covey defined in his work, *The Seven Basic Habits of Highly Effective People*. Covey taught that in an "interdependent reality," a "win-win" solution is the only solution that enables the relationship to endure. Isn't the description of an "interdependent reality" a core element of America as "one nation...indivisible"? Referring back to Lincoln's quote above, it is very likely that our country cannot long sustain our historic elements of strength and unity without a recommitment to sustaining that interdependent reality, and a new commitment to embracing the "win-win" approach to governing.

The social, economic and military challenges of the past 20 years have put our core principles and values under a "stress test" in America. In this new century, we've had two decades of slow economic growth, while we've had essentially no growth in the incomes of almost 60% of American households for almost 50 years before the pandemic of 2020. The size and prosperity of the middle class is shrinking, along with the quality of life in the average middle-class household. That term, "middle class," refers primarily to the "middle" 40% of Americans, from data of income trends by quintile, or groups of 20%, of American households. But the bottom 20% of American households have also seen no increase in average income growth over this same period.

As a result, too many families are living from paycheck to

paycheck, even with two or sometimes even three breadwinners, and are unable to accumulate any savings for emergencies, college or retirement. Many cannot afford basic healthcare, and live under the threat of financial ruin in the event of a serious illness or injury. Costs for everything rise consistently, as does the difficulty of making ends meet. And many households in the middle class worry constantly about losing their jobs, as there is no financial safety net for tens of millions of families.

These changes have resulted from a range of difficult and diverse challenges in the past several decades. We had a moderate recession in 2000 and then the largest recession and worst global financial crisis since the Great Depression less than a decade later. Our homeland was attacked for the first time since World War II in the first year of the new century and we've been at war in the Middle East for two decades. In combination, these events have put significant stress on our government's financial resources, and our ability to deal effectively with these internal and external crises.

Unfortunately, our government leaders have not responded well to these circumstances. Instead of working together to solve these issues for the benefit of the American people, they seem to be focused on meeting the needs and desires of donors and their own group of partisan supporters, and on protecting their own longevity in office and in power. Rampant partisanship, rigid ideologies, career self-interest, intolerance of differences, and fear of the change in our national identity are weakening our ability to address these societal and economical challenges effectively. These factors are also weakening the unique position of positive influence America has held in the world in the nearly 75 years since World War II.

It was during and after World War II that the United States became not only the strongest country militarily; at that time in history, as a nation we chose to use our strength to become the major force for good in the world. We helped other countries defend their own freedoms and independence, and improve their own economies and the health and educational standards of their people. Where and when possible, the USA has encouraged other countries to adopt greater levels of individual liberty and freedoms for their own citizens. There are American cemeteries in many other countries where Americans fought and died for the liberty and freedom of others. The citizens of very few countries have sacrificed themselves for the freedom of countries not their own.

These actions did not just benefit other countries, and they were not handouts; they were investments that also benefited our country. We are more secure in a world of strong economies and just and peaceful societies than in a world of broken economies and failing societies. We are also more secure in a world of free and democratic countries than in a world of authoritarian dictatorships or in societies suffering from Fascist tendencies.

In a recent article published on BigThink.com, the Charles Koch Foundation asserted that: "America's Greatest Foreign Policy Successes Are from Diplomacy, Not War." The article included a list of the top five accomplishments that diplomacy has contributed to the peace and security of the world, and of course of the United States. Number 5 is the Marshall Plan and the rebuilding of the post-war world after World War II, which directed investments in rebuilding not just our allies but our enemies in that war as well. It is still today the most uniquely selfless action ever undertaken by the victorious country in a major war against other countries; but it is totally consistent with the historic values and principles of America.

Our economy is also stronger when we can sell our products and services to 100% of the world's consumers instead of just the 4% that American consumers represent. This focus on a global trade policy creates many more high-paying jobs in our country; and our companies are made stronger by competition in the world than by isolation, so American consumers also benefit from increasingly better products with better values.

Another challenge we face today is the concentration of wealth at the top of our society that has greatly increased within the past 30 years. The incomes and wealth of the top 20% of citizens have grown immensely as the size, incomes and wealth of the middle class have shrunk. Is this a good trend for the health of our democracy? Consider how wealth has been concentrated in government systems and cultures in other countries and in different periods of history. Where is the concentration of wealth in monarchies? In theocracies? In dictatorships? In Communist countries? Haven't all these other governments and societies concentrated wealth at the top? Has concentrating wealth at the top made those governments and societies great societies with a high quality of life, freedom and liberty, and opportunity for the majority of their citizens?

If you wonder if this is a relevant factor in the United States, consider where the concentration of wealth has historically been in democracies, including our own. How has it changed over time? Where was it in the 1950s–1990s when most of America's current national wealth was built? What drove that amazing growth in wealth? What made the USA the greatest economy in the world? Was it only the actions and prosperity of the top 1%–10%? Did they do it alone? Has any country, government, society or culture ever become a truly great society solely by growing the prosperity of only the wealthiest class?

In fact, wasn't it the development of a growing and prosperous middle class that generated the wealth in America that our major companies and their leaders enjoy today? Could Amazon, Microsoft, Google, Apple, Facebook, P&G, GE, Boeing, Ford, GM, Delta Airlines, or even Walmart be the companies they are today without tens of millions of prosperous middle-class families during the 1970s–2000s buying bigger houses, nicer furnishings, air conditioners, multiple cars, multiple color TVs, computers, laptops, tablets and cell phones, cable TV and internet services, and taking more vacation trips, than the average household could afford in the 1950s and 1960s?

These changes that took place in the years between 1950 and 1990 in the average American household, not just the top 1%–10% of households, are the key drivers of the overall wealth in our country today. Could our country and these companies have seen the growth in the economy and wealth in that period if just the top 1%–10% of the households were able to purchase those items? I believe history and facts show clearly that the wealth and equity growth of these companies, and of the country's economy overall, could not have been achieved without the growth in the size and prosperity of the middle class driving that growth, via the spending provided by increasing middle-class incomes.

While the brilliance of a few people may have led to the creation of these inventions, would they have generated great wealth without the work of purchasing, manufacturing, distribution, and sales employees to produce and sell the products, and millions of consuming households to purchase them? But as these companies have seen incomes and profits rise, we have seen that most of the profits generated were allocated to the few executives in the company or, more recently, the shareholders. We have not seen most of the workers who contributed to the generation of these profits sharing in those profits. That has been a major factor in the rising wealth and income gaps we are faced with today.

Closing the gaps in wealth and income requires a focus on community—economic community—that makes countries and societies stronger and healthier. The growth of the size and prosperity of the middle class has been the key driver of economic growth, better education and health levels, and the level of peace of the society in many other countries, from the newly democratic nations in Europe to the newer emerging democracies and globally significant economies in Japan, Korea, Taiwan and China.

If these issues are so key to our economic growth and the health of our society, as the facts and history would indicate, why are they not more the focus of pro-growth economic policies by either major party? What has to change in how Congress operates so that important national policies that benefit the country overall can be developed from facts, data, history and objective analysis, and not partisan ideology or donor interests?

This is the great challenge America faces today. Will we succeed in maintaining the values and principles of our Forefathers and our Founding Documents in the face of the challenges of greater diversity and societal change? Will our leaders, operating under today's congressional rules and partisan political environment, be able to come together and act for the interests of the country overall, instead of acting in their own career self-interests or in the interests of their donors and their party?

If the past few decades indicate that this outcome is in doubt, then what changes would provide for a Congress that better serves the national and the public interest? If relying on congressional members to make the "rules" for how government operates is not working, then perhaps it is time for a "constitutional renewal" by enacting Amendments to incorporate "Citizen Rules" in the Constitution for how "We the People" want our Congress and our government to work. That is what this book will explore.

Will today's citizens be willing to accept a renewed commitment to serving the nation and others? Will today's citizens become the generation that will readily volunteer to be the foot soldiers in facing this challenge? It is perhaps a greater challenge to the existence and nature of America than the external threats of Fascism in World War II, Communism in the Cold War, or radical religious terrorism in today's world. Why?

Because these threats, these challenges, are *internal* threats; they are of our own making. But the fate and future of our country, and perhaps the world, is no less at stake on the outcome of how we respond to these challenges; on whether we choose to rise to meet the challenge together, as our Founders did, and as the Greatest Generation did before us. Or whether we let our fears and our self-interest permanently divide us.

This is America's Turning Point. We need to find out if there is a majority of Americans today who are willing to work together in a movement to "repair and restore" our Constitutional Republic, by asserting for ourselves as citizens the authority for making the rules for how we want to be governed, reclaiming it from the coalition of career legislators, political parties and their donors, and special-interest groups; to end this era of divisiveness and become "one indivisible nation" once again, united behind "win-win" policies that address the needs of all Americans, not just those of half of America; and to restore the principles of citizen legislators who will seek public office to serve the country in the way that was preferred by many of our Founding Fathers.

* * *

The next chapter will begin exploring what changes to the Constitution we might consider that would result in providing America with a more bipartisan, perhaps even a non-partisan government, in the future; that would result in a new government that truly reflects the principles of being "of the people, by the people, and for the people" and not the influences of career self-interest, partisan interest or donor interest; a government that is guided in *how* it operates by "Citizen Rules," not by rules that are designed to sustain the role and power of career politicians.

Chapter 2

Questions to Frame the Changes We Might Want to Consider

Many experts, pundits, authors and even independent non-profit and citizen groups have called out many of the problems facing the USA, tracing them to the rampant partisanship, the influence of money since the Citizens United decision, and the resulting divisiveness and dysfunction in government that exist in our country today. But few if any writers or political commenters have sought to develop and suggest non-partisan, workable solutions that could reverse these influences and reunite the country. My personal experience with developing solutions for complex but under-performing organizations has shown me that this is usually best achieved by taking a comprehensive approach, involving the following four steps:

(i) First, looking at where the desired outcomes are not being realized;

(ii) Next, identifying the barriers and root causes of the unrealized outcomes;

(iii) Then, defining and exploring solutions to overcome the barriers and address the key root causes of the unrealized outcomes;

(iv) Finally, developing an action plan to implement the solution with specific measures to determine if the solution actions are working.

Before beginning to apply this approach to some of our key problems, this chapter will give readers the opportunity to evaluate their own thinking with regard to the problems in how Congress and our political leaders are acting today, and their own preferences for how to best address changing these actions. We will present 13 questions about these key areas where the outcomes we expect from Congress in our Constitutional Republic are not being realized, without regard to party or partisan ideologies. In each question, readers will be presented with two choices for potential changes to address these areas. At the end of the chapter, we'll suggest what the readers' choices indicate about their openness to change, or their satisfaction with the current environment.

These questions and responses have been collected from nearly two years of presenting and discussing this topic with about 200 members of several university lifelong learning classes from three different universities, in five different counties and four congressional districts in southwest Ohio. Three of these districts tend to lean Republican, and one tends to lean Democrat, based on their voting history in recent elections. These questions have helped people understand their current thinking and opened up their thinking to alternative points of view.

Thirteen Questions

1. What is your definition of a national leader? What do we expect of our national leaders?

In a democratic republic, where our national leaders take an oath of office only to the national Constitution, don't we as citizens expect that those who are elected, regardless of their home state or party, will see their primary duty as serving the needs and interests of the country, of all citizens, whether those citizens voted for them or not? Or do we expect those we vote for to serve only our interests, only those of our party, and only those of our state, even if they take actions that undermine the interests of the country overall?

We have three co-equal branches to our national government.

The President is elected nationally; the Congress is elected from the states; and the national judiciary, the Supreme Court, is not elected but appointed and ratified by the other two national branches. Regarding the Congress as a national leadership body begs the question, what is your definition of a national leader, if elected by the states and not by a national vote?

We only have 535 members of Congress—100 Senators and 435 Members of the House of Representatives—in a government that serves nearly 330 million citizens. They represent the national legislative branch that has separate powers from the President and the executive branch, with oversight authority for the executive in the implementation of laws and the conduct of global affairs, and for the judiciary in the confirmation of the judicial appointment process. But given that they are elected by states, what is your definition of a national leader in Congress?

(a) Someone who focuses only on the policy needs and concerns of the people who voted for them? Someone who advocates for national policy based only on the ideology of their party, and the interests of their state's voters, and of their donors?

(b) Someone who puts country over party, and service to country over self-interest or party interest? Someone who advocates for the needs and concerns of their state and of their voters within the construct of national policy that accommodates the needs and concerns of others outside their state and partisan base as well?

2. Should we consider a change to the Electoral College to minimize or eliminate the winner-takes-all allocation in presidential elections and the outcomes it leads to in governing?

Under our Constitutional Republic, Presidents are elected not by the raw national popular vote but by a majority of votes in the Electoral College. In the national popular vote of citizens, we rarely see an election with a margin of victory as large as 60%–40%. More often, the differences are 45%–55% or 49%–51%, reflecting the level of diversity of political preferences, and life experiences, and of needs and concerns in our wonderfully diverse country. Is this narrow difference reflected in how our national campaigns are conducted, and how the policies emerging after an election are developed to govern the country overall?

In two of the past five national elections for President, the candidate who won the popular vote nationally did not win the Electoral College vote, and therefore the candidate with the lower popular vote total nationally became President. In nearly all states, a candidate could win the state's popular vote by the slimmest of margins, 0.1% of the total vote, and be awarded 100% of the state's Electoral College votes. This winner-takes-all aspect of our presidential elections seems today to lead to a win-at-all-costs approach to elections, and a focus on partisan messages and "getting out the party's base" instead of developing policy ideas that can appeal to the majority of voters.

With a predominance of states—about 37 in the past 20 years—where the popular vote has consistently favored either Republican or Democrat candidates, there are only a few "swing" states—only about 13 where the popular vote majority could favor either Republican or Democrat candidates in a given election. This situation results in four key problems with our elections:

- Major party candidates tend to maximize campaign time and messages in these states and minimize or avoid campaign time and messages in the states where the candidate's party either dominates or is at a significant disadvantage in the popular vote.

- The winner-takes-all aspect of the Electoral College leads to a win-at-all-costs approach to elections from candidates of both parties. Both parties have adopted a redesign of congressional districts in states they dominate, called "gerrymandering," to provide an advantage in elections for their party's candidates, and an almost guaranteed favorable outcome. This is a process that clearly violates the Constitution's implicit guarantees of free, fair and unbiased elections. It also essentially disenfranchises voters who prefer the minority party in the state; and leads to the impression that individual votes don't count, resulting in lower voter turnout and even fewer candidates standing for competitive election in many states.

- The winner-takes-all aspect of the Electoral College also leads to a greater focus by the candidates on policy proposals that appeal only to the partisan base of their party, to ensure they "get out their own base" in elections, instead of advocating policies that appeal more broadly to all the citizens in each state and the country overall. This focus follows the winning candidate into office and often results in major policy initiatives being passed by a compliant Congress controlled by the President's party, without the input of or a single vote from the minority party.

- But most importantly, this win-at-all-costs aspect of our elections too often results in candidates from both parties employing untruthful, unfair or misleading ads and messages, and "dirty tricks," to tip the election in a state by just that small percentage. And after winning all the Electoral College votes in individual states and the national majority, there is little incentive to develop policies that address the needs of all citizens, each state and the country overall. Sadly, this not only leads to greater divisions in the country, but candidates from both parties essentially ignore the needs and concerns of citizens in the other party and other parts of the country that don't align with the needs and concerns of their party's base voters.

Given these outcomes, perhaps we should consider whether or not the current method of allocating a state's Electoral College votes based on the winner-takes-all approach is fully consistent with the desire to have national policies that reflect the preferences of both party's voters. Do we feel that winner-takes-all elections in the Electoral College, voting by state, are providing the outcomes desired in our Constitutional Republic? If the "winners" represent between 51% and 59% of the country's popular vote preferences, but when elected they set priorities and policies only based on their own party and partisan base, ignoring the needs and concerns of 41%–49% of citizens, does that lead to a united and strong country, or a divided and weak country?

As a potential remedy, how might "proportional" allocations of Electoral College votes by state be more consistent with the principles of our Constitutional Republic? In other words, if the state's popular vote split 52%–48%, the candidate in the majority would receive 52% of the Electoral College votes in that state instead of 100%, and the candidate in the minority would receive 48% of the Electoral College votes instead of 0%.

Might such an approach lead to candidates from both parties allocating campaign time to most states, and developing policy positions and messages more broadly focused on the interests of most voters, rather than focusing primarily on the interests of just their partisan voter base? Might this approach also lead to the need for the parties to collaborate in setting policies and priorities that work for most of the citizens in each state, instead of just seeking a bare majority? Might this also lead to more citizens feeling that by being involved in elections and with their elected leaders, their voices will be heard and their votes can make a real difference?

Predictably, there is today an emerging number of candidates and partisan political analysts now calling for elimination of the Electoral College completely and electing the President solely on the basis of winning the national popular vote. Such a dramatic change to one of the core elements of the "balances" put into the Constitution by our Founders seems to represent an undue risk of "unforeseen consequences" at the core of our constitutional political processes. This seems to be a very short-sighted, essentially partisan response to the situation without much consideration of the broader impacts of such a change to the Constitution. And it is unnecessary. Perhaps there is a change that might be worthwhile considering, short of full repeal, as discussed below.

(a) There should not be any change to the Electoral College at all, neither eliminating the Electoral College and replacing it with the popular vote, nor changing how Electoral College votes in each state are allocated. This is too fundamental an element of our Constitution, which is there to ensure that the influence of a few large-population states cannot control presidential elections by their dominant population numbers.

(b) We should consider a change to the Electoral College to allocate votes in each state to candidates on a proportional basis to their share of the popular vote in that state. This would make it important for candidates to consider the entire electorate in each state, even those states where polling indicates they might only win 30%–40% of the popular vote. Today they might ignore that state entirely. But under proportionality, they could still gain an important number of Electoral College votes, instead of anticipating no Electoral College votes unless they can win 50.1%. This allocation approach would result in the Electoral Vote totals by state being fully representative of both the majority and the minority voter preferences in each state. And it would substantially lessen the winner-takes-all aspect of our presidential elections, and might encourage governing more to the country overall and less to partisan bases.

3. Should we alter the process for translating each state's popular vote into Electoral College votes, by eliminating the step of each state's legislature naming individual electors who are selected to vote in the Electoral College as indicated by the popular vote, and the step enabling Congress to challenge the certification of the Electoral College votes in the states by the Congress?

Elections for President and Vice President are conducted by the individual states, under the constitutions and the election laws of each state. The popular votes of the citizens in each state are counted, most often by bipartisan teams of election officials and citizen volunteers, at the precinct level, then aggregated to the county and then the state level. The total votes are then certified by the state election officials, the State Attorney General and the Governor. These vote results determine the number of Electoral College votes, and states proceed to appoint an equivalent number of "electors," allocated to the winner of the popular vote, or proportionally allocated to each candidate under the proposal in paragraph 2(b) above.

Today, the electors appointed by the states physically meet and cast votes for President and Vice President. Some states require the electors by law to cast their votes for the candidate who won the majority of the popular vote. But some states have no such legal retirement, which has occasionally led to so-called "faithless" electors voting against the candidate who won the majority of the state's popular vote.

After the Electoral College vote, the Constitution currently calls for the Electoral College votes of each state to be sent to Congress for a final count and certification in a presidential election. Election law passed by Congress gives Congress the authority to object to the Electoral College vote from an individual state, and question the validity of the elector slate presented by an individual state. If signed by a single member of both the House and Senate, the objection is debated separately in each House. If a simple majority in both Houses agrees, the electors chosen based on the vote of the people can be discarded. These "rules" essentially enable one party in Congress to overturn an election if their party has lost. These are not constitutional requirements — they are rules made by the members of Congress, and they are most certainly not consistent with the principles of the Constitutional Republic envisioned by our Founders.

By replacing Electoral College votes with electors, and having Congress review the qualifications of electors, there are now two steps in the process after citizens have voted where partisan politics can play an undemocratic, partisan political role in overturning the votes of the citizens.

Thus, the question is, do these two steps that are currently required by law between the votes of the citizens and the certification of the Electoral College votes strengthen or weaken the power of the people in each state to have their votes aggregated as voted to determine the election of President and Vice President?

(a) Because of the importance of the Electoral College process in our presidential and vice-presidential elections for over 230 years, there should be no changes to how state legislatures select and appoint electors, and how Congress reviews and confirms the validity of the certificates of Electoral College votes before being counted for the purpose of formally electing the President and Vice President.

(b) These two steps which follow the formal certification of the popular vote in each state should be replaced by a simple translation of the proportion of the popular votes to the appropriate number of Electoral College votes certified by the states, without any role for the Congress in challenging or objecting to the certified voting results in any of the states, nor the number of Electoral College votes for any candidate, when properly certified by the states when presented to Congress. There is ample time between elections in early November, and the certification of the final popular vote count and Electoral College vote allocations by the states in mid-December, for the candidates, parties or Congress to request or conduct investigations of any irregularities before the Congress meets to certify the national count in early January.

4. Do we expect our congressional members and the political leaders of the major parties to follow the principle of "serving the nation"?

Congressional leaders take an oath of office to support and defend the Constitution, not an oath of loyalty to a state or a region, or to a party. Is acting to favor partisan interests ahead of the national interest, when no party represents more than 40% of the country, consistent with that oath? Is it an oversight on the part of the Founders that the word "party" does not exist in the Constitution, that it is not part of the constitutional obligations of our elected or appointed leaders?

What are the expected actions that define "serving the nation" for congressional members who take the oath of office? There are two possible sets of actions that we as citizens might like to prescribe for our elected officials. Which of the two options below do you think is most desirable for the country?

(a) Today, beginning from the date they take office, our elected officials are focused primarily on winning the next election. It is reported that some members spend up to 40% of their time in Washington out of their office, raising funds and seeking votes. They work in a system, defined and controlled by the senior party members, that assigns leadership positions based on the amount of money raised for the party and for their own and the party's re-election. They have limited or no time or any incentive to work with members of the other party. Thus, most tend to focus on meeting the needs and concerns of only those citizens who are in their party's base.

These actions are necessary for members of Congress to continue to serve the people who elected them. The interests of the citizens who voted for them are their first and only priority. And there is no need for any changes to this process.

(b) Tomorrow, we prefer our elected leaders to spend their time in office focused on serving the interests of the country. They would work to understand the needs and concerns of their base, and they would collaborate frequently and openly with members of the other party to understand the needs and concerns of other Americans different than their own or their base in developing policies. They would readily and routinely spend most of their time in Washington working together with the members of the other party who represent other districts and states, to accommodate their needs and concerns in developing policies that work for most Americans. They would spend no time while in office on raising money or campaigning for their next election.

Our elected leaders would conduct legislative affairs

with a high level of transparency and accountability for results, by setting clear goals for the outcomes of public programs prior to approving spending, and would demand the same of their fellow members, regardless of party. They would require and follow up on an analysis of program performance with a public report on the results of the program's implementation versus goals, before seeking to recommit additional funds in the following fiscal year.

5. How do we want our congressional members to govern, to make legislative policy on key issues?

There are many procedural "rules" that have been institutionalized by the elected officials in Congress, and which party has been in control has had little effect on these rules. These rules have given total control of the legislative processes in both Houses of Congress to the party which is in the majority. In part, these rules give total authority to the senior members of the majority party to control most of the legislative processes:

- To determine which legislation will be permitted to come to the floor for a debate and vote, and which will not come to the floor for a vote;
- To determine the authority of the committee chairmen to control the actions of each committee (agenda, issuing of subpoenas, calling of witnesses, consideration of legislation, etc.);
- To determine the assignment of committee chairmen;
- To determine the committee assignments for all other members of their parties; and
- To control whether Congress will provide effective oversight of the executive Administration—whether they will act to obstruct an Administration of the other party with investigations, or whether they will simply rubber-

stamp the actions of an Administration of their own party.

The majority party generally does not need minority-party support to enact their decisions. The majority party has the ability to carry all votes by having more members on each committee, and having a majority of members in the overall House, than the minority party, where only simple majorities are needed to approve actions. Only the filibuster rule in the Senate, when 60 votes are required, provides any incentive for the majority party to interact at all with the minority party.

In our wonderfully diverse country, where diversity is a key source of our uniqueness and core strength, can the ideology of either party alone ever unite our country? What happens if we do not unite the country behind "win-win" policies that reflect the needs of both parties and of a large majority of American voters? If we become more divided and more dysfunctional in our policies, will we weaken our economy and society, weaken our national defense and our ability to contribute to good in the outside world, and thus become less secure? Is there any alternative to uniting the country other than by policies that reflect the needs and concerns of the country overall, *both* parties, and *both* sides of the political spectrum on key issues?

We are asking in the questions below if this current system represents the legislative process "We the People" support and want to continue; or do we want a different system, one where congressional members work together on all legislation and program development for the benefit of the country?

(a) We believe single-party policies are the best for the country. We believe that when one party has a majority in both chambers of Congress, and is able to control the legislative process, the potential delays of gridlock can be avoided or minimized. We want congressional members to work only within their own party, to set legislative policy only based on the needs, concerns and ideologies of their donors and their voter base.

(b) We believe that bipartisan policies are the best for the country. We believe that these policies are likely to be the only solutions that will work for most Americans, as opposed to solutions driven by the ideas of only one party. We believe these are the only policies that can unite most of the country. We want congressional members to set legislative policy by working together; to work to respect, understand and accommodate the needs and concerns of both their party *and* the other party, so that the country's overall needs and concerns are reflected in national policies.

6. Each of our congressional members is of course a member of a political party. Once elected, how do we want our representatives to act?

Elected officials are selected from the members of their party in their district or state to stand for election. While they are elected by a majority of the citizens in that district or state, they are primarily supported by voters from their own party. But as we've discussed earlier, in our Constitutional Republic we expect our elected officials to govern by representing all citizens in their constituency, and not solely to represent the citizens or the party that voted for them.

If this is the behavior we expect from our elected leaders, then how do we view those who confidently assert a political ideology about what is best for the country, even if it does not represent the needs and concerns of all citizens, but only those of their party? Are they deserving of our vote? Can we as citizens also respect and even care about others who don't share our beliefs or ideas of what's best for the country? Is a country where citizens and elected leaders are so passionately committed to their own partisan beliefs, without respect for or accommodation of others who have beliefs and needs different from their own, that much different from countries where citizens are so passionate about their own religious beliefs that they cannot respect or accommodate the beliefs and needs of fellow citizens of other religions or sects? Because of the violence that has always followed that kind of religious divisiveness in several countries, might we want to consider carefully where continued partisan divisiveness in our country might take us?

(a) We want leaders who stand firm on the principles and ideologies of their party or their party's base voters. Since each party and their voters believe that their ideologies and beliefs about what is best for the country are "right," and the other party's ideologies and beliefs are "wrong" for the country, we do not want our representatives to compromise or collaborate with those who represent a "wrong" point of view.

(b) We want leaders who, while confident in their own beliefs, have enough humility to realize that others' beliefs might have validity, enough empathy to care about the beliefs of others, and who understand that their role in governing is to serve *all* the citizens, not just those who share their partisan beliefs. We want leaders who understand that their views may not be best for those who have different life experiences and situations, and therefore different needs and concerns, than their own. We want leaders to have respect for the views of others who think and believe differently than they do, and look to accommodate those needs of other citizens along with their own.

7. How is the amount of money in politics and the nature of the undisclosed "dark" money contributions to Political Action Committees (PACs) impacting our elections? A Supreme Court

decision (Citizens United) essentially removed most of the Federal Election Contribution limits on donations by stating that "money is speech," and thus could not be regulated by Congress.

But how do average citizens feel about this influence? Do large money contributors have an advantage over ordinary citizens in gaining access to and influencing the thinking and actions of their representatives in Congress? Have the wealthy contributions to candidate campaigns or to the inaugural committees of elected candidates led to appointments of "ambassadors"? Have these contributors been able to receive support for their business or investment properties?

Does this special access to elected officials once in office undermine the "one person, one vote" principle behind our democracy, where every citizen's vote should have essentially equal impact? And should citizens have access to and the opportunity to petition and influence their elected representatives on an equal basis, without regard to their party affiliation, and whether and how much the citizens have contributed to their campaigns?

So the question is, should Congress be able to limit the amount of money that citizens, companies and organizations can donate to political candidates, elected officials, and political issue advocacy groups? Should every donation made and received be made public, so there is no "dark money"?

(a) No, the Supreme Court decision that "money is speech" should be upheld, and individual companies and issue advocacy groups should be able to contribute as much money as they choose to the candidates, elected officials and issue advocacy groups that they support.

(b) Yes, the Supreme Court decision equating money to speech should be overturned with a Constitutional Amendment that states clearly that "We the People" do not believe money is speech, we do not believe that unlimited donations should be allowed. We believe that the political and campaign donations from groups and organizations such as corporations, associations, unions, issue or political action groups, or non-profits should be limited to the same amount as an individual citizen. Money should not be able to derive more access to and influence on elected officials. These groups should be required to disclose all donations received and funds contributed to any candidate, party, or other organization.

Congress should be required to pass Election Finance Laws to implement these new campaign finance limits and requirements. Companies and all organizations with limited donations can still distribute their points of view on candidates and issues to their employees, members and other citizens who "opt in" to receive them. Their employees and members, of course, can contribute as individuals. And every donation made and received should be a matter of public record by those organizations both making and receiving political and campaign contributions.

8. Has the rise of elected leaders becoming career politicians helped undermine the focus on serving the country in Congress?

It seems that for nearly all our elected leaders, the focus today has become winning the next and future elections, so that their careers as elected officials can continue. In order to achieve this goal, elected leaders need to raise funds for campaign expenses from donors; and they need to have the support of their party for both monetary and campaign staff contributions. Securing these elements requires a pretty strict compliance to the priorities of major donors, and of party leaders.

Thus, the focus of these leaders becomes: (1) winning the next election; (2) raising contributions from major party donors, by addressing their priorities; and (3) following the priorities of party leaders. Research indicates that an average Congress member spends almost 40% of their time while in Washington working on re-election, not working on legislation, addressing the needs of their constituents, or serving the country overall. There is little or no incentive in achieving these goals to work with the other party to address the needs and concerns of voters other than those of their party. In fact, the incentives are to undermine the initiatives of the other party, and to treat their members as the "enemy."

In addition, over the past 30+ years, members of Congress have only averaged 145 days in Washington each year. The remaining 220 days are spent primarily working in their local districts or states, with occasional trips to domestic and international locations to research issues related to legislation or natural disasters in their state, or on vacation. But while in their home districts or states, considerably more time is spent on campaign fundraising than working to address issues with groups of citizens in open formats like town-hall meetings.

If the career interests of elected officials are one of the major barriers to a focus on serving the needs of the country over party or donor interests, perhaps limiting the terms of congressional members to eliminate that career interest should be seriously considered. On this issue, the key factor is to eliminate the need or ability to run in the next election, so that the focus of elected officials is only on working together to serve the country. The specific proposal would provide a limit of one six-year term for Senators and one four-year term for House members. One-third of Senators and one-half of House members would be elected every two years. This would largely eliminate seniority as the key factor in selecting congressional leaders as well. Since no member could run for another office while serving, there would be a two-year gap before a member could run for a different office, if they desired. But no member could serve in an office for more than one term in their lifetime.

The question then becomes, is this an action that could have a major impact on the negative influences of self-interest, donor interest and partisan interest beyond enacting term limits on Congress? More specifically, might the prohibition on running for election while in office help minimize the influences of donors and party leaders, and increase the focus on working together for the overall benefit of the country? Might the limit of a single term of service help to attract only those citizens to run for Congress who desire to serve the country rather than serve their own career goals?

(a) No, we should not enact term limits on Congress members. We would lose the expertise that senior members gain by serving many years in Congress. If members only serve one term, the unelected congressional staffs would be able to exert undue influence over the elected members in what legislation should be passed and how the process of passing legislation works. Finally, this would deprive citizens of the right to vote for the congressional members they choose to represent them.

(b) Yes, limiting Congress members to a single term would likely be a major factor minimizing the impacts of donors and partisan influences on our members of Congress. Without the need to be re-elected, congressional members would not need to respond to the needs of donors and partisan influences after being elected. Without the time spent on running for the next election, congressional members would have more time to spend working on legislative initiatives, and would have no disincentive to work with members of the other party to do a better job of addressing the country's real needs. Thus, the quality of legislative policies enacted in this environment would likely be better for the country than the current highly partisan and often dysfunctional system. And without the path to a career as a member of Congress, we might well find that the people choosing to run for office are likely to be those with an honest and selfless desire to serve the country, not a desire to build their own career.

9. How do we as citizens want to define the procedural rules for how Congress will operate the legislative and other approval processes, including the authority of oversight and accountability for the executive Administration, that determine how the country is governed?
The rules of congressional legislative procedures are not prescribed in detail in the Constitution. As discussed earlier, the Constitution currently leaves the definition of these rules to the members of each House to set for themselves, relying on the citizens to act to remove congressional members who don't serve the country, by election or impeachment. But in the past several decades, the rules made by the congressional members seem to be made for the benefit of the majority party and the elected members themselves. Today, the majority party has full control over the legislative process, and many of the key policies enacted by both parties over the past two Administrations have been developed and passed on to the country by only the majority party. This might seem to be in conflict with the principle of representing a democratic republic.

For example, under rules made by the members of both Houses, the majority party controls what laws are voted upon in each House—the Senate Majority Leader and the Speaker of the House control the legislative and voting agendas. The majority party controls every committee, and the committee chairmen control what bills are approved, what investigations are pursued, what witnesses are called, what subpoenas are issued, and the conduct of the committee meetings. All these important actions of a committee in our Congress are controlled by a single person.

In addition, if the congressional majority party is different from the President's party, they can block the desired policy directions of the President. Or if the majority party is the same as the President's party, they can rubber-stamp the President's policy directions and actions without providing any degree of a "check and balance" or oversight function. Neither actions would seem to be consistent with putting the needs and interests of the country over the political interests of the party.

The Senate majority of both parties has delayed or rejected presidential appointments in past years for partisan political reasons. But in 2016, partisanship reached a new level of political "malpractice" when the Senate Majority Leader on his own effectively blocked the Senate from performing its consideration of an appointment of a Supreme Court nominee by the President as required in Article 2, Section 2 of the Constitution, who was from the other party. The Senate Majority Leader refused to schedule either a hearing for the nominee or a vote on the appointment by the full Senate, even though the "advice and consent" specifically required by the Constitution "of the Senate" can only be fulfilled by a vote of the full Senate. In doing so, the Senate Majority Leader placed partisan political advantage above his and the Senate's constitutional duty—and undermined the strength of our Constitutional Republic.

Of course, the Senate is not required to approve any appointment, but its members are required as a body to provide "advice and consent" via an up-or-down vote. There is no sense of the full Senate's "advice and consent" constitutional role when there is not a vote but only a decision by one Senator or even only by the majority party. By the way, the office of Senate Majority Leader is not a position even mentioned in the Constitution, let alone granted any powers to interpret or override this constitutional provision.

Are our leaders fulfilling their oaths of office when not one of the other 99 Senators, the 435 Members of the House, or the President or any Cabinet-level officers, who all have pledged to "support and defend the Constitution against all enemies, foreign or domestic...," would even speak out against this action at the time, except in terms of partisan fairness? Doesn't this action represent a prime example of putting "party over country"? Should Congress continue to make its own rules to define the processes for governing?

(a) Yes, we want to continue to have the elected members of Congress make their own rules for the legislative and other approval processes that determine how the country is governed.

(b) No, we want some key Citizen Rules, defined and approved by citizens, to determine how Congress will govern; how they will operate the legislative and other approval processes, including the oversight and accountability functions of the executive Administration.

10. Do "We the People" want to see a stronger provision for "checks and balances" on the actions of one branch of government by the other?

One of the points of genius of the Founding Fathers in structuring our government under the Constitution was to add a system of "checks and balances" between the separate and independent branches of government. That system protects our freedoms and liberty by preventing one branch from becoming too powerful and corrupted through lack of oversight of and accountability for their actions. But recently, party loyalty across the branches of government seems to have undermined the protections of "checks and balances" that our Founding Fathers built for us. Congress instituted the role of independent Inspectors General to provide a professional, non-political oversight role across the government. Most of these "IGs" are appointed to their roles by the President with the advice and consent of the Senate, although some are appointed by executive department directors. As with all presidential appointments, these IGs serve "at the pleasure of the President," which essentially removes their ability to be fully independent in their roles.

The Supreme Court recently stated that the strengthened independence that Congress wrote into the law expanding the IGs' role, limiting the President's authority to remove IGs only for poor performance of duties or moral or ethical behavior violations, was an unconstitutional violation of the "separation of powers" principle. Apparently this was not seen as an appropriate protection against the potential corrupt action of the President by removing IGs conducting an investigation that might have an adverse personal effect on the President or any of his appointees, thus undermining the important principle of "checks and balances" between the branches.

How do we as citizens feel about the need for objective, unbiased and independent "checks and balances" between the branches of government? Do we favor a more powerful and perhaps unchecked executive branch that can operate more independently of congressional oversight, with little ability of Congress to hold the executive branch accountable for acts of poor performance of their duties, or moral or ethical violations? Or do we favor more congressional oversight and accountability checks on the Administration's actions?

(a) The strengthening of congressional oversight would represent a weakening of the strong executive branch that the country's security requires. Since the IGs and key executive department directors and secretaries serve at the pleasure of the President, the President must have the ability to remove any person in whom he has lost confidence or for any reason he chooses.

(b) It is important that Congress is able to provide a strong and effective "checks and balances" role, as the Founding Fathers intended, on the powers of the executive branch. To accomplish this role, Congress needs to be empowered to exert effective oversight of and accountability for executive actions through the fully independent operations of the Inspectors General, and to protect an appropriate level of independence in the operation of key executive departments.

For this role to be effective, Inspectors General should be able to conduct investigations freely and without undue influence, and should not be removed by the actions of the President alone. Similarly, operations of the Justice Department, the key intelligence agencies, top military leadership, the Treasury and the IRS must be protected from undue political actions or influence from the President to perform their important roles for the country. Thus, any removal of an IG or director or secretary of a specified executive department must be confirmed by the Senate. These appointments must be confirmed by the Senate to assume the role, so providing for an open process to determine whether the removal of a confirmed appointee from that role is justified and free from corrupt intent, seems fully appropriate.

11. Should we consider an action to reduce partisan influences in the judiciary?

In our government, the principle of the "rule of law" means that no one in our country, and no one in our government, even the President, is above the law. This principle is protected by the existence of an independent Justice Department, including the Attorney General, the US Attorney offices, and the judicial system. The only action that can compromise this principle in

Justice Department operations is the interference of the President in the independent operation of the Attorney General or the US Attorney's offices, either to cause investigations to be started or stopped, or to remove an Attorney General or US Attorney from their positions, without an appropriate, unbiased justification.

The potential undermining of the independence of the judicial system can happen through excessive partisan actions in the nomination and the congressional approval processes of federal judges and Supreme Court justices. With lifetime terms for federal judges and Supreme Court justices, the impact of partisan influences in the selection of nominees and in the appointment process could lead to long-term partisan impacts on the independence of the judicial branch. Should party loyalty take the place of seeking to appoint unbiased judges, and focus instead on appointing judges with a judicial ideology that is consistent with the partisan ideology of the President and majority party in the Senate? Could the result be a judicial system that becomes overly politicized instead of being independent of the partisan actions of Congress and/or the executive branches?

(a) No, the lifetime terms of federal judges and Supreme Court justices should not be replaced with shorter terms. This is a key provision in the Constitution that is designed to ensure that federal judges and justices are removed from the potential political influences of being judged for their performance and having to go through another appointment and confirmation process.

(b) Yes, the lifetime terms of federal judges and Supreme Court justices should be replaced with shorter terms. People live much longer today than on average in 1789, and a lifetime appointment of an ideologically biased judge or justice can have a long-term adverse impact on the country. The proposal would be to establish a ten-year term for the federal judges and justices. At the conclusion of each ten-year term, a judge or justice could be renominated, obviously by a different President, and reconfirmed by the Senate, which would be a Senate with totally new members (who under the Citizen Rules would be limited to a single six-year term). So an unbiased judge or justice may well provide a lifetime of service via successive ten-year terms. But a judge or justice who exhibits too much partisan ideology in their decisions over a ten-year term would be subject to not being reappointed or reconfirmed.

12. How do we feel about the "gerrymandering" of voting districts by both parties for state or congressional elections?
Should party voting patterns be a consideration in the demographic balances in district boundaries, or should it just be limited to other factors, such as race, income, age, rural/urban mix, and so on? Or should districts only consist of nearly equal populations of adjoining and contiguous regions without regard to any other demographic issues?

Equal population between districts is the only specified constitutional requirement. The other elements may vary by the nature of contiguous districts with very different makeup in other demographics. If state political leaders from the majority party alone remain empowered to draw new district lines, should there be a separate non-partisan citizen review board in each state to provide oversight, with the authority to reject the proposed new district alignment from a one-party-only redistricting process and require that the district lines be redrawn?

Whatever process is used, the opportunity for bias in terms of party, race or ethnic issues is great with the degree of citizen and voting data available today. Would it be important then to have a non-partisan, unbiased commission to provide oversight of district alignments by the states, with authority to require the redrawing of voting-district lines found to be biased? Oversight authority would not include the authority to redraw district lines themselves, and all oversight decisions by the commission would be subject to a challenge in federal court. Would such a commission help ensure fair, unbiased and non-partisan congressional district boundaries?

(a) Since the Constitution doesn't prescribe a process for drawing new congressional district boundaries after each mandatory ten-year census, it is appropriately left up to the state legislatures to draw the new district lines based on any criteria that they choose. No other oversight is appropriate or should be instituted.

(b) Because drawing voting-district lines to favor one party or the other can impact the outcomes of elections in an unfair way, there should be an unbiased, non-partisan process to ensure that the drawing of new district boundaries is fair and free of partisan bias after a census. Congress should be required to establish a separate unbiased, non-partisan citizen commission to review state voting-district alignments, with authority to require states to redraw any district alignments found to be biased. In doing so, the commission should be required to state specifically the basis for the finding of bias and supporting data, and to provide a suggested remedy to the states. These findings will be released publicly when provided to the states.

The history of gerrymandering by both parties is a prime example of political leaders acting in their own interests, against the interest of the country overall and outside the intention of our Constitution. The single purpose of gerrymandering is to define districts that give one party an advantage over the other for winning more easily in future elections, making it more difficult for different groups to have their voices and votes impact the choice of their leaders.

13. With the increase in spending on political advertising and the advent of social media, the opportunities to spread false or misleading messaging in an election campaign have risen dramatically. What changes, if any, are needed to ensure fair elections that would be constitutionally appropriate?
Existing law requires commercial speech to meet the standard of "truthful and not misleading" messages. This is a reasonable limit to free speech that has passed Supreme Court reviews and has been in place for decades. Commercial messages influence consumer purchase choices, and it would create an unfair advantage if businesses could use misleading or false messages about their own or competitors' products. The losers would be consumers potentially damaged by poorer products, and employees and shareholders of the "maligned" businesses damaged by business losses—each put at risk by an unfair and dishonest tactic. Without this protection, businesses who "cheat" might well prosper over businesses who are honest, and even put the honest businesses out of business.

Is it important for our democracy that citizens can trust that the messages being received from any and all sources in an election are also "truthful and not misleading"? Are political candidate or campaign issue messages mostly "truthful" and consistent with facts today? Do you trust the campaign messages you see and hear? Or do they too often take content out of context and send "misleading" messages, or just make totally false statements? Are there any penalties for using messages that are false or misleading to influence an election? Is this fair to voters? Is it good for the country? Can we have fair elections and a truly democratic government if our elections can be manipulated by false and misleading campaign messages?

We have now had decades of effective reviews of truthful commercial speech, and all advertising and labeling messages, by an unbiased non-governmental review board. This board, the National Advertising Review Board (NARB), does not have the power to require changes to commercial advertising, but can require that advertisers provide supporting data for any advertising claims or messages that they make. After review, the NARB can ask for changes to or deletions of commercial messages they judge to be false or misleading. If these requests are not complied with voluntarily, the NARB publishes their review results, their decision, and the agreement or refusal to comply. If there is no agreement to comply, the NARB turns the file over to the Federal Trade Commission (FTC) for prosecution under the law. A new Political Messaging Review Board could operate similarly with regard to political messages from all groups and in all channels directed to the voting public.

Many students who have heard this suggestion in my previous classes have asked, "How can any review board be totally unbiased in reviewing political advertising or speech?" It really is very straightforward. Any claim about what a candidate has said, written or "believes" about an issue must be supported by facts. As in the case of commercial speech, to make statements in political speech, a candidate, person or organization must be able to have a supporting fact that shows the point is true. If there isn't such support, then the claim would not be considered truthful. It's up to the "speaker" or the "sender" to ensure they are making a truthful statement about a candidate or an issue that can be supported. There's no subjectivity or bias involved on the part of the media channel or platform—there are either facts that support the message or there aren't.

As in the case of commercial speech, the speaker or initiator of the message must be able to present factual information on which the message is based. The responsibility of any distributor of the message, including broadcast, print and social media platforms, is to ask for and review the factual information that supports the truth of the message, and agree that it represents appropriate verification of the truth.

Political speech is even more critical to the country and the effective working of our democracy than commercial speech, as it influences our choice of leaders in a self-governing society, not just our choice of products. The NARB provides an effective model for the voluntary compliance of such a board's rulings, with the opportunity to resort to a court resolution if there is a complaint of bias or refusal to comply. A Political Messaging Review Board would allow for quick action to enable the removal of any intentionally false political messaging, and would increase public awareness of the objective review process.

Thus, the question is, should there be a non-partisan, unbiased citizen review of political advertising messages to ensure that voters hear truthful messages about candidates and issues?

(a) No oversight is required or needed. Under our Constitution, free speech by individuals can't be reviewed or limited. Political speech is likewise protected and can't be reviewed by anyone without introducing bias that could compromise our democracy. Voters have to take individual responsibility to "fact check" the candidate and other political messages they receive via any and all sources.

(b) We should have an Amendment to the Constitution that states clearly that untruthful commercial and political speech can be subject to limitations under laws designed to support free and fair commerce and elections in America. This can be accomplished by Federal Election Laws establishing an unbiased, non-partisan citizen review board for political messages in a campaign year, for the messages from candidates, parties and political issue groups distributed in all media sources.

Review Your Preferences

If you tended to favor the responses to the above questions in the (a) group, then you may be pretty comfortable with the partisan divisions that have been dominating how political leaders are governing today, and comfortable with the legislative rules that Congress has set for itself. You may feel that these actions are not only currently *permitted* under the Constitution; you may believe they have been and will continue to be *beneficial* for the country. As a result, you may see little or no need for major changes to how Congress operates. While that is a position I, as the author, don't agree with, I don't expect every citizen to support any or all of the changes that will be proposed in this book.

If you favor the way Congress makes policy today, I encourage you to think back to previous years when whatever party you support was not in the majority. I hope you might come to agree that the best interests of the country cannot be served by single-party partisan policies from either party in the majority. And when the party you favor has not been in the majority, I'm sure you were not in favor of most of the policies enacted under such a Congress or Administration. A Congress that makes national policies which ignore the needs and concerns of nearly half the country is hardly the kind of Congress that our Founders hoped to pass on to future generations of Americans.

In the following chapters, there will be much discussion on specific individual issues and policy suggestions where you, as the reader, may hopefully see a non-partisan, win-win approach presented that is totally new to you. You may see that the details of the policies outlined with this approach may in fact address the needs and concerns you have on this issue, while also addressing the major needs and concerns of the party you favor. Citizens in the "other" party are simply fellow citizens who may think and believe differently than you, and may have a totally different life experience than your own. But isn't it true that all citizens should be able to expect their representatives and government to be willing to look for ways to address their needs and concerns, whether or not they are members of their elected representative's party?

In addition, you may see that the country would be more united, stronger, with less divisiveness and rancor among our leaders and citizens, if the suggested win-win approaches were considered. So I hope you will be interested enough in this possibility to continue reading, and to participate in the issue discussion blogs at www.citizenrules.blogspot.com to share your ideas as part of the process.

On the other hand, if you tended to favor the responses in the (b) group, then you are likely to be open to major changes in how Congress operates. We will explore those potential changes in the chapters that follow. We will also explore what non-partisan, "win-win" solutions to many of the problems and issues that divide us today might look like, if the proposed changes were enacted. In the current partisan environment in the country, many of these problems and issues are not being solved in any way that is satisfactory to most Americans, so some change seems to be appropriate.

In either case, on whatever side of the "change" issue you find yourself, I hope you will continue reading through the following chapters. They will include non-partisan, fact-based discussions of the major issues the country faces routinely and provide examples of what win-win solutions might look like, for your consideration. And at the end of the book, I hope you will objectively consider the specific changes presented to certain sections of the Constitution that would implement these changes, with the goal of lessening the impact of divisive partisanship, resulting in more adherence to the principles of serving the nation, and providing greater accountability and transparency in how Congress operates.

There are specific changes proposed that are designed to improve the focus of governing in the national interest and to limit the focus on the self-interest of members, or the interest of donors or partisan special interests. The goals of other changes would be to minimize the impact of control by the majority party and of the seniority of members on the governing process, making that process less partisan and more "democratic"; to increase the accountability of Congress in spending public money; and to increase the transparency of how congressional members are voting on individual tax, spending and other critical program issues.

* * *

If these overarching goals are of interest to you, I invite you to continue reading.

Chapter 3

What Are the Current Problems with Congress Today and Their Root Causes That We Might Want to Address?

Issues to Be Addressed—Which Are Key?

This chapter will identify many of the key problems in how Congress operates and governs today that seem to be in conflict with many of the principles of the Constitution and/or the intent and perceived expectations of our nation's Founders, even if these intentions and expectations were not stated in the Constitution but were stated in other sources. Many of these problems result from the excessive influences of party and partisanship today; of the influence of money and donors over votes and voters; and of rules that Congress has set for the benefit of its own members.

These rules seem to have come about with the rise of lifetime "career" legislators that has taken place largely in the last 150 years or so, and the recent trends in executive leadership departing from the expected norms of appropriate actions on several fronts, including areas of ethics and conflicts of interest. All of these problems seem to be undermining the very quality and effectiveness of our democracy, and essentially replacing the focus of our elected leaders and citizens on loyalty to the Constitution and to serving the nation, with loyalty to party and individual leaders.

The Concept of "Citizen Rules"

In order to develop a set of "Citizen Rules" that a large majority of "We the People" might agree to enact to replace the rules that Congress has established for its own operations, we need to consider the problems that the existing rules are causing to our Constitutional Republic, and the potential non-partisan solutions, as objectively and creatively as possible.

As a reminder, the steps we will take to identify problems and eventually propose solutions are as follows:

(i) First, looking at where the desired outcomes are not being realized;

(ii) Next, identifying the barriers and root causes of the unrealized outcomes;

(iii) Then, defining and exploring solutions to overcome the barriers and address the key root causes of the unrealized outcomes;

(iv) Finally, developing an action plan to implement the solution with specific measures to determine if the solution actions are working.

Step 1—Desired Outcomes Not Being Realized

Here is a list of some of the desired outcomes that are not being realized in how Congress operates today.

1. Congress in too many ways does not operate by putting the country's interest over their party's interests, their personal career self-interest in being re-elected, the "demands" of major donors, and the needs, concerns and demands of their party's base in their home district or state. In addition, the minority party seems to be rooting for the majority party to fail, rather than seeing working with the majority party to develop effective policies as indicative of success for the country, rather than success for the majority party. The political calculus seems to be that since our party is always right, and the other party is always wrong, the country only benefits if our party wins. And the electoral calculus is that there is no appreciation from their party's base voters for working with the other party, involving collaboration and compromise instead of conflict

and obstruction. As a result, we see some of these perhaps undemocratic actions happening very frequently:

- Members of Congress in the majority party seem most often to exclude the minority party from major legislative and policy deliberations, preferring to develop policy via a one-party process. This has taken place on major national policies such as the healthcare system overhaul under Democrats and the tax system reform and rate cuts under Republicans.
- Members of Congress in the minority party always seem to be rooting for policies of the majority party to fail. Having been largely excluded from major policy deliberations, their posture is to oppose the changes that ignore their needs and concerns, and obstruct the processes in which they were not able to participate.
- The Constitution sought to set up a system of checks and balances between the three branches of government. One element of this balance is the "check" on the power of the executive branch via congressional oversight of the administrative actions and policies. However, members of Congress in neither party practice unbiased oversight of the Administration when the Presidency is held by their own party. Then, both parties practice almost no oversight and in fact act to block any attempts by the other party to provide oversight of the Administration. When the Presidency is held by the majority party in Congress, the minority party seems to forego all sense of unbiased oversight in their quick and public denunciation of almost any administrative actions, while members of the majority party vigorously defend the actions of the Administration, no matter the circumstance.

2. Members of both parties in Congress have enacted rules to

place control of the key processes of government in the hands of senior members of the majority party; such as:

- Many pieces of major legislation are now developed by "select committees" of the majority party in private sessions, without any public hearings from relevant experts, without the input from a standing committee with members of both parties, and without any minority-party input at all. Debate on the benefits and risks of specific bills has been drastically curtailed.

- No matter how many House Representatives or Senators would like to see a debate and vote taken on a particular piece of legislation, the majority party's Speaker of the House and Majority Leader in the Senate can on their own stop any legislation from coming to the floor for discussion or vote, and set the rules for the length of time for debate and consideration before voting. Thus, voting is essentially limited to those bills the party leaders favor and believe will pass. So we've seen 2,000-page legislation on major policy issues required to be voted upon within a few days or even a few hours of being presented to members of the House or Senate.

- Under existing congressional rules, there is significant deference and consideration given to members based on seniority, not on relevant skill or experience, on competence, or on accomplishment; and congressional committee chairmen, always members of the majority party, are essentially in total control over committee operations. For example, the committee chairmen alone decide what legislation or topics will be considered or investigated by the committee; what witnesses to call when considering legislation or conducting an investigation; what subpoenas will be issued or not issued; and which bills will be reviewed by and voted on by the committee.

3. A concerning outcome of the flood of money contributions to congressional members and parties is that members of both parties seem to give higher priority, in terms of who they choose to meet with, listen to and respond to in the choice of legislation they support, to major donors and representatives of a party's special-interest support groups, than to individual constituents. The interests of these groups seem to have more influence over the attention, the decisions and the actions of members of Congress than do citizens' interests or the national interests.

For example, it has been reported that some members of Congress will meet in person only with constituents who have donated to their campaign. And that recently, some members of Congress have chosen not to hold public meetings with constituents in their districts just to avoid having to address questions from constituents who may feel current policies are not addressing their needs and concerns. But they will meet often with donors and voters from their own party.

4. As we've discussed previously, members of Congress from both parties spend a considerable amount of time while in Washington focused on their own re-election activities and raising campaign funds versus time spent working on issues related to governing.

Specifically, it has been reported that members of the House of Representatives, starting on the day the new Congress is sworn in, spend as much as 40% of their time in Washington out of the House Office Building. Since the law prohibits them from engaging in campaign or fundraising activities in federal office buildings, both parties provide call-center offices located across the street for members to work on re-election and fundraising activities while in Washington. Those days are of course meant to be days working to serve the nation. As a result, citizens pay the salaries for members of Congress while they spend a great deal of their limited days in Washington campaigning and raising funds for their own re-election.

5. Instead of acting as citizen legislators, as it seems many of our Founders preferred, our representatives today seem to act as the "governing elite." To paraphrase Benjamin Franklin's statement at the Constitutional Convention cited earlier, they act as the masters, not the servants, of the public.

For example, Congress has the authority under the Constitution to set its own salaries. The members have extended that authority into setting their own healthcare and retirement benefits, and to provide nearly unlimited staff, office and travel expenses for themselves. They also have explicitly exempted themselves from many of the laws and rules that they have enacted for the country. And though the compensation for members of Congress in the early years was limited to a modest daily allowance for days they worked in Congress, congressional members today earn a full-time salary, even though Congress is only in session for about 145 days a year. Many representatives today enter "public service" as members of the middle class and leave personally very wealthy, as the facts below suggest.

- Between 1789 and 1855, Congress was paid $6 per day that Congress was in session. Beginning in 1855, Congress members started paying themselves an annual salary, initially $3,000.
- In 1955, congressional salaries were $12,500. By 1985, they had increased to $75,000, an increase of 600%. By 2002, the salaries had doubled to $150,000. Salaries were raised to the current level of $174,000 in 2009.
- The growth in average net worth from 2004 to 2012 for congressional members was $591,000. In the same period, the average American citizen's net worth increased by $60,000. This is nearly a tenfold advantage in average

household net-worth increases over the average citizen for our "citizen legislators."

6. As discussed earlier, the winner-takes-all rules under which our government operates today encourage a lot of behavior that ordinary citizens would consider undemocratic and unethical.

- These rules undermine the willingness of the majority party to even consider, let alone respect and accommodate, the needs, concerns or ideas of the other party. The majority makes up rules that guarantee that the majority party can govern as a one-party dictatorship instead of a republic, if they just have one more seat in either chamber of Congress. This can lead to essentially no representation for up to 49% of the citizens represented by the minority party.
- These rules can also lead to many citizens believing that unless the party they favor is in the majority in their state, their vote will not matter in presidential elections, and their needs and concerns will not be represented or considered after the election. We should not be surprised, then, that over time, this can lead to a low approval rating for Congress and a low voter turnout rate in most elections. This very much undermines the strength of our democracy.

7. Gerrymandering of congressional districts by both parties has been a regular practice of the majority party in nearly every state following a new census every ten years. The new census each decade triggers the redrawing of congressional district boundaries. But in too many states, the state legislative officials with the power to draw the new voting-district boundaries use the new census data to provide an advantage to the majority party over the minority party in every election for the next ten

years. This is a prime example of both parties, where they are the majority party in the state legislature, putting self-interest and partisan interest over their oath of office to serve the public interest.

As an example of how such an action can enable politicians to maintain their positions as career politicians, consider the following facts:

- The public's approval rating of Congress has for more than a decade been in the range of 9%–19%.
- But over the same period, 90%+ of members of Congress seeking re-election have succeeded in being re-elected.
- This re-election rate compares to less than 50% for incumbents choosing to run for re-election from 1798 to 1900.

8. Regardless of the party that has been in the White House or in the majority in Congress, we have seen Congress engage in deficit spending, continuously raising the national debt. Specifically, the accumulated deficit from 1787 to 1998 was $5,600 billion ($5.6 trillion). This is an average of $28 billion annually over our first 200 years, including the impacts of two world wars and the Great Depression. We had a balanced budget in 1999–2001. Beginning in 2001, the following trends have transpired to add $10,331 billion ($10.3 trillion) to the accumulated debt:

- Under a Republican Administration from 2001 to 2008, upon inheriting a balanced budget, $2,006 billion ($2.0 trillion) was added to the deficit, an average annual deficit of $250.8 billion.
- Under a Democrat Administration from 2009 to 2016, following the greatest economic decline since the Great Depression, $5,727 billion ($5.7 trillion) was added to the deficit, an average annual deficit of $715.8 billion.

- Under a Republican Administration in the first year, 2017, $665 billion was added to the deficit.
- Under the tax cut passed in December of 2017, $833 billion was added to the deficit in 2018, and $1,100 billion ($1.1 trillion) was added in 2019.
- Since 1998, there have been *no* formal annual budgets enacted by Congress before the start of the fiscal year. The last fiscal-year budget enacted on time was in 1997.
- As a result, the accumulated debt of the US government was $22.7 trillion through 2019, pre-pandemic. In this century, in just the past 19 years, we have increased the total accumulated debt by over $15 trillion, an average of $750 billion per year, and a fourfold increase in average annual deficits over the first 200 years.

In reviewing this data, it's important, for context, to remember that we began the 2001 fiscal year with a balanced budget, in fact a small surplus, from 1999 to 2000. Then the Iraq War began in 2001 without any additional revenue added to pay for the additional unplanned expenses of the war. In fact, there was a tax rate cut enacted in 2003 with the purpose of growing the economy enough to pay for itself and the war spending, which did not happen.

In the 2009 fiscal year, in addition to continuing the Iraq War expenses, we suffered the most serious recession to the economy and the financial system since the Great Depression of the late 1920s to early 1930s. Deficit increases reflected the government's financial support for the economy and financial system that peaked in 2011, and then was gradually reduced until 2015.

The tax cut passed in December of 2017, yet again an action designed/promised to increase economic growth more than enough to pay for itself, once again failed to achieve that expected goal. The immediate loss of revenue increased the annual deficits to the highest levels since we came out of the recession. The economic gross domestic product (GDP) growth rate in 2017 was 2.2%, 2.9% in 2018, and 2.3% in 2019. At the time of this writing, the majority of forecasts predict a GDP growth rate of less than 2.0% in 2020—before the coronavirus crisis had impacted economic growth results.

Thus, in the 2017–19 period, deficit spending rose by $2.5 trillion while GDP economic growth averaged 2.6% versus the average 2.3% in the 2013–16 period before the tax cut. So, for a deficit increase of over $2.5 trillion, which is debt that future generations will need to repay, the economy grew only 0.3%, which seems like a pretty bad return for the US taxpayers.

9. As we've noted, Congress has routinely failed to propose, debate and pass a budget before the start of the fiscal year. For at least the past 30 years, under the majority control of either party, Congress has been taking the following actions instead of setting a budget with proper deliberation of both parties in planning the fiscal year's spending:

- Spending for key programs has been approved based on separate continuing resolution bills without an overall budget plan, nor with any accountability for the impact of taxes or spending on the deficit, nor with any detailed analysis of economic trends and factors.
- For most years Congress has been passing spending bills to support government programs without setting expected outcomes, and renews the spending authorization for programs without analyzing the effectiveness of results achieved versus expected outcomes.
- A common practice has been for the majority party in Congress to develop large spending programs for multiple items and the single appropriation bill required to fund them, in a single-party conference of a small number of

the majority party's members. Often, no interaction or consulting with the minority party takes place. Then a comprehensive spending bill, often encompassing as many as 2,000 pages, might be introduced on the floor for a vote by the full House or Senate to approve, with no time for members to read the details of the bill, let alone providing for a meaningful review or debate of the details outside of the partisan committee that drafted the bills.

• When the two parties do compromise, it is often a political bargain to accommodate the special interests of both parties' donors, special interests, and voter bases. The spending increase interests of the Democrat party base and the tax-cut interests of the Republican party base are often combined in a compromise, without regard to the impact on the deficit or overall economic growth. These compromises add to the accumulating national debt which future generations of Americans will be forced to pay interest on and eventually have to pay down, putting the future economic and national security of the country at risk.

10. There is little accountability for the spending on most government programs, or the implementation of legislative programs as intended by Congress and an Administration. Rarely, if ever, will Congress set a specific goal for public programs to achieve, define a specific benefit to be delivered for a specific segment of the public, or predict what the expected outcome of reaching that goal would be, beyond allocating an amount of dollars to businesses or households. And almost never will the performance of public programs be publicly reviewed versus the goals and expected outcomes, before renewing the spending on the program for another fiscal year. Most of the programs are developed and implemented based on ideological goals, and are continued year after year without ever analyzing

or reporting the actual results being achieved.

The major element of oversight for both the Administration and Congress in terms of investigating the misuse of government funds, the abuse of elected and appointed positions, and unethical conduct or conflict of interest, is the office of Inspectors General. However, these roles currently can be too easily dismissed by the President if an investigation touches on the behavior of himself, his family or friends, members of his own party, or his appointed officials in key Administration departments.

11. There is a lack of personal ethics and professional conflict-of-interest standards exhibited by many members of Congress, and elected and appointed members of the Administration. Some examples of these behaviors are as follows:

- First and foremost, putting loyalty to party over country. The members of one party will rarely if ever speak out publicly about the ethical misdeeds, conflicts of interest, or false statements of a member of their own party. This amounts to a failure of ethics in putting their oath of office to the country over their partisan loyalty interests, in protecting majority control for their party at all costs, and in prioritizing their personal need for the party's support for their re-election to continue in office.

  Whatever your view of the processes and the resulting charged offenses and outcome of the recent impeachment trials, it is hard to credit most participants, from either party in either chamber, with putting the interests of country over party, or honestly adhering to their special oaths to "do impartial justice" as jurors. These events seemed to begin and end largely on the basis of party loyalty alone.
- Making false and/or misleading statements to the public

in campaign messages about key issues and other candidates. It has become all too common for members of both parties to make exaggerated charges against individuals of the other party and the other party's policy proposals or actions, based on false or misleading "evidence" or conspiracy theories with no basis in fact. This is considered "politics as usual" in the win-at-all-costs battle between the parties for majority control of government every two years.

- Using their position to provide benefits and advantages to individuals, companies, or associations who make large donations to their campaign. Recently, members of Congress and Cabinet officials have exempted themselves from avoiding conflict-of-interest situations, where these officials have established or maintained a personal financial interest in companies or industries in which they have oversight powers and responsibilities.

12. There is a "revolving door" between politicians and lobbyists that benefits the self-interest of the individuals and special-interest groups in both parties, and their non-governmental special-interest clients. This relationship leads to at least the appearance of a level of corruption in our political processes, given the large contributions to the campaigns and re-election funds of parties and elected officials from lobbying groups, and the number of former elected officials who earn big lobbying income after leaving elected office.

- When elected officials lose elections or choose to leave elected office, many of them simply move to the "other side" of the lobbying process, and begin lobbying elected officials for major individual, company or association donors.
- Due to the familiarity with current elected officials, in

Congress and in the Administration, and their staffs, it is relatively easy for former elected officials to obtain meetings and to understand how to leverage contributions from lobbying clients to obtain special considerations from elected officials to benefit their clients—whether these considerations are in the best interests of the country or only in the interests of the lobbying client, the lobbyist and the elected official.

- Lobbying activities are required to be reported quarterly by clients and lobbying companies. Donations received by elected officials and staffs are required to be reported under Federal Election Laws. But it seems that these reports are so dispersed in official records that they have limited visibility to the public. Also, there are "lump sums" donated by individuals to elected officials that are apparently not required to be tied to specific issues or legislation.

- In the previous Administration, there have been four Cabinet-level officials overseeing industries where they have previously served as major industry lobbyists. It seems fair to question whether in such cases, the loyalty of those folks is to the country, to their own financial interests, or to the companies and leaders of the industries where they have realized substantial financial gains.

There may well be other actions that are of concern to citizens in how the government operates. The purpose of this book is not to provide a detailed cataloging of all problems, but to provide a solution that could help minimize the problems listed as well as the unlisted ones. These problems are numerous enough in quantity and comprehensive enough in scope to provide the basis for a separate rich discussion, in other books, of changes in how Congress operates. But hopefully, the solutions presented herein will succeed in providing a meaningful improvement to the focus of Congress on serving the nation instead of their own interests, their party's interests, or the interests of special-interest donors.

* * *

The next section of this chapter will open a discussion on the root causes of these actions, an important understanding to have before the options of specific changes to be made can be defined as objective, non-partisan and effective for the country.

Step 2—Identifying the Root Causes of Unrealized Outcomes

1. Money in politics. Major donors and lobbyists have too large an impact on how Congress governs—career politicians enter Congress as middle class, and leave as multimillionaires.

- The Federal Election Commission, independent and bipartisan, cannot limit contributions of individuals to PACs, and contributions of groups to parties and congressional members.
- Donations by individuals to PACs and other issue advocacy groups are not required to be disclosed, creating a huge source of "dark money" influencing our policy and election decisions. This lack of required transparency makes it easy for excessive contributions, including those coming from foreign sources, to exert unfair influence on our elected officials and our government.
- Campaigns seem to start for the next election within weeks of completing the most recent election. This results in almost no break in campaign spending, increasing the emphasis on raising money constantly and leading to election-messaging "burnout" among many voters.
- When under the majority control of either party, Congress

has consistently failed to manage the federal budget responsibly. Since the parties worked together to balance the budget in 1999–2000, both parties have responded to the demands of their bases—one to lower taxes and one to raise spending—without regard for the impact on the national economy or debt. Spending and tax programs are passed and continued without accountability for whether they are achieving the goals or purposes intended.

- The operating and travel budgets for the Administration and members of Congress and their staffs are rarely reported or specifically debated and approved publicly. This leads to little or no public accountability for the size or growth of these budgets, nor for the compliance of individual members of Congress with guidelines for operating within the budget.

2. Partisanship. Elected officials put party loyalty and self-interest above fulfilling the oath of office and serving the nation.

- Each party has locked itself into narrow ideological beliefs about the policies and ideologies that are best for the country overall. Each party regards its beliefs as the only "right" policies, and the other party's policies as "wrong" or even dangerous for the country.
- Major policies impacting the entire country are often drafted by small committees of one party without the input of the other party. Bills proposed by members of the minority party can be blocked by the Speaker of the House or the Senate Majority Leader from coming to the floor.
- The competition for power and control between the parties has reached the point in the past few decades where "winning at all costs" has become the driving force on both sides. The focus is not on competing for the best

ideas to serve the nation, but on competing for the control to implement ideas targeted to their own partisan and donor bases.

- Politicians from both parties seek to unfairly rig election processes when they have majority control in state legislatures. They seek to provide an unfair advantage for candidates from their party, by "gerrymandering" district boundaries, to sustain their positions without really competing for them or having to serve the needs of all citizens.

- There is little or no willingness to hold members in their own party accountable for any policy or personal actions while in office. The loyalty to party seems to exceed loyalty to law, expected standards of ethical behavior, and avoidance of conflict of interest.

- Congressional members support the party leaders and the Administration when the President is of the same party, and they tend to oppose the majority party and the Administration when the President is not of the same party. There is little effort to work together on policies for the benefit of the country overall.

- Congressional members who don't support the party leaders or the Administration of their party will likely find themselves facing a primary election challenge from within their own party.

3. Career self-interest. Politicians focus on their own re-election over serving the country.

- Many elected officials know that to protect their careers from election to election, they need the following:
  - Support of the party leaders to receive committee assignments;
  - Party support in primary elections (i.e. no challenges

from within the party);

- ○ Support of donors and party leaders to fund re-election campaigns.
- As a result, individual members generally follow the lead of the party leadership in voting on legislation as a united party, failing to represent the interests of constituents from the other party.
- Individual members in each party will rarely meet with or work with colleagues from the other party in developing or supporting legislation, so bipartisan legislation is extremely rare.
- Members meet within party caucuses and support party priorities in legislation to the 90%–95% of votes, too often developing legislation without input from the other party. These actions set up partisan conflicts that are played out with the press and the public to strengthen positions appealing to their base voters.

The next step in the process is to analyze the root causes listed above and identify potential solutions to overcome the root causes. The options discussed below have been developed with as much objective, non-partisan analysis as possible related to each of the key root causes listed above.

Step 3—Identifying Potential Solutions to Overcome the Root Causes

1. To overcome the root causes of **money in politics**, we might consider the following actions to be part of the new "Citizen Rules" to be included as proposed Amendments to the Constitution:

- Declare that money is not speech, extending the principle of "one person, one vote" for access to and influence of elected officials. This would involve setting limits on political contributions each year for all individuals based on a reasonable and affordable percentage of average middle-class income.

○ This could be accomplished by enabling the Federal Election Commission to set limits on all contributions from individual citizens to any political entity each year—to a party, a member of the Administration or of Congress, or to any issue action group or Political Action Committee (PAC).

○ The new laws would also prohibit contributions from non-citizens, and limit contributions from companies, associations, unions and any political issue group to all candidates and to any political entities involved in supporting candidates in federal elections. This limit would be equal to the limit set for individual citizens.

○ This law would also require that all donations by individuals to candidates for or members of Congress, to associations or unions, and to political issue groups and PACs be maintained and publicly disclosed by all those entities accepting such contributions.

○ Finally, this new law would require that all companies, associations, unions and political issue groups and PACs maintain records of all contributions made to candidates, parties, political issue groups, PACs, and so on.

• Limit the period of campaign message spending by all federal election candidates to the calendar year in which the election will be held. Certainly ten months of campaign messages is sufficient for candidates to make their cases and voters to make their choices in November elections.

• Establish an independent non-partisan commission to oversee the fairness of congressional districts and require revisions to politically, racially, or otherwise biased congressional district boundaries.

- Require more accountability and transparency in how Congress spends public funds; specifically:
  - ◦ A balanced budget each fiscal year, except when a declared state of war or national emergency is passed formally by both Houses of Congress and signed by the President.
  - ◦ That spending be set first based on national needs, including a target for economic growth and employment levels, and then that the required taxes to provide the required income to fully fund the spending be set afterward.
  - ◦ Pass separate bills for each major spending program, and for separate items in the tax plan to provide federal income; prohibit the packaging of separate issues into one bill.
  - ◦ All programs spending public money must have annual goals, expected outcomes, and transparent discussion of benefits versus costs, all reported to the public, and an annual review of all programs spending public money must be reported to the public and used as the basis for continuing, changing or stopping them in succeeding years.
  - ◦ Provide separate transparency and public accountability for Administration and congressional operating and travel budgets. Hold individual elected and appointed officials accountable for improper management of public budgets.
- Prohibit members of Congress, their staffs and Administration officials from working as paid lobbyists when they leave office.

2. To overcome the root causes of **partisanship**, we might

consider the impact of the following actions:

- Political leaders from both parties would need to focus primarily on their oath of office to support and defend the Constitution, and to serve and unify the nation. The only way to unite the country is behind policies that represent the diverse needs and concerns of the country overall. Focusing on policies that appeal only to one party's base will never unite the country, nor develop the policies that would be effective for most of the country.
- Congress would be required to operate under a new set of "Citizen Rules." In part, these rules would require a specified number of session days between a bill coming to the floor and taking a vote, to allow time for reading and understanding of the bill by members, and for debate on the floor. Also, the rules would require that bills proposed by a small group of members of either chamber must be brought to the floor for a vote within a specified number of session days to allow time for review by committee. These actions would remove the absolute power of majority-party leaders in the House and Senate to control which proposed bills are brought to the floor for a vote.
- These new "Citizen Rules" would further require that in order to pass legislation in either chamber, Congress would need a bipartisan majority vote, not just a majority vote of one party. Specifically, the rules would require that the majority vote to approve or pass any legislation would include a minimum number of the total approval vote to come from the minority party. While this action would give the minority party the power to block or obstruct legislation, it would also require the parties to work together to pass any legislation. And it would prevent any major "one party" policies from passing that would address the interests of the majority party but not

address the concerns of most Americans.

- Since the need to have party support for the next election seems to result in most members placing loyalty to party above a willingness to work with the other party, and refusing to hold their own party members accountable for improper actions, the new "Citizen Rules" would limit congressional members to serving only one term and they would be prohibited from running for any other office while serving. This would help ensure that elected officials would have only one focus after taking the oath of office, that of serving the country. They would also have the 40% of time spent today on campaigning while in office to spend working on legislation with the other party to serve the overall needs of the country.

The key benefit we are seeking in reducing the period of service to one term—a four-year term for House Members and a six-year term for Senators—is to limit the influence of donors, party loyalty and career self-interest on the actions of elected officials while in office. A two- or three-term limit would still result in members spending time seeking donations and support for their next election while serving, until their final term. Only a one-term limit will ensure that congressional members do not spend time focused on their next election while in office instead of being focused entirely on serving the country.

Since there would not be the opportunity for a political career and a path to wealth from a career in Congress, perhaps we might get candidates who choose to make the sacrifice to serve in Congress out of patriotism, like those who serve in the military. That would seem to make it more likely that these new and different congressional members could put country over party and work together to solve our key issues. Imagine what innovative approaches to solving our major national issues might result.

3. Here are some additional specific issues to be addressed and the changes that would help overcome **career self-interest**, ensuring that our elected members of Congress would work on addressing the needs and concerns of the nation, versus their own careers and donor and partisan interests:

- Congress should not continue to set their own compensation, health, and retirement benefits. New "Citizen Rules" would define a process for setting the compensation and benefits for members of Congress and other government executives and employees.
  - Tie congressional compensation to the military pay scale. They only get a raise when the military gets a raise. Other politically appointed officials would have compensation scaled appropriately versus the selected congressional pay levels.
  - Congressional healthcare benefits for members and their families would need to be acquired in the same way and from the same sources as those used by the American people for independent healthcare; this would also prohibit Congress from setting up their own healthcare benefits.
  - Since Congress members would only serve for one term, there would be no need for a retirement program involving a pension or lifetime benefit. Congressional members would be expected to add to their own retirement accounts, IRAs and 401(k)s during their one term in office.
- How do we avoid or at least minimize conflicts of interest with members of Congress?
  - Candidates would be required to release ten years of tax returns upon filing as a federal candidate, and to put all financial and commercial property assets into blind trusts with third-party trustees before taking the

oath of office.

- Would these concerns extend to the Administration and executive officers as well?
  - Yes, from President, to Vice President, to senior non-professional staff, to Cabinet and sub-Cabinet-level officials who require Senate confirmation.

4. Should congressional members continue to set their own rules of operation of the legislative process for Congress? Or should the new "Citizen Rules" coming from a citizen-led movement define new rules for how legislative processes should operate?

- What changes in the legislative process rules would make Congress more effective in working together, avoiding one-party governing, and in serving the country overall instead of just one party's base?
  - As suggested earlier, we could consider requiring all legislation passed by a majority vote to include a minimum of 5% support from the minority party. This would eliminate one-party control over the legislative process and require that the parties work together to get results for the American people. Since members would be volunteering to serve just a single term in choosing to run for elected office, it is unlikely they would make the sacrifice to serve and make no impact during their one term by merely obstructing all legislative proposals.
- Should there be more votes and fewer caucus and committee meetings about who will vote how?
  - Consider that without spending 40% of their time focused on the next election, congressional members would be able to be more productive in developing effective policies for the country.
  - The new "Citizen Rules" would require that

congressional committees should provide reviews of and recommendations on proposed legislation in a timely manner prior to being considered by the full chamber for a debate and vote, but should not be able to block votes on legislation.

- Should the majority party and senior members have complete power over what laws come to the floor for a vote?
  - No, the new "Citizen Rules" would require proposed bills with at least 10% of the chamber members as co-sponsors to be reviewed by the relevant committee and presented on the floor within 20 session days, and voted on no earlier than three days after being presented on the floor to provide time for reading and understanding the bill, but no later than six session days after being presented on the floor.

5. Should we modify the congressional budgeting and spending processes?

- Is a balanced budget important as a requirement?
  - Consider that, at present, the interest on the national debt takes up 7%–8% of the total federal budget, even at historically low interest rates of about 2%. If interest rates rise to 5% or even 8%, levels seen in the not-too-distant past, then interest on the debt could rise to a staggering 15%–25% of the total federal budget. Interest on the debt would then become the single biggest expense in the federal budget. This outcome would either cripple our country with much higher tax rates or reduce our ability to fund necessary programs.
- What does it mean to say: "We can no longer afford to..."?
  - Consider that we built the world's leading economy after World War II with a top personal tax rate of 91%

for the 15 years from 1948 to 1963, and a business tax rate of 50%. With those funds, under both Democrat and Republican Administrations, the country sent over 4 million World War II veterans to college to provide a skilled and educated workforce; built the interstate highway system to provide a twentieth-century infrastructure; paid down most of the World War II war debt, instead of passing the debt forward to our generation; and invested in rebuilding the economies of our World War II allies and enemies, setting the foundation for a more peaceful world after two world wars over just three decades.

Doesn't "we can't afford to" mean that "we don't want to" spend money on a program? It means the majority party does not see that the need being addressed is important to their base, but may or may not be important to nearly half the country. We should not be reluctant to provide the federal income for major, important needs of the country overall. Unless we are in a time of declared war or national emergency, we should be willing to pay for the programs needed by the country overall or by large segments of the country, and should not borrow for necessary spending, passing that debt on to future generations to pay. Over the past 70 years, the economy in many decades has grown significantly during periods of higher tax rates than we have today or have seen in recent years. The key is whether the tax revenues are allocated to programs that actually benefit the country and the overall economy, or not. And whether or not the programs that receive public funding are effective in the positive impacts they are designed to achieve.

6. Should we handle multi-year programs like military weapons and infrastructure differently than planning for this year's

spending needs?

- Consider that military weapons and infrastructure programs invest in resources that have a useful life many years after they are purchased, while many other programs, such as education and welfare benefits, have a benefit that only lasts during the same year of the spending. Thus from a budgeting standpoint, it may make sense to budget for those longer impact expenses to be paid over the expected life of the weapon or infrastructure element, and budget for other programs to be paid in the current year.
- Are we transparent enough in publicizing the budget once approved, and the progress in managing the budget versus the approved targets, during and at the end of the year?
  - Consider a possible new requirement that the budget must be made public in a very simple overview format, not just at the beginning of the fiscal year, but updated after each quarter, showing the actual results versus the planned budget for the key categories of federal income and spending by major category, and the net surplus or deficit. The public would then be able to easily see the specifics of any changes in spending levels versus budget by category, in the changes in income levels versus budget by category, and of the impact of these changes to the deficit versus the budget.
  - With this information, the sources of variances to specific spending categories and in different economic situations would be clear, and remedial actions could be more objectively developed, discussed, and agreed upon by the Congress, with the full transparency for and understanding of the public that can lead to united

support for subsequent actions.

- What about the bundling of unrelated appropriations and policies together in one "omnibus" bill? How to best address a change to this practice—by line-item veto, or single-item rules?
  - ○ Consider requiring all bills with distinct issues to be voted upon separately. A line-item veto still shields the congressional members from individual public accountability for their votes on each issue, and shifts it to the President. Holding separate votes on each distinct issue of spending and revenue would prevent the bundling of special-interest bills in with major bills for the country and forcing approval without a separate public vote.

7. Is it important to improve the fairness, honesty and integrity of federal campaigns?

- How do we feel about the unlimited money, from unlimited donations, being spent during campaigns? What changes might help improve fairness?
  - ○ We have previously mentioned changing the Constitution to declare "money is not speech" and to require limits on both the amounts of contributions and the duration of campaign spending in election years. But even with limits on money, there are other issues to consider regarding the fairness of elections, as discussed below.
- Are we concerned that candidates, parties or special-interest groups run false or misleading messages about opponents and policy issues?
  - ○ It seems that false messages have become the major tactic used by candidates in both parties. It's not only that the messages are negative about their opponent

instead of positive about their own ideas; too many of the messages are intentionally false, or edited to be misleading. This seems to be more like manipulation of voters rather than enabling educated decisions by the voters based on truth, facts, and better understanding.

- What about providing fair and equitable access to voter registration and voting processes, while also ensuring no significant level of election fraud that would unfairly change election results?

  ◦ It seems that with the technology available today, which provides identity security for individuals in many areas such as credit cards, social security, direct mail, computer platforms, utility billing, and so on, it would be fairly easy to design a voter registration and identity confirmation system that makes access equitable for all citizens and secure from fraud.

  ◦ Recently we have seen many states change their voting laws under the premise of enhancing election security. However, none of these changes are based on any factual evidence of problems or significant fraud levels in recent elections. Since the equity of access to voting is a core right in our democracy, shouldn't states be required to present specific evidence of problems or fraud in elections and clear definitions of the causes to be "fixed" by the changes in election law being proposed? Should changes to these important laws be made based on proven facts, not unfounded partisan claims, rumors or theories?

- What about conflicts of interest, or elected officials realizing personal financial gains from their actions as elected officials? Are we concerned about these actions?

  ◦ Just as with our military service people, don't we expect our elected officials to act without corruption? Don't we expect them to put their oath of office to serve

111

the Constitution and the country ahead of their own self-interests, and not seek to profit personally from their positions? Isn't *not* doing so the very definition of corruption?

○ We mentioned earlier the changes that would minimize these potential conflicts: (a) requiring the release of tax returns when filing as a candidate for federal office or when nominated for a position in an Administration post requiring Senate confirmation; and (b) requiring investments, commercial property assets and business ownerships to be placed into a blind trust administered by a third-party trustee before taking the oath of office.

○ However, history has shown that this requirement alone will be a major benefit but probably not sufficient for combating conflicts of interest. We should also require that new ethics laws be passed to provide significant financial penalties and loss of office if a person is guilty of such action. For elected federal officials, actions that involve personally benefiting from official decisions would need to be specified as a "high crime and misdemeanor" in the Constitution by amendment.

Step 4—Developing an Action Plan to Implement the Best Solution Options

Key question: Are there new solutions for getting better results from Congress that are *not* based on the political ideology from just one side of the political spectrum? What would non-partisan, "win-win" solutions require of congressional members? What might these solutions look like?

• "Win-win" solutions are the only solutions that will build a strong, united country. Partisan solutions may appear to be lose-win or win-lose between the parties, but over the long term, they are actually lose-lose, when the country's unity depends on the parties to act interdependently with each other. "Win-win" solutions require both sides to care that the other side has a "win" in the solution as much as they care about a "win" for themselves. Isn't that the principle recorded in the last sentence of the Declaration of Independence, that the strength of our country depends on a commitment to our *inter*dependence?

- Military units and teams reflect that sense of putting their unit, team or country above personal gain or benefit. If we can remove the influences of money, partisanship and career self-interest from our elected leaders, and have Citizen Rules made for how Congress operates that encourage working together, then perhaps we can reclaim a government that serves the nation, minimize divisiveness and reunite our country.

In Which Areas of the Operation in Congress Would We Like to See Changes?

We've reviewed several area of problems that have arisen from the influences of money, partisanship, and career self-interest, combined with the power of our leaders to make the rules for how Congress operates. What follows now is a suggested list of specific changes in the rules for how Congress operates that will eliminate or minimize these influences in our politics and should result in members of Congress who choose to run for election out of a desire to serve, instead of to be served.

All these changes will be resisted by the existing parties, members of Congress, politically appointed executives, and most political issue groups and PACs, and of course wealthy donors who consistently make large donations; essentially all the people and organizations who benefit from the current system. All of these changes will need to be implemented as

Amendments to the Constitution for them to be permanent. And since several involve changing existing elements of the current Constitution, they must be ratified as new Amendments or they would be subject to the judgment of the Supreme Court versus the current Constitution. We will discuss *how* these changes can be implemented after reviewing *what* the specific changes are.

Reviewing the "Citizen Rules" Changes We'd Like to See Happen

Here is a review of the key changes first listed in the Introduction that, if implemented together, would put in place new "Citizen Rules" for the operation of Congress to more strongly support the national interest:

1. Setting term limits, compensation, and health and retirement benefits for members of Congress and senior Administration officials
2. Defining new rules for the legislative processes to limit partisanship; confirming primacy of "Citizen Rules" in the Constitution over procedural rules enacted by members of Congress
3. Defining timing requirements for Senate votes on treaties and presidential appointments; limiting the duration of acting presidential appointments; limiting absolute presidential reprieves and pardons
4. Strengthening congressional oversight of executive implementation; strengthening the independence of Inspectors General and key executive departments in the Administration
5. Defining rules for budgeting, taxing and spending processes: balance, timing, accountability, transparency, and effectiveness
6. Prohibiting Congress members from paid lobbying roles after serving in Congress or the Administration

7. Prohibiting laws exempting Congress from laws enacted on citizens

8. Changing the allocation and certification of Electoral College votes in presidential elections

9. Limiting the terms of Supreme Court justices and federal court judges

10. Ensuring fair and equitable access to registration and voting for all citizens, and elections free from fraud

11. Defining rules for campaign financing — donation limits and disclosure requirements

12. Defining rules for truthful messaging and timing of campaign advertising

13. Providing an independent council to oversee voting-district alignments after census

14. Defining rules for ethical behaviors and financial conflict of interest, and for handling non-salary personal income for President, Vice President, and all senior elected and appointed officials

15. Defining a non-partisan judicial process for impeachment and actions considered as impeachable offenses

16. Establishing a program of required national service for all citizens between the ages of 18 and 29.

Each of these changes will be discussed in some detail in the following chapters. We will attempt to look at both the benefits and the risks of each of these changes, so the reader has an opportunity to consider the value of each change independently, versus maintaining the existing situation, and to see how by working together they might provide the benefits to the country we've discussed above.

But Congress is not the only element of our society where service to self-interest has replaced service to country. Our freedom as a country and as citizens is not free or guaranteed to survive without the constant attention to serving the country's interests, not just by elected and appointed leaders, but by citizens as well.

Thus, in addition to ensuring that our elected representatives choose to run for office for the primary purpose of serving the country, there is another group critical to the quality of our democracy that we must address as well—our citizens. For as we quoted in the Introduction, President John F. Kennedy reminded us that "the kind of government we get depends upon how we fulfill those responsibilities [of the office of citizen]."

So the final change on our list is to formally require all citizens between the ages of 18 and 29 to complete a two-year period of public service. Citizens can choose to serve in the military; as police, firefighters or first responders; as teachers in under-resourced and poorly performing schools; as doctors, nurses or other healthcare providers in under-served communities; as lawyers or legal counsel to community service organizations; or in other local community service roles. This service can be completed anytime after high school graduation, or after college graduation, after attaining skilled certification, or after completing graduate school education, as long as the service commences no later than the twenty-eighth birthday and is completed no later than the thirtieth birthday.

These roles are not volunteer roles; each role would require meeting entry-level qualification requirements; would provide training and build skills, resulting in personal development; would include accountability for meeting expected results; and would provide appropriate compensation and benefits, including the opportunity for college or trade-school tuition support after service. Naturalized citizens who attain their citizenship after their eighteenth birthday but before their twenty-first birthday would also be obligated to complete the National Service Program requirement.

In the next chapter, we will explore details of how these

changes could impact the operation of Congress in governing the country, and the overall nature of our politics.

Chapter 4

Looking at the Details of the Changes

In this chapter, we will explore in more detail each of the 16 changes that collectively represent a major portion of the proposed Citizen Rules for how Congress operates. These would replace many of the rules that elected members have defined in order to sustain the influences of partisanship and seniority in how Congress governs. We will also discuss additional changes that are outside of the rules defined by Congress, but will have a strong positive impact on achieving the overarching goals of reducing the influence of career self-interest, partisanship and major donors on congressional members and across government.

1. (a) Setting term limits for members of Congress

- Eliminate the impact of re-election so that officials focus on serving the country instead of party interests, special interests and career self-interest. Running for re-election brings in the influences of money, partisanship and career self-interest during the time members are supposed to be serving the country. Even if limited to two or three terms, much of the first one to two terms will be taken up in raising funds and campaigning for the next election. With a single term, all fundraising and campaigning would be done before taking the oath of office, so all time and decisions while in office can be focused on serving the country. And there would be no influence exerted by having to run in a primary that might limit the intention to work collaboratively with the other party and risk not being re-elected. In addition, the preferences given currently to the seniority of members in filling congressional leadership roles would be greatly reduced. But a single two-year term for House members would be too short. Thus, the proposal would be to set term limits to one six-year term for Senate members, electing one-third every two years as we do currently; and one four-year term for House members, electing one-half every two years instead of electing all members every two years.

1. (b) Setting compensation levels for members of Congress and senior Administration officials

- Remove the ability of Congress to set their own pay levels. Tie congressional pay levels to the military pay scale. Remove special pay and benefits for congressional leaders except officers named in the Constitution. Future congressional raises will only come when Congress raises the military pay scale. Politically appointed senior Administration executive pay levels would be indexed to the congressional pay level.

1. (c) Defining health and retirement benefits for members of Congress

- Healthcare benefits
  - Remove special healthcare benefit programs for Congress. Congressional members would be required to obtain healthcare benefits from their salaries in the same marketplace as individual Americans who are not covered by a corporate, organizational or union benefit program. This will greatly increase the personal understanding by members of Congress of the impacts of the national healthcare system that most citizens must operate within.

- Retirement benefits
  - Members of Congress would not receive any retirement benefits, as they would only serve one term and cannot run for election to any other office while serving. They would participate in individual, private IRAs and 401(k)s as the majority of Americans do, but receive no lifetime retirement benefit. They would be eligible for a matched contribution limit set by Congress that is consistent with the average matched compensation levels existing in the private sector. They would also receive a modest "relocation allowance" to return to private life after serving their term.

2. Defining new rules for the legislative process to limit partisanship; strengthening congressional oversight of executive implementation

- Require single-issue legislation, and prohibit omnibus bills. Require each bill to include only one issue to be voted on and approved separately by both Houses and signed by the President. Budget bills should be voted on to provide overall goals for spending, revenue and deficit levels for the fiscal year, before individual spending and tax bills are approved. The programs that require government spending and the tax programs that provide the revenues for these programs should be voted on as individual elements of each package.
- Spending and tax proposals during the fiscal year should be consistent with the overall goals on spending, taxes, and deficit levels approved in the fiscal year's budget.
- Reduce the power of the committee system, and that of individual majority-party leaders, in controlling which bills come to the floor for a vote. Require any bill that is co-sponsored by at least 10% of the members in each

chamber to be brought to the floor of that chamber for a vote within 20 session days. Once introduced on the floor, a vote must follow no sooner than three session days, to allow time for members to read bills and debate. A vote must be held no later than six session days after its introduction. The 20 session days allows time for a committee hearing and recommendation for the full chamber before coming to the floor.

- Require that a minimum of 5% of the majority votes to approve all bills, and to confirm all presidential appointments or removals of appointed officials, be from the minority party or parties. This requirement ensures that all legislation passed in Congress will have to consider the needs, concerns and interests of the overall country and not just one party. This ensures that bills are not passed with just the majority party's votes. If the minority party's input is not included, then the input from representatives of perhaps 40%–45% of the citizens would be excluded. While this requirement also enables the minority to block legislation, by having eliminated or reduced the influence of career self-interest, extreme partisanship and major donors on members under the single-term limit, we should have an environment where collaboration between the parties should prevail.
  - Each House may determine the details of other rules of its proceedings for areas that are not defined within the Constitution or Amendments as new "Citizen Rules." By including the Citizen Rules as Amendments to the Constitution, both Houses are required to adhere to the Citizen Rules in their proceedings as constitutional obligations.
  - The Inspectors General role is to provide non-partisan professional oversight of the administrative departments in implementing congressional laws

via regulations and enforcement, and compliance of officials with conflict-of-interest laws, or to investigate possible abuses of positional authority. This element will provide a level of protection from political interference in their activities by requiring that any removal of an Inspector General by the President be confirmed by the Senate, providing a measure of congressional oversight of the President's power to replace Inspectors General.

3. Defining timing requirements for Senate confirmation voting on presidential appointments; limit the duration of acting presidential appointments; limit absolute presidential reprieves and pardons

- Require the Senate to bring all nominations made by the President for appointments required in the Constitution to the floor for a vote of the full Senate within 60 session days of the nomination.
  - ○ The Constitution requires the Senate to provide "advice and consent" to key presidential appointments. This requirement doesn't require the Senate to approve any individual nominee. But it does require the Senate to hold hearings (necessary for advice) and provide an up-or-down vote (necessary for giving or withholding consent) within the 60 session days of the nomination. The Constitution, in Article 2, Section 2, does not give the Senate majority party leader the authority to withhold a vote by the full Senate. This element adds clarity to that section of the Constitution and avoids false interpretation by elected officials.
  - ○ The 60-day session period allows time for full committee and individual Senator reviews of each candidate before voting. If a vote does not occur

within the 60-day session period, the Senate members will permanently forfeit all pay for each day the vote is delayed. Forfeited pay will *not* be reinstated after a vote is held if beyond the 60-day session period.

○ All Senate confirmation votes are approved by a majority vote, with the requirement that at least 5% of the approval vote comes from the minority party or parties.

○ No Supreme Court justice or federal judge appointments should be made by the President within 120 days of the date of a national election for President. Any vacancies that occur after that date will require a nomination by the succeeding President and confirmation by a new Senate.

• Limit the time to serve for an "acting" Cabinet or key Administration position requiring a Senate confirmation to 60 days without a formal nomination for the position being announced by the President. "Acting" roles are designed only to provide limited continuity between confirmed appointments, and should not be used to circumvent the oversight that a formal Senate confirmation provides.

• The presidential authority to grant pardons and reprieves for offenses against the United States was established as an absolute power of the President, to be exempt from oversight by Congress. However, this absolute power has led to several questionable pardons and commutation of sentences for presidential friends and acquaintances in past years, by presidents of both parties. Without oversight, this authority could be used in a corrupt manner to pardon people who are involved in unethical or illegal actions at the direction of, or in partnership with, the President.

○ There would be a new requirement that presidential

pardons, reprieves and commutation of sentences must be reviewed and confirmed by the Senate. This would provide a degree of oversight for the pardoning process, limiting the prospect of potential corruption on the part of any President in using this power for his own personal benefits and friends.

4. Strengthening congressional oversight of executive implementation; strengthening the independence of Inspectors General and key executive departments within the Administration

- Provide protections for the independence of key executive departments specified below from interference by the President for reasons of personal or political benefit.
  - Traditionally, all presidential appointees in the executive departments of the Administration serve at the pleasure of the President. For over 200 years, there has been respect for a "firewall" between the President and the operation of the justice and the military departments, and more recently, the national security and intelligence agencies, and the Internal Revenue Service under the Department of the Treasury.
  - As a nation, we have realized that if the President were to directly interfere in the investigative decisions in the Justice Department, we could lose the principle of "fair justice applied impartially and without bias to all citizens." In addition, there would be too great an opportunity for corrupt action from the President to stop investigations against his interests, family or friends, and to start investigations against political opponents or the companies that support them or that they represent. A similar concern exists with the operation of the Internal Revenue Service and the

private information they hold on citizens, and the decisions they make to investigate citizens' financial activities.

○ Thus, key positions within the executive branch will be provided with an extra degree of independence in the conduct of their positions. Specifically, once appointed and confirmed by the Senate, any actions involving removal and/or reassignment of these officials shall be reviewed by the appropriate Senate committee, and shall only be carried out with the advice and consent of the full Senate. The positions covered by this requirement are as follows:

  ‣ The Attorney General of the United States, the Directors of the FBI and CIA, and all appointed US Attorneys;

  ‣ The senior military officers who serve as chairman and members of the Joint Chiefs of Staff, and the senior officers of each of the military services branches;

  ‣ The Directors of National Intelligence and the National Security Agency;

  ‣ The Treasurer of the United States and Commissioner of the Internal Revenue Service.

• Inspectors General are appointed by the President with the advice and consent of the Senate. Their role is to serve in every Administration department to oversee the appropriate implementation of legislative programs and accountability for public spending and budgets, and to conduct investigations when appropriate into possible offenses of ethical or moral violations, legal offenses, conflict of interest, or abuse of position offenses.

  ○ The independence of the Inspectors General from partisan political influences is key to the effective oversight they are appointed to provide. While part of the executive branch, and part of each department's leadership team, no Inspector General can be removed only by the President, but any removal will require the advice and consent of the Senate. All charges of poor performance or unethical offenses by Inspectors General must be brought before the Senate committee for review. The removal of Inspectors General recommended by the President must be approved by a majority vote of the full Senate (with the 5% minority participation requirement in the majority as discussed above).

∘ When recommended by the President, the Senate must conduct a review of the reasons for dismissal or reassignment of an Inspector General, and a vote to confirm or reverse the removal or reassignment must be held within 30 session days of the President's recommendation of the removal or reassignment. If a vote does not occur within the 30-day session period, the Senate members will permanently forfeit all pay for each day the vote is delayed. Forfeited pay will *not* be reinstated after a vote is held beyond the 30-day session period.

∘ Each Inspector General must provide at least an annual report to the Congress, the President and the public on the effectiveness of administrative executive departments, on the implementation of legislation, and the results versus expected outcomes for all programs that involve the spending of public funds.

5. Defining rules for a budgeting process — balanced, transparent, timetabled, accountable, effective

• Require that each new Congress, elected every two years, develop and approve a two-year budget bill before the start of the next fiscal year. This bill would set the overall spending and taxing revenue targets in each major category, and the resulting surplus or deficit target for the fiscal year.

○ This budget bill would include the official forecast of the target deficit for the fiscal year, and would be added to the accumulated debt level from previous years to determine the new debt-level target for the government, as a required element of the budget plan. The debt limit is not subject to a separate process apart from the formal fiscal-year budget process establishing spending, revenue, and annual deficit or surplus targets for the coming fiscal year.

• Require that annual fiscal-year spending and tax bills be presented and voted on separately to implement the actions outlined in the two-year budget bill. In spending bills, each major program should be presented in its own bill, including specific goals and benefits for the program to achieve, and voted on separately. In tax bills, each major tax program should be presented in its own bill and each tax voted on separately, including taxes that are tied to specific spending bills.

○ These annual fiscal-year spending and tax bills must fit within the targets of the approved two-year budget and deficit targets, or a new two-year budget and deficit target, which must be approved in a separate preceding vote. Long-term military and infrastructure program spending would be proposed with total spending and expected lifetime, with the projected spending plan over time to complete the total funding needed. This projected spending plan would be used to set the annual spending for the appropriate year of the budget being authorized.

○ All programs that spend public money must be

presented with clear goals, objectives, benefits to be provided for the country or to specific groups of citizens, and the expected outcomes to be realized, including the efficiency of the program in achieving the desired outcomes. At the end of each fiscal year, results for all spending programs will be evaluated and compared to the objectives and desired outcomes defined and publicly reported, before any continuation or reauthorization of spending.

- Require that all budget, spending and tax bills be approved by a simple majority, with a minimum of 5% of the majority votes from the minority party or parties. As with element 4 above, this bipartisan approval requirement is designed to ensure that the federal budget, spending, tax revenues, and deficit or surplus plans are not developed based on the priorities of a single party, but reflect the overall needs of the country, as represented by the input of both parties.

- Require that the tax code eliminate all existing special deductions and credits, so that the actual tax paid by individuals and businesses would essentially be the same as the published tax rate. Short-term adjustments to tax rates could be passed in exchange for specific investments that will benefit the overall economy. When published tax rates are set comparable to the actual effective tax rates actually paid by individuals and businesses after current deductions, the published tax rates will be lower than the published rates today.

  ○ Eliminating deductions and credits, the major source of special-interest lobbying and major donor contributions to campaigns, will ensure that any business making a profit pays some level of federal income tax. Today we have over 50 major companies who collectively reported hundreds of billions of profit, yet paid no federal income tax. Many others pay a lower effective tax rate than much smaller businesses, and some even lower than their employees who earn much less income.

∘ In addition, this action will reduce the special interest and major donor influence on members of Congress. Elimination of deductions would also simplify tax return preparation and increase transparency of business profitability and business and personal tax liability. In business taxes, the extensive and complex list of deductions and credits results in an advantage for large businesses over small businesses. The large businesses can afford specialized tax advisors to enable them to minimize their tax liability, which small businesses cannot afford. As a result of simplifying business taxes, the disadvantage for small businesses, the drivers of job and economic growth, would be removed.

• Replace "continuing spending resolutions" with the requirement to issue a two-year budget at the opening of each new Congress, to be approved *before* the start of each fiscal year. Specifically, Congress would be required to approve budgets for each fiscal year at least ten session days before the start of the fiscal year.

• Require that congressional pay be forfeited if the budget is not passed on time. For each day beyond the ten-day session requirement that the budget is not passed in advance of the start of the new fiscal year, members of both Houses will permanently forfeit all pay until the budget is passed and sent to the President. Forfeited pay by congressional members will *not* be reinstated after the budget is approved, but pay of staff and contractors would be reinstated if the delay in any spending programs resulted in layoffs of staff or contractors.

- Require that the budget be balanced, except when there is a declared war or national emergency. New spending approved during the fiscal year that increases the deficit level must be offset by revenue increase or spending reductions within the two-year budget, or a new budget and deficit level must be approved. The final budget must be balanced in both planned and actual results at the end of the period.

- Require that the staff and travel expenses for Congress be voted upon as a separate spending bill, and that congressional members' results in managing expenses within those budgets be published at the end of each fiscal year with the report of the performance of all spending programs as discussed above. Require that funds collected for Social Security and Medicare *not* be used for any other purpose or program, and that surpluses in these programs *not* be used to offset a deficit in other programs, or to purchase Treasury Bills, except under a formally declared state of war or national emergency by the House, the Senate and the President. The spending, tax revenues, and deficit or surplus for these programs shall be managed and reported separately from the country's operating budget for all other programs. Further, Congress is required to return any surpluses that should have accumulated through the years prior to the ratification of these Amendments, but were used for other purposes than the appropriate funds assigned for exclusive use in these programs.

6. Prohibiting congressional members from paid lobbying roles after serving in Congress

- This requirement would prohibit congressional members from being paid to directly lobby any sitting members of Congress, or any member of the existing executive or congressional staffs, after serving in Congress. This is a lifetime prohibition. Volunteering as an advisor or providing expert opinion to an existing appointed or elected official or congressional committee, and receiving an appropriate travel expense reimbursement, is not prohibited by this requirement.

7. Prohibiting laws exempting Congress or congressional members from laws enacted on organizations and citizens

- This requirement would prohibit congressional members from exempting themselves as individuals or as an organization from obligations they pass that are required of organizations and citizens. This is a simple requirement that confirms that members of Congress are citizens whose temporary role is to serve the country, and that they, as individuals and an organization, are subject to the same laws and obligations that apply to all organizations and citizens.

8. Changing the method for allocating and certifying Electoral College votes in the states

- This requirement changes the allocation of Electoral College votes in each state, from a winner-takes-all basis to a proportional basis for each candidate, reflecting their percentage of the popular vote won in each state.
  - This approach would minimize the Red State/Blue State division in presidential election results, and encourage presidential candidates to campaign in all states and to adopt campaign platform proposals that address the needs and concerns of the country overall.
- This requirement also changes the steps for the counting

of Electoral College votes in each state to protect the votes of the people from being replaced by the intervention of politicians or elected officials. After the certification of the popular vote by the state's election officials, the state's Electoral College votes will be allocated to each candidate based on the proportion of the state's popular vote each candidate received. The state's electoral vote certificate will be prepared by the state's election officials, signed by the Governor and the Secretary of State.

Each state's certified election results will include the total popular vote, the popular vote recorded for each candidate, and the proportion of the total popular vote, and the resulting Electoral College votes allocated to each candidate (President and Vice President) and the proportion of the total Electoral College votes awarded to each candidate. These certified results are then presented to Congress, for the sole purpose of certifying the report from the states, including the required information, without challenging the results as certified by the states, and counting the total Electoral College votes won by each candidate in the nation, and formally affirming the next President and Vice President.

○ The timing of popular and Electoral College vote certification by each state should be completed no later than six weeks after the election (i.e. mid-December), and counted and confirmed as the national result by Congress no later than nine weeks after the election (i.e. early January). Specific dates will be set by Congress before the start of each federal election year.

○ Any concerns with or challenges to the initial vote count following the election will be investigated and, if appropriate, the vote will be recounted, as prescribed by state law. All such actions will be completed within the timing specified above. After certification by the states in mid-December, the sole role of Congress is to count and certify the total of the Electoral College votes for each candidate, determined by the states on the proportional share of the popular vote for each candidate, with no authority to challenge the vote counts.

9. Limiting the terms of Supreme Court justices and federal judges

- Set the terms of each Supreme Court justice and all federal judges to ten years. As discussed in the previous chapter, the lifetime terms for justices and judges was set in the Constitution for the purpose of removing these senior roles in the judiciary branch from the influences of elections, politics and partisanship. However, the lifetime appointments do not seem to be very effective in achieving this goal at this point in our history.
  - With the ability to approve judiciary appointments by a vote of only one party, and the willingness and ability of the Senate Majority Leader by himself or herself to withhold a Senate "advice and consent" process from a presidential appointment from another party, even the judiciary branch processes have now become politicized. While only about one-third of Supreme Court decisions have split along ideological lines closely aligned with partisanship differences, these cases have often been the ones that have the greatest impact on the country's societal and civil liberty issues.
  - To minimize the impact of political and partisan compromises on the independent judiciary over the long term, this requirement would replace the lifetime term with a ten-year term. These terms could be

renewed for multiple ten-year terms if reappointed by a different President and reconfirmed by a different Senate.

10. Ensuring fair and equitable access to registration and voting processes for all citizens; ensuring elections are free from fraud

- Require that Congress establish a citizen-led, independent, unbiased and bipartisan Federal Election Oversight Board with the authority to review state laws and results in the areas of fair and equitable access to registration and voting processes for all citizens. Board members shall be appointed by the Federal Election Commission and consist of citizens who are not and have never served as elected or appointed officials or political party officials at the federal or state level, or as a paid lobbyist, with an equal number of members from each major political party.
  - The Fourteenth and Nineteenth Amendments include very straightforward and clear requirements that the right to vote shall not be denied or abridged by the Congress or the states on the basis of race, creed, ethnicity, or sex. But states have for decades provided voting registration or voting access based on other factors, from payment of a poll tax, to the recitation of governmental facts, to the requirements of identification that are not available to all citizens on an equal basis. The Federal Election Oversight Board would provide ongoing oversight of state laws in these areas to provide timely revision or removal of any laws or processes that undermine the principles of fair and equitable access to all citizens in each state.
  - If election results indicate that these processes are not equitable, that citizens in some precincts have longer

voting lines or limited access to registration, or if new laws seem likely to erode equitable access in these areas, the Board shall investigate and if appropriate require the states to revise the laws, or operational siting, staffing or hours of service for registration and voting locations. The states may challenge Board rulings with the Federal Election Commission and ultimately in federal court.

- The Board will also have authority to review states' results in investigating and documenting evidence of election fraud and state laws to minimize election fraud; shall require that new laws are based on evidence or facts of fraud levels and causes; and shall require that the new laws relate to the specific levels and causes of election fraud documented by investigations.

11. Defining rules for campaign financing—donation limits and disclosure requirements

- Clearly specify within the "Citizen Rules" Amendments to the Constitution that "money is not speech, and companies and organizations are not citizens." Require that Congress pass Federal Election Laws to set specific limits on the level of contributions, in terms of money or gifts of value, from each individual citizen allowed each calendar year to all candidates, parties and issue action groups, based on an amount a citizen with average income could reasonably afford.
- Require that all contributions to every candidate, party and issue action group be publicly reported. Prohibit anonymous contributions to any political group, campaign, candidate, inauguration committee, political action committee, or non-profit that engages in political activities.

- Limit contributions from companies, unions and all organizations to any political group, campaign, candidate, PAC, political issue group or non-profit that engages in political activities to the same levels as for individuals.

12. Defining rules for truthful messaging and timing of campaign advertising

- Require that all messages about a candidate from whatever source during an election year must meet the test of being "truthful and not misleading" in content and presentation. No messaging can be utilized or publicly distributed that cannot be supported by facts. The responsibility for providing credible and factual information to validate the truth of messages rests with the candidate or person making the statement. The distributor of the statement has the responsibility to request the supporting information, and agree that it credibly supports the statement, or refuse to distribute the statement or withdraw it from distribution.
- Require that Congress establish an independent, non-partisan and unbiased Federal Election Message Oversight Board with authority to review all candidate and campaign messages, including messages from parties, PACs and political issue groups, in all forms and distribution channels, and to request support for the truthfulness of messages. The Federal Election Message Oversight Board will have the authority to require either revision or removal of candidate, campaign, party, and political issue group messages from public distribution if found to be in violation of the "truthful and not misleading" standard.
  - Extend this authority to all messages distributed to the public during an election year, including those

messages originated in, repeated by, or distributed by any media sources or social media platforms.

○ Require that all such reviews be made public, and that the initiator of the ad or message has access to a public appeal process, overseen by the Federal Election Commission.

○ The members of the Federal Election Message Oversight Board shall be appointed by the Federal Election Commission. The Board members shall be citizens who shall not have served as elected or politically appointed officials at the federal or state level, nor served in any role in a political party or as a lobbyist. There shall be an equal number of Board members who identify as a member of each major political party.

• Require that campaign spending on ads or targeted voter contacts of any kind be limited to the calendar year in which federal elections are held. No public broadcast, delivery or posting of any election or campaign-related messages or targeted voter contacts by or about candidates or potential candidates in an upcoming national election, or the primary elections to select candidates for national elections, may begin before January 1 of the year of the election.

13. Providing a process to oversee state voting-district alignments after census

• The independent Federal Election Oversight Board, defined in rule 10 above, shall also have the authority to provide a review of congressional voting-district maps drawn by the states. Any degree of partisan, racial, ethnic or other demographic-based bias evident in the drawing of congressional district boundaries would be prohibited in the "Citizen Rules" Amendments to the Constitution.

- This Board would have non-partisan citizen members appointed by the Federal Election Commission. The Board members shall be citizens who shall not have served as elected or politically appointed officials at the federal or state level, nor served in any role in a political party or as a lobbyist. There shall be an equal number of Board members who identify as a member of each major political party.

- The Board would have authority to request states to redraw any congressional district boundaries judged to be biased based on partisan, racial, ethnic, or other demographic data. States would have the ability to appeal the request in a public review by the Federal Election Commission, and ultimately a federal court, if the state legislature disagreed with the determination of the Board or the Federal Election Commission.

14. Defining rules for avoiding financial conflict of interest with all elected and appointed officials, and clarifying rules for handling personal income for the President, Vice President, and all senior elected and appointed officials

- Require that the President and all members of the Administration and Congress and their senior staffs adhere to the same standards of ethics and conflict-of-interest policies while in office. These standards require the disclosing of personal income tax records and placing personal assets in blind trusts, thus suspending any direct business ownership or realization of any commercial benefit accruing during their service. The President is confirmed as subject to the Ethical Behavior Laws enacted by Congress for all senior elected and appointed officials.

- Require that all candidates for federal elections (President, Vice President, Senate and House), and all senior appointed officials, release the most recent ten years of federal tax returns when they file papers as a candidate or when their appointment is announced by the President, prior to the Senate confirmation process.

- Require that all candidate-elects who win national elections, and senior appointed officials confirmed by the Senate, put all personal financial, business, investment and commercial property assets into blind trusts managed by third-party (i.e. non-family or non-connected) trustees *before* taking the oath of office.

- Provide a legal process for investigating and determining if a violation of the personal interest aspects of ethical standards by elected officials has occurred, by specifically defining such a violation as a "high crime" under the constitutional standards for an impeachable offense.

- Clarify and extend the Emoluments Clause by requiring that all personal income received by the President, Vice President, and all senior appointed and elected officials in Congress while in office be directed to their blind trusts without any information of the amount of income or the impact on the blind-trust value of transactions by the third-party (non-family, non-connected) trustee being communicated to the official or any family members while in office.

15. Defining a non-partisan judicial process for impeachment and specific actions considered as impeachable offenses

- Confirm that the constitutional requirements for impeachment charges, trial and judgment involve a judicial-based process which supersedes the extension of the authority of Congress to make the rules for proceedings in the House and Senate, to the processes of impeachment and trial.

○ Preparation of impeachment charges by the House will involve both public and secure hearings, employing full discovery and subpoena powers and governed by the normal processes and standards established by law for an investigative body. The standard for this process is the action of prosecutors in seeking an indictment, and the protection of the rights of accused persons in the Constitution.

▸ The outcome shall be determined by a majority vote of the House deciding if the "preponderance of evidence," and witness testimony if any, indicates the likelihood that an impeachment offense has been committed, and that the accused person is likely to be responsible. In this case, an impeachment indictment would be approved.

▸ As in the approval of bills and appointments, the approval by the House of an impeachment indictment requires a minimum of 5% of the voting majority to be from the minority party.

○ The trial of an impeachment indictment in the Senate will involve a public trial governed by the rules of evidence and witness testimony admissibility, and the conduct standards of jurors, to ensure the same unbiased deliberations that exist in judicial rules and courtroom procedures.

○ When the impeachment trial shall involve the President or Vice President, the impeachment trial will be presided over by a three-justice panel including the Chief Justice as presiding justice. The other two justices will be Associate Justices of the Supreme Court, each of whom was originally nominated by a President of a different party. Judicial decisions and rulings shall be those agreed by two of the three justices. The Senators shall serve only as jurors, and shall have no authority to challenge, question or overrule the decisions and rulings of the three-justice panel on any issue, including, but not limited to, witness testimony or evidence admissibility.

- For impeachments involving all other elected or appointed federal officials, the trial in the Senate shall be presided over by the senior justice of the District Court of Appeals from the District of Columbia, and two who shall be associate justices nominated by Presidents of different parties—excluding the sitting President—who will be selected by the presiding Chief Justice. This three-justice panel shall exercise the same judicial authorities as in the trial of the President.

The House prosecutors, the accused, their attorneys and all Senators will be required to refrain from any public statements, from the beginning of the impeachment investigation in the House through the completion of the Senate trial and decision. After a vote of impeachment in the House, the Senators will serve as jurors in the trial, and will continue not to speak publicly on any issue related to the impeachment, nor will they discuss any aspects of the impeachment charge and trial with other Senators.

- Prior to all impeachment trials, the Senators will each take an oath to do "impartial justice" as currently required in the Constitution, based only on the evidence and testimony presented in the trial. Conviction shall require the approval of two-thirds of the Senators sitting as jurors, as currently defined in the Constitution.

16. Establishing a required program of national service for all young citizens

- Require that all citizens, between the ages of 18 and 29, complete two years of national service in a full-time paid position. The purpose is to strengthen the sense of national service as a part of citizenship in our society, and to expose citizens of different backgrounds to each other in their service roles.

- Define national service roles as military, first responders (police, fire, emergency medical technician (EMT)), teaching and medical professional roles in under-served areas, and several other roles that would fill key needs in our country and communities.

- A five-member National Service Board shall be established by Congress to oversee the National Service Program. The five Board members shall be former senior officials from each of the following professional career ranks: (1) military; (2) police; (3) fire or EMT; (4) teaching; and (5) medical. These members will be nominated by the President with the advice and consent of the Senate, and may only be removed with the advice and consent of the Senate.

- There are no exemptions or waivers, except for obviously limiting physical, mental, emotional, or other medically certified conditions. If service does not begin by the twenty-eighth birthday, citizens would be assigned to a mandatory role. All decisions of the National Service Board are reviewable in an appropriate court of law.

Chapter 5

Background and Details of Key "Win-Win" Policies

This chapter will explore how the changes outlined in the previous chapters above could lead to a "win-win" approach in congressional governing processes and legislation development, reflecting the approach of "country over party." Such a change in governing could lead to new and innovative policies that better address our key problems, which seem unsolvable under the divisive influences of money, partisanship and career self-interest, and a one-party majority governing to its base.

Policy 1—Economy: Economic Growth, Middle-Class Income Growth, Narrowing the Income Gap, Job Growth, Reducing the Deficit

First, as a starting point for discussing an innovative, comprehensive, pro-growth economic policy, let's review some facts and history to inform the discussion, rather than looking at these topics via partisan ideologies. Let's start by asking some key questions.

Part 1. Some questions, facts and history on economic growth, taxes, budgets and deficits

Do higher tax rates always mean lower economic and job growth?
Many citizens, and one of our major political parties, have voted and legislated on the belief, the ideology, that cutting taxes will grow the economy and reduce the deficit. The belief is that cutting taxes will increase business profits, which is a true fact. But to result in economic growth, businesses need to use

the increased profits to grow their business, by making business investments and hiring more workers, and paying higher wages and bonuses to employees to contribute to middle-class income and overall economic growth.

If these were the actions that resulted from tax cuts, then economic GDP would increase. But if the extra profits are primarily used to pay executive bonuses and buy back stock, and there's no significant increase in business investment or hiring, or in salary increases or bonuses to middle-class workers, these actions will have a minimal effect on economic GDP growth.

Why? Because the single largest factor driving economic GDP growth is not business profitability or stock price; it is middle-class spending and income, which drives 70% of economic GDP growth. Thus, if working middle-class incomes and spending are not growing as a direct result of economic and tax policy, it is almost mathematically impossible for the overall economy to grow more than 1%–2% at most.

So let's look at a series of questions that would perhaps help us understand, objectively, the relationships between tax rates, business profits, overall economic GDP growth and working middle-class incomes:

- Do the facts indicate that we have historically high tax rates today? Are they the highest in the world? Were they the highest tax rates in history before the 2017 tax cuts?
- Were taxes and regulations significantly hurting company profits before the 2017 tax cuts? How are company profits doing today? How have they done in the past six to eight years?
- How has economic GDP growth been impacted by the tax cuts and deregulation actions of 2017? Has economic growth significantly increased in the past two years since the tax cuts (and before the pandemic year impact) over the previous four years?

- Have we ever had strong economic growth rates at higher tax rates than we have today? Have our strong economic growth rates in our recent past been achieved at higher or lower tax rates than today? How many years of annual economic growth rates greater than 3% have been achieved at top personal tax rates below 40%?
- How many years of annual economic growth rates greater than 3% have been achieved at top personal tax rates greater than 40%?
- What are the economic risks, if any, to consistent annual deficits and an ever-increasing national debt?

The following discussion will provide the answers to these questions and help inform our understanding of which policy elements would provide the best approach to economic GDP growth.

What economic factor has the greatest impact on economic and job growth?

The greatest factor in our nation's economic security and our ability to provide a high quality of life for our citizens is the level of the ongoing average overall economic GDP growth rate. The economy is typically the most important issue to voters in most elections and is a top priority in the policy of almost every Administration, regardless of the party in the majority. All personal income, all jobs, all federal and state funds ultimately come from the profits generated by a growing commercial sector. And a growing economy depends on two factors that are codependent: (1) increases in real commercial profitability, and (2) increases in working middle-class incomes.

However, both parties have advocated and, when possible, implemented economic growth policies based on partisan ideologies and not based on analysis of what are the most significant factors that drive economic growth. Republicans typically advocate driving economic growth through business profit growth stimulated most often by cutting taxes. While business profit growth is a prerequisite, by itself it is not a large factor in overall economic growth, and is therefore not sufficient by itself. It is *how* profits are invested that determines the degree of economic growth.

By contrast, Democrats typically advocate driving economic growth by raising taxes and spending government money to provide benefits and services to specific under-served demographic groups. While this may have an important social justice aspect and can be somewhat stimulative, it often has only a small impact on the overall working middle-class income growth in the country. So these policies by themselves have historically not been large factors in overall economic growth.

Here are some questions about the beliefs that many people hold concerning economic growth, and the facts that might help develop objective answers:

- *Have strong economic growth rates always existed with low tax rates? Do high profits drive economic and job growth directly?*
    - Overall annual economic GDP growth rates have slowly declined considerably over the last two decades. Do the facts indicate that company profits have grown or declined at the same time? Do the facts indicate that stock market prices have risen or fallen over the last two decades? Do the facts indicate that overall middle-class incomes have increased or decreased over the last two decades? Do the facts indicate that tax rates have risen or fallen over the last two decades?
    - Which factor has changed in a direction that would relate to the decline in economic GDP growth rates? Company profits have grown, stock market prices have risen, middle-class incomes have been stable, and tax rates have decreased. Which of these factors,

therefore, seems to have the greatest impact on economic growth—company profits, stock market prices, middle-class incomes, or tax rates?

As mentioned earlier, neither of the partisan policy approaches directly addresses the single factor that accounts for 70% of economic GDP growth. That factor is overall middle-class spending and income. When middle-class income is not growing, middle-class spending can't grow without increasing average household debt levels—which of course is not a path to sustaining long-term economic growth.

- Since middle-class incomes have the greatest impact on economic growth, should government set wages for businesses in order to drive economic growth? Or should government increase taxes on upper-income households and businesses, and cut taxes on middle-class households? Or is there a policy approach that could increase middle-class incomes without a "tax and spend" approach from a new government program to essentially reallocate incomes? Are there any actions that have been done in the past that we could adopt?

Next, let's look at the underlying data on past economic policy results (see the following table).

Trends in Annual Economic GDP Growth

Historic GDP Growth, Top Personal Tax Rate, Business Tax Rate, Annual Deficit

Year	GDP Growth	Top Tax Rate	Bus. Tax Rate	Deficit/Surplus $MM
1945	-1.0%	94.0%	38.0%	-47.6
46	-11.6%	86.5%	38.0%	-15.9
47	-0.9%	86.5%	38.0%	4.0
48	4.3%	82.1%	38.0%	11.8
49	-0.5%	82.1%	38.0%	0.6
1950	8.4%	91.0%	42.0%	-3.1
51	7.5%	91.0%	50.8%	6.1
52	3.8%	92.0%	52.0%	-1.5
53	4.5%	92.0%	52.0%	-6.5
54	-0.6%	91.0%	52.0%	-1.2
55	7.0%	91.0%	52.0%	-3.0
56	2.0%	91.0%	52.0%	3.9
57	2.0%	91.0%	52.0%	3.4
58	-0.9%	91.0%	52.0%	-2.8
59	6.9%	91.0%	52.0%	-12.8
1960	2.4%	91.0%	52.0%	0.3
61	2.3%	91.0%	52.0%	-3.3
62	5.9%	91.0%	52.0%	-7.1
63	4.3%	91.0%	52.0%	-4.8
64	5.6%	77.0%	50.0%	-5.9
65	6.2%	70.0%	48.0%	-1.4
66	6.3%	70.0%	52.8%	-3.7
67	2.5%	70.0%	52.8%	-8.6
68	4.7%	75.3%	52.8%	-25.2
69	3.1%	77.0%	52.8%	3.2
1970	0.2%	71.8%	49.2%	-2.8
71	3.3%	70.0%	48.0%	-23.0
72	5.2%	70.0%	48.0%	-23.4

Year	GDP Growth	Top Tax Rate	Bus. Tax Rate	Deficit/Surplus $MM
73	5.6%	70.0%	48.0%	-14.9
74	-0.6%	70.0%	48.0%	-6.1
75	-0.2%	70.0%	48.0%	-53.2
76	5.2%	70.0%	48.0%	-73.7
77	4.5%	70.0%	48.0%	-53.7
78	5.4%	70.0%	48.0%	-59.2
79	3.1%	70.0%	46.0%	-40.7
1980	-0.3%	70.0%	46.0%	-73.8
81	2.5%	69.1%	46.0%	-79.0
82	-2.0%	50.0%	46.0%	-128.0
83	4.4%	50.0%	46.0%	-207.8
84	6.9%	50.0%	46.0%	-185.4
85	4.1%	50.0%	46.0%	-212.3
86	3.4%	50.0%	46.0%	-221.2
87	3.1%	38.5%	40.0%	-149.7
88	4.0%	28.0%	34.0%	-155.2
89	3.5%	28.0%	34.0%	-152.6
1990	1.9%	31.0%	34.0%	-221.0
91	-0.2%	31.0%	34.0%	-269.2
92	3.3%	31.0%	34.0%	-290.3
93	2.8%	39.6%	35.0%	-255.1
94	4.0%	39.6%	35.0%	-203.2
95	2.5%	39.6%	35.0%	-164.0
96	3.7%	39.6%	35.0%	-107.4
97	4.4%	39.6%	35.0%	-21.9
98	4.3%	39.6%	35.0%	69.3
99	4.7%	39.6%	35.0%	125.6
2000	4.1%	39.6%	35.0%	236.2
01	1.1%	38.6%	35.0%	128.2
02	1.8%	38.6%	35.0%	-157.8
03	2.5%	35.0%	35.0%	-377.6
04	3.4%	35.0%	35.0%	-412.7
05	3.0%	35.0%	35.0%	-318.3

Year	GDP Growth	Top Tax Rate	Bus. Tax Rate	Deficit/Surplus $MM
06	2.6%	35.0%	35.0%	-248.2
07	1.9%	35.0%	35.0%	-160.7
08	-0.3%	35.0%	35.0%	-458.6
09	-3.5%	35.0%	35.0%	-1,412.7
10	3.0%	35.0%	35.0%	-1,294.4
11	2.5%	35.0%	35.0%	-1,299.6
12	1.6%	35.0%	35.0%	-1,087.0
13	2.2%	39.6%	35.0%	-679.5
14	1.7%	39.6%	35.0%	-484.6
15	2.6%	39.6%	35.0%	-438.5
16	2.9%	39.0%	35.0%	-584.7
17	2.2%	37.0%	35.0%	-665.4
18	2.9%	37.0%	21.0%	-779.1
19	2.3%	37.0%	21.0%	-984.2
2020	-3.5%	37.0%	21.0%	-3,100.0 (Pandemic Year)

Source: US Office of Management and Budget

What has happened in history after past tax cuts?

Did we get stronger long-term economic growth? Did they pay for themselves in economic growth, with no increase in deficits?

The following are a series of questions regarding economic growth and related issues that are often never asked and therefore never answered specifically in policy development processes:

- What has happened after past tax cuts? What actions were taken by business with the higher profits that resulted? Did middle-class incomes grow? Did the economy grow in the long term? What has changed? What increased, what declined?
- What happens when the deficit grows after tax cuts? What is the next action that is usually taken by the Congress? Is it then to cut important programs that support sustained

economic growth and/or overall quality of life?

- Is there a tendency to cut spending after tax cuts raise deficits? What spending is usually cut? Does that cycle tend to lead to lower infrastructure and education spending? Does that support or undermine sustained business growth?

- How did the tax reform/cuts in 2017 impact the overall annual GDP economic growth results and deficit versus the expected outcomes? How much has the economy grown since the tax cuts? Data shows only a 0.3% GDP growth in 2018–2019 versus the last four years before the tax cut. So, did the tax cut "pay for itself" or did it result in greatly increased deficits? Data shows that the combined annual deficits in 2017–2019 exceeded $1.5 trillion over those two years. Is that what was expected?

- What has happened to planned investments in infrastructure and workforce education? Have we had major government investments in these key programs that actually support overall GDP economic growth since 2017? What is likely to happen to healthcare funding, to social security funding, and infrastructure and workforce development if deficits continue to grow?

- Does history show us that we can sustain a higher tax rate than we had in 2017 and still have a growing economy? Would increasing working middle-class incomes grow the economy even at modestly higher tax rates?

If the answers to these questions might help us better understand which factors have the greatest impact on economic and job growth, would it seem that understanding these answers would be helpful to developing more effective economic growth policies going forward?

Let's look at some of the data that helps answer the above questions.

- **What actions did businesses take after the tax cuts in 2003?** Those tax cuts were intended to "free up" capital for the job creators and businesses. But as the data seems to indicate, this did not lead to the creation of a great number of new jobs. How then did most businesses use the capital created by the tax cut?

  - Between 2005 and 2007, over $1 trillion in business capital was invested in buying back stock. Statistics tell us that there was an additional $2–$3 trillion of capital sitting "on the sideline" and in overseas markets before the tax cuts. If you recall, the tax cuts provided incentives for businesses to repatriate those funds into the country, so they could be invested in hiring new employees and investing in growing their business and the overall economy. But beyond strong economic GDP growth in 2004–2005, annual deficits rose and overall economic GDP declined, culminating in the recession of 2008–2009. But business profits stayed high and an additional $6 trillion was invested by companies in buying back stock. Since investments in business expansion and employee wages increased only modestly, it is likely that much of this overseas capital was invested in buying back company stock.

  - Why would businesses invest in stock buybacks instead of business expansion? Stock buybacks increase stock price for a short period by inflating the earnings per share data by reducing the amount of stock in the market. But they do not create one single job, nor generate real future growth opportunities for a company, nor result in the opening of one new market, nor lead to the development of one new product, nor contribute to the increased competitive position of the business.

  - The very prosperous economy we have enjoyed overall

for most of the past 60 years grew out of the Great Depression and the end of World War II, primarily because we created a large, prosperous and growing middle class after the end of World War II, even though we had record *high tax rates* to fund infrastructure and workforce education investments.

º It is the consumer spending increases fueled by a growing and prosperous working middle class that created the wealth that all classes have enjoyed over the past 70 years.

º There has been no positive economic "trickle down" effect in the history of prosperous societies. There is only a "trickle up" benefit for all classes when there is a prosperous and growing middle class to fuel consumer demand. As we stated, data clearly shows that the biggest factor (at 70%) impacting GDP economic growth is working middle-class spending and income. If we do not enact business policies that restore that prosperity to the middle class, then eventually the overall prosperity of all classes will be impacted as well.

• **What did our grandparents and government leaders do with the debt from World War II?** Did they ignore the needs of a world-class infrastructure to support a world-class economy? Did they fund the investment with debt, or with tax revenues? Did our grandparents and government leaders act with the belief that just cutting taxes and increasing profits would spur economic growth after World War II? What were the top tax rates then? What did they do with government spending during that period?

Here are the facts that answer those questions. After World War II, beginning in 1949, our government leaders:

- ° Invested in new infrastructure (interstate highways) and expanded the nation's electric grid to support new economic growth;
- ° Invested in free college education for about 4 million World War II veterans to support skilled workforce development;
- ° Invested in foreign development aid and development to our enemies and our allies;
- ° Did not fund these investments with deficits. These investments were funded primarily out of current revenues *and*, at the same time, most of the World War II debt was paid down, instead of passing all of the debt forward to the next generation.

Here is a summary of some of the details of those actions and the facts behind them:

- The highest personal income tax rate during World War II was 79%, to help pay for the wartime expenses without building too much debt. Then in 1945, the top personal income tax rate was increased to 94%, then reduced each year in 1946–1949 from 86% to 82%.
- But in 1950, the top personal tax rate was increased to 91%–92% and remained at that level until 1963. This generated the income to help pay down World War II debt and invest in the transition of the economy from war time to peace time, and create new jobs for returning veterans of the war. The major infrastructure spending on transportation and energy resources in those years built the foundation upon which our economy and quality of life grew consistently for nearly 50 years.
- In addition, our leaders showed they had learned the lessons of World War I, when the USA became isolationist and left the economies of Europe, both allies and enemies,

in ruin—which only served to fuel social unrest and the rise of extremist movements. So, after World War II, the USA also funded investments to help rebuild the economies of both allies and enemies, in Europe and in Asia, to reduce the risk of extremism rising again in these destroyed countries.

- As a result, except for active regional wars in South-East Asia (Korea and Vietnam), and the Cold War with Russia, most of the world experienced seven decades of relative peace and economic growth after two world wars in the previous three decades. It's important to note that our previous enemies in World War II have become some of our strongest allies (Germany, Italy and Japan) and business trading partners. Even Vietnam has become an economic trading partner today.

Have we always had large annual deficits? Does a large debt matter to economic growth?

Many experts and most political leaders act on the belief that the amount of US debt that has grown immensely since the mid-1970s is not of major concern for US economic strength or security. While the kind of large deficits we have experienced over the past 40+ years or so may not now be impacting the day-to-day economic life of the US or its citizens, can we be sure that these beliefs are well founded in facts and can be trusted over the long term?

- Have large annual deficits always existed? Has the budget ever been balanced? When was that? How did we balance the budget? What happened since we had a balanced budget?
- What percentage of the budget today is allocated just to pay interest on our debt? What is the current interest rate on the debt? Is it historically high or low? What

would be the impact on our economic security in the future if the interest rate rises two or three times and the deficit continues to rise? Are we placing our children and grandchildren, and the future of our country, at a significant risk?

A chart showing the changes in the size of the annual deficits each year (not the cumulative debt) is included below. This chart indicates that annual deficits were very minimal from the 1960s (actually from the 1950s following the end of World War II) through the early to mid-1970s, but began a steady increase through the late 1970s to the late 1990s.

Trend in Annual Deficits—Impact of Tax Policy (2016 Data; 2018–2020 Est.)

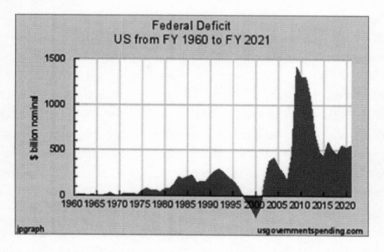

Tax cuts since 1950: 1964: **91–>77**; 1970: **77–>70**; 1982: **70–>50**; 1987: **50–>38.5**; 1988: **38.5–>28**; 2003: **38.5–>35 (small increases in 1952, 1990, 1993, 2013)**

Note that this period includes several successive tax cuts initiated in the 1980s that initially reduced tax rates and federal revenues, and significantly increased the deficit. Again, these tax cuts were based on the "theory" that reducing taxes would increase GDP economic growth rate, which would increase federal income by amounts greater than the losses in revenues from lower tax rates. Unfortunately, this did not happen, as the tax cuts were not directly tied to increase the one factor that has the largest impact on GDP economic growth, as we'll discuss below—middle-class income and spending. This growth in deficits ended with a bipartisan agreement to balance the annual budget in 1998 by raising taxes and cutting spending. This achieved a balanced budget and a small surplus in 1999–2000, a period of strong economic growth.

The history of highest personal income tax rates since 1945 is summarized in the chart below.

Historical Highest Personal Income Tax Rates

Year	Top Rate	Year	Top Rate
1945	94.00%	1970	71.75% Tax Cut
1946	86.45%	1971–1980	70.00%
1947	86.45%	1981	69.13%
1948	82.13%	1982–1986	50.00% Tax Cut
1949	82.13%	1987	38.50% Tax Cut
1950	91.00%	1988	28.00% Tax Cut
1951	91.00%	1989	28.00%
1952	92.00%	1990–1992	31.00%
1953	92.00%	1993–2000*	39.60%
1954–1963	91.00%	2001	38.60%
1964	77.00% Tax Cut	2002	38.60%
1965–1967	70.00%	2003–2012	35.00% Tax Cut
1968	75.25%	2013–2015	39.60%
1969	77.00%	2016–2018	39%–37% Tax Cut

*Note: After the balanced budget in 1999–2000, spending

157

increased in 2001 to fight terrorism. But we didn't pay for it. In fact, we cut taxes further in 2003, creating major deficits until 2008 when the financial system collapsed and deficits in 2009 increased significantly as revenues declined and spending grew. *Sources: Eugene Steuerle, The Urban Institute; Joseph Pechman, Federal Tax Policy; Joint Committee on Taxation, Summary of Conference Agreement on the Jobs and Growth Tax Relief Reconciliation Act of 2003, JCX-54-03, May 22, 2003; IRS Revised Tax Rate Schedules*

Summary of historical data

Our average annual GDP economic growth rates have fallen steadily by decade since 1950. At the same time, stock market prices and corporate profits have increased significantly, while personal and business tax rates have declined. Overall middle-class incomes since 1967 have seen essentially no growth for nearly 50 years.

If the key drivers of economic GDP growth are low tax rates and high corporate profits and stock market prices, shouldn't we also have had record high levels of economic GDP growth in this period? But if the key drivers are *not* low taxes or high profits and stock market prices, what should our key policy focus be to drive sustained economic GDP growth for the country?

Part 2. New idea—achieve economic growth, middle-class income growth, job growth, narrowing the income gap, reducing the deficit concurrently

New economic growth policy idea—incentivize companies to share earned profits with all employees

This policy idea is not based on any partisan ideology or theory. As we have shown, it is based on the fact that the factor with the largest impact on GDP economic growth rate is middle-class income and spending. The new aspect of this policy idea is *how* best to increase middle-class income. Since strong economic GDP growth requires sustained growth in company profitability *and* growing middle-class incomes, might it make sense to link a growth in middle-class income to the growth in company profitability by incentivizing companies to share profits with *all* employees?

But is there evidence or data that indicates the sharing of profits with employees can help sustain positive company profit growth?

- A small test of knowledge—facts and history on profit sharing:
  - Q: The first profit-sharing program for employees started when?
    - A: 1887
  - Q: Where did it start?
    - A: Cincinnati
  - Q: Who started it?
    - A: Procter & Gamble (P&G)
  - Q: How has it impacted the company's success?
    - A: P&G was added to the Dow Jones 30 Industrials Average in 1932; only IBM, Coca-Cola and P&G remain in the list as of August 2019
    - A: P&G has 131 years of consecutive dividend payments, and 65 years of consecutive dividend payment increases to shareholders.
- In considering a policy that would encourage companies to allocate a large portion of a company's earned profits to employees, perhaps we should look at how profits are allocated today to see if there might be a negative impact on a company's ability to generate profits. To help the overall economy as well as the individual company, we would hope to see a major portion of annual profits invested in actions to grow the business, make it more competitive,

add new products, open new markets, modernize old plants, build new plants—and of course, create more jobs, hire more employees, and share increasing profits with the employees who are contributing to the profit growth.

In the past 50 years, an increasing amount of annual profits has been invested by most companies in raising salaries, bonuses, and profit sharing, but only for senior executives. This has helped fuel the growth in the income and wealth disparity in our society that we'll look at shortly in data.

And in the past 20 years, trillions of dollars in company profits have been diverted from investments in actions that would drive long-term company growth, to driving short-term stock price growth via buying back their own stock. Taking shares of stock out of the market, even with no increases in actual company sales or operating profits, increases one of the key factors driving stock price— earnings *per share*. If earnings are difficult to increase in the short term, reducing the number of shares of stock in the market increases the numerical value of earnings *per share*. But as we have discussed earlier, this action will not add one extra dollar in product or service sales; it won't open one new market; it won't build one new plant or modernize one old plant; it won't develop one new product or service; and it won't add one new job, or help grow the overall economy.

A Reuters analysis in November 2015 found that many iconic US industrial companies were spending more on stock buybacks and dividends than they were investing in research and innovation. And many companies were even spending *more* in stock buybacks than they reported in net profit, borrowing money at the low prevailing interest rates and increasing debt to do so!

How the cult of shareholder value has reshaped corporate America

Combined stock repurchases by U.S. public companies have reached record levels, a Reuters analysis finds, showing that many companies are spending on share repurchases at a far faster pace than they are investing in long-term growth through research and development and other forms of capital spending.

Almost 60 percent of the 3,297 publicly traded non-financial U.S. companies Reuters examined have bought back their shares since 2010. In fiscal 2014, spending on buybacks and dividends surpassed the companies' combined net income for the first time outside of a recessionary period, and continued to climb for the 613 companies that have already reported for fiscal 2015.

In the most recent reporting year, share purchases reached a record $520 billion. Throw in the most recent year's $365 billion in dividends, and the total amount returned to shareholders reaches $885 billion, more than the companies' combined net income of $847 billion. Among the 1,900 companies that have repurchased their shares since 2010, buybacks and dividends amounted to 113 percent of their capital spending, compared with 60 percent in 2000 and 38 percent in 1990. And among the approximately 1,000 firms that buy back shares and report R&D spending, the proportion of net income spent on innovation has averaged less than 50 percent since 2009, increasing to 56 percent only in the most recent year as net income fell. It had been over 60 percent during the 1990s.

"A SCARY SCENARIO"

In theory, buybacks add another way, on top of dividends, of sharing profits with shareholders. Because buybacks increase demand and reduce supply for a company's shares, they tend to increase the share price, at least in the short-term, amplifying the positive effect. By decreasing the number of shares outstanding, they also increase earnings per share, even when total net income is flat. Over the years, a belief has taken hold that companies' primary objective is to maximize shareholder value, even if that means paying out now through buybacks and dividends money that could be put toward long-term productive investments.

"Serving customers, creating innovative new products, employing workers, taking care of the environment … are NOT the objectives of firms," Itzhak Ben-David, professor of finance at Ohio State University's Fisher College of Business and a buyback proponent, wrote in an email response to questions from Reuters.

WEALTH BENEFIT

Share repurchases have helped the stock market climb to records from the depths of the financial crisis. As a result, shareholders and corporate executives whose pay is linked to share prices are feeling a lot wealthier. That wealth, some economists argue, has come at the expense of workers by cutting into the capital spending that supports long-term growth—and jobs. Further, because most U.S. stock is held by the wealthiest Americans, workers haven't benefited equally from rising share prices.

Maximizing shareholder value has "concentrated income at the top and has led to the disappearance of middle class jobs", said William Lazonick, professor of economics, University of Massachusetts-Lowell. Thus, said Lazonick, maximizing shareholder value has "concentrated income at the top and has led to the disappearance of middle-class jobs..."

Excerpted from "The Cannibalized Company," an online article published by Thompson Reuters, November 15, 2015, by Karen Brettell, David Gaffen and David Rohde

When experts argue that this policy is "good for shareholders," they are taking an extremely short-term view, because billions of dollars are not being invested in innovation or research to improve a global competitive position, to develop new products, to open new markets, or to improve operational efficiency. And many of these companies are now seeing their growth decline after several years of this policy, while some have seen hundreds of millions of dollars of profits invested in buying back stock totally disappear following declines in the stock price, after buying back their stock at higher prices.

In addition, this policy "inflates" share prices above what would be "deserved" by earnings growth alone. The inflated stock price raises the stock's price-to-earnings ratio (P-E), and encourages investors to increase borrowing on margin to buy more shares in anticipation of further short-term share price growth. This is in fact happening again, since the 2009 recession dropped the record peak of P-E ratio levels in 2008, just prior to the recession, and history shows the inflation in P-E ratios and higher investor margin utilization can eventually lead to huge stock market corrections at best, and serious recessions at worst.

As we've observed, history shows that a growing stock market is not a major factor driving economic and job growth.

The number-one factor driving economic growth is middle-class spending, driven by middle-class incomes, which have not risen substantially for almost 20 years. The Reuters article found that the policy of buying back company stock as a major use of profits has come partially from an expectation of slower economic growth and demand driving the investment of profits in places where there are greater short-term returns. The increased focus on continuing high levels of stock buybacks since the 2017 tax cuts has only exacerbated this situation, and may hasten the time when a major stock market correction, triggering the next potential recession, could occur. These continued stock buybacks are probably a major factor driving the "Trump Bull Rally" since the 2017 tax cut policy was enacted, as the largest use of incremental company profits generated by the 2017 business tax cuts has been to buy back company stock.

What should be done to restore a long-term focus on overall economic growth by both companies and Congress?

The Democrat party actions to ban stock buybacks by law, as reported in the Reuters article, charging this action as stock price manipulation, are short-sighted as a solution to address the problem. Legislation to prevent stock buybacks by itself will have no benefit to the economy and drive more divisiveness in Congress. If Democrats were to propose, as part of a simpler tax code, to incentivize sharing profits with *all* employees via a low tax rate on earned operating profits allocated to sharing profits with *all* employees, and the highest tax rates on profits allocated to stock buybacks, then companies could earn a lower tax rate by choosing to invest profits in their employees, growing middle-class incomes, without undermining the profitability of the company. If middle-class incomes were to grow, then the economy would grow at a faster rate, more jobs would be created, and the incentive to invest in innovation and research and new products would be greater than today—and federal revenues would grow as the economy and incomes grow, to help us achieve a balanced budget *and* provide support for needed programs, even at lower business tax rates overall.

If Congress could come together and enact an innovative policy to benefit the country, based on facts and not ideologies, this could be a time when tax, deficit and economic growth policy can all come together, to help businesses focus on long-term versus short-term investments, help them be more competitive on a global basis, avoid the risk of a market correction and recession, and improve the quality of life for many millions of middle-class workers.

There's another value to individual companies and the overall economy in employee profit sharing: this would help lower the income and wage gap in our country. There have been many societies throughout history that have concentrated wealth in the top 10% with huge income and wealth gaps — monarchies, dictatorships, theocracies and Communist countries. What has happened to these societies when the wealth gap reached a critical point? Can we have a free enterprise economy that "works for everyone" if the workers who help create the profits of companies do not share in the profits they help create?

Why doesn't this receive more focus from Congress and the Administration? Could it be that so many big donors and large investors in congressional leadership are benefiting personally from the current actions?

Part 3. Growth policy—approach to taxes, spending and deficits

Below is a suggestion for legislative actions to balance the budget and grow the economy—details that are not part of a Constitutional Amendment, but that could result from legislation developed by new members, who are serving only one term without the influences of partisan and donor interests, and will work together under the Citizen Rules described in previous chapters.

- Start the budget-planning process by setting an overall economic growth and deficit target for the fiscal year.
  - We have not achieved a 3% annual GDP growth rate since 2010 and only three years in this decade;
  - A 3% annual GDP growth rate would provide the increased federal tax revenue at lower tax rates to support the needs for investment in infrastructure, education, and retraining for future jobs.
- Set spending to meet the country's needs and set tax structures and rates to provide the necessary income, considering the need to focus on the drivers of economic growth, specifically on middle-class income, including expected profit sharing and expected competitiveness of business tax rates with global competitors to maintain profit levels and US jobs.
- Establish a new tax code for both individuals and businesses with graduated tax rate levels based on personal and operating business income, with either no or only a minimal number of deductions allowed. This would lower the published tax rates to be essentially equal to the effective tax rates paid, simplify filing, and substantially reduce lobbying for individual and industry tax preferences, a major source of money and contributions in politics.
- Establish more tax brackets, not fewer brackets, so that the tax impact on increased earnings levels is gradual as incomes increase, and is not a barrier to growth.
- Justify all spending programs with a specific, measurable goal to achieve behind the spending, and an annual review of existing program results versus goals before approving new spending. Cut or reallocate spending that's not adding real value.

- Determine the spending level needed to provide for real needs in the budget areas currently supported, such as required military upgrades to existing equipment and military living standards, VA benefit improvements, existing social service programs, and so on.
- Add the new spending levels needed to support investments to sustain economic growth, including infrastructure investments, and skilled workforce development (education, training and retraining programs).
- Based on economic forecasts, project revenue to come from the simplified tax code with minimal deductions, considering the historic allocation of income tax revenues between personal income and business tax streams. See if the revenue targets can be met with a personal top tax rate below 40% and an average top business tax rate below 30% (average of the four tax rates in each bracket).
- In personal tax rates, set higher tax rates for investment-only income (i.e. not earned income), but lower tax rates for earned income, to reflect a higher "valuing" of work by the middle class.
- Set four business tax rates in each operating income tax bracket. Set lowest business tax rates on income used for profit sharing; middle rates for investing in the business; higher rates for executive-only bonuses or salary increases; and highest rates for stock buybacks. Set small business tax rates as business tax instead of pass-through earnings on personal tax rates.
- Set an overall budget target that links overall spending and tax plans with the targets for overall annual economic GDP growth, middle-class incomes and business profit growth, and annual deficit and debt targets. As spending and tax programs are passed during the fiscal year, they must stay within these targets, or new overall budget targets in each of these areas must be passed concurrently.

- Above all, avoid cutting taxes and raising spending in an existing deficit environment, and use "forecast growth" with modest economic growth increases to offset the deficit cuts. Increase economic growth first via overall middle-class income growth and sustained company profit growth rates at higher tax rates, then cut taxes when solid economic growth is achieved and surpluses result.

The outcome of this approach would likely be to raise middle-class incomes for employed workers faster than incomes can rise via wage increases that could undermine the sustained profitability growth of companies and limit the country's overall GDP growth. If you don't believe it is important for companies to be profitable, let's consider a couple of facts:

1. In the history of the world, the wealth of a nation has always depended on the profitability of the commercial sector. Whether that was based on agricultural or natural resource products that could be sold or traded with other nations, or later based on manufacturing of new products and new technologies, the commercial sector wealth represented the wealth of the nation, and the economic and physical security of that nation.

2. It is a fact that every dollar of federal or state tax revenue, and every dollar of employee wages and salaries, comes ultimately from the profitability of our commercial sector. Commercial profits generate tax revenues directly, and some of these revenues pay for salaries of government employees. Commercial profits of course also pay wages and salaries to their employees, whether they make and sell products and services to other businesses or to consumers. And commercial profits generate the funds for investing in growing the business and, as a result, growing the overall economy, creating jobs, and increasing overall working middle-class incomes and wealth

via sharing of strong profits with *all* employees.

Without sustained and growing business profitability, we won't continue to be a strong and secure nation with a high standard of living for citizens. It is not *whether* businesses are profitable that is the issue, but *how* those profits are invested that determines the economic strength and security of the nation, and the quality of life of our citizens. Those outcomes can be achieved *if* a major portion of the business profits are shared with *all* employees, so that overall middle-class incomes grow, helping to sustain economic growth, minimizing the income growth gaps between the middle and top income segments, *and* increasing the quality of life of our citizens.

What is shown in the table below are the actual trends in average income levels by quintiles (five equally sized segments of 20% of households) from 1968 to 2016.

Trends in Average Household Income — by 20% Quintiles and Top 5%

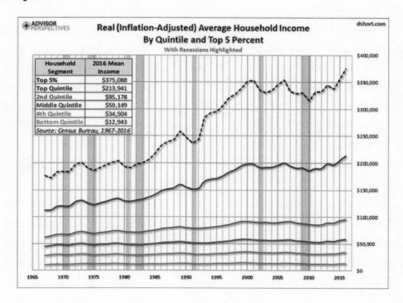

What this data indicates is that since the mid-1960s, the incomes of households in the bottom 40% of the USA have essentially not changed on an inflation-adjusted basis for nearly the past 50 years!

The middle quintile 20% of households, the middle 40%–60% group, have increased income only modestly—from about $45,000 to about $55,000 annually, or $10,000 over 50 years, an average of about $200 per year, or less than half of 1% per year on average above inflation. That is obviously a minuscule increase over 50 years for 60% of households. The next 20% of households, the second quintile, the top 60%–80% group, have had income growth of about $35,000 over 50 years, an average of about 60% over the past 50 years, and an average of about 1.2% per year or $700 per year above inflation.

In contrast, the top quintile, the top 20% of households, the top 80%–100% group, have had income growth of about 91%, about $100,000 annually, or about $2,000 per year, nearly doubling and increasing about 1.8% per year above inflation. Within this group, the top 5% of households, the group from 95% to 100%, have had income growth of about 110%, increasing by about $200,000 annually, or about $4,000 per year, more than doubling and increasing about 2.2% per year above inflation.

So it seems that for most of the past 50 years, working middle-class incomes, represented by the 40% and 60% groups, have experienced very little income growth. If we expand the view to the full bottom 60% of households, then over half of the country's households have not really participated in the economic and profit growth of the companies they have helped generate. And since 70% of GDP economic growth is dependent on middle-class income and spending growth, we can see in the chart below that average GDP growth by decade has generally trended downward over the past 50 years, while tax rates have declined to record low levels, while business profits and stock market valuations have risen to record high levels before and after the 2008–2009 recession, and while deficits have skyrocketed.

Historic GDP Growth, Top Personal Tax Rate, Business Tax Rate, Annual Deficit

Decade	Avg GDP	Avg Per Tax	Avg Bus. Tax	Avg Ann. Deficit	
1945–49	-1.9%	86.2%	38.0%	-$9.4 B	
1950–59	4.1%	91.0%	51.0%	-$1.8 B	
1960–69	4.3%	80.3%	51.7%	-$5.7 B	
1970–79	3.2%	70.2%	47.9%	-$35.1 B	
1980–89	3.0%	48.4%	43.0%	-$1,56.5 B	
1990–99	3.1%	37.0%	34.7%	-$13.4 B	
2000–09	1.7%	36.2%	35.0%	-$31.8 B	
2010–17	2.2%	37.6%	35.0%	-$881.7 B	
2018–19	2.6%	37.0%	21.0%	-$1,096.2 B	
2020	-3.5%	37.0%	21.0%	-$3,100.0 B	(Pandemic Impact)

The extent of the potential problem that our ever-increasing debt represents to the economy is infrequently raised in our debates on economic policy. Voters who did realize a small decrease in their tax burden in 2018 most often seem happy about the extra money they retained, without any sense of understanding that this extra money essentially has come from the increase in the national debt. So these funds were essentially borrowed from our children and grandchildren, who will at some point have to deal with the impact of paying interest on the debt on our future economic and national security.

We saw how our parents and grandparents responded to the end of World War II. They invested in infrastructure— the interstate highway system—and in building an educated workforce—sending 4 million veterans to college for free. They did not pass on massive debt from World War II, nor borrow for infrastructure and education investments, passing on the accumulated debt to our generation and future generations.

Rather, they accepted the high personal tax rates needed to pay for these investments. As a result, they passed on the greatest economy in the world to us, the current generation.

Today, we seem incapable of putting the future of our country, or the security of our grandchildren, ahead of our own short-term desires for a somewhat better economy and quality of life today. We are increasing debt not just to recover from a dangerous recession, as we did in 2008–2010, but simply to boost short-term company profits with the hope that this will also result in higher economic growth rates. But like some companies who have sought short-term stock market gains by investing hard-earned profits in buying back stock and then seen the profits evaporate in stock price declines, our country is increasing our debt significantly and putting our long-term economic security at risk.

How does our accumulated debt load represent an economic security risk?

Let's look at the interest on the debt we need to pay out of the current budget. Through 2019, the accumulated debt is $21.6 trillion. With interest rates at all-time lows, the interest rate on the debt was just 2.2% in 2019. With that low an interest rate, the interest payments represent about 9% of total federal spending. However, interest rate payments were the fastest-growing part of federal spending in 2019, up 15% despite lower interest rates (down about -24%) due to higher debt balances (up about 26%). In comparison, other major elements of the budget rose about 6% overall. It is projected by the Congressional Budget Office that interest payments could more than double in the next ten years.

Interest rates on the debt are at near record low periods, reflecting the overall low interest rates we are experiencing currently. But 30 years ago, interest rates were five times higher than they are today. As we are at record low rates today, it is reasonable to expect that interest rates are likely to increase substantially in the future. They may not increase by five times, but they could easily double or triple, from about 2% to 4% or even 6%, in just a few years. Should that occur, even without any further increases in the debt balance, interest payments could easily double to 18% of the budget, or even to 24%–27% of total spending. Rising interest payments on such a large and increasing debt balance represent a "ticking time bomb" on the economic and national security of our country. We cannot control when and by how much interest rates may rise in the future, so the potential impact of this "time bomb" exploding in our economy is not under our control.

As the percentage of our spending required for interest rate payments increases, it will be harder to fund important programs without raising taxes. Both of these outcomes represent a significant risk to the future economic growth and security of our country. For example, this potential 9% increase in the percentage of the budget for interest rate payments is more than the percentage we allocate for all veterans and transportation infrastructure expenses combined. It is also greater than the amount we allocate for education, international affairs (including the State Department), housing support, energy, and science development combined.

The larger the debt balance grows, the more difficult will be the challenge of reducing the deficit. In 1998, we balanced the budget in 1999 and 2000 by a combination of raising taxes and cutting spending. These actions resulted in surpluses, not deficits, over two fiscal years, with continued economic growth. Then in 2001, we began a pattern of increasing spending and cutting taxes, resulting once again in growing deficits.

For fiscal year 2019, the annual deficit represents almost 9% of the total spending. So, to balance the budget by spending cuts alone, we'd have to cut about $380 billion out of a $4.2 trillion budget. When we look at the current allocation of spending in the chart below, we would have to cut out nearly all discretionary spending except food and agriculture, transportation, and veteran programs. Such action would seriously weaken key aspects of our economy, our national security, and the quality of life in our communities. As well, the investments needed for growth, as we've discussed, would not be possible, likely leading to a significantly lower annual GDP growth and higher unemployment.

Percent of spending, including discretionary and mandatory

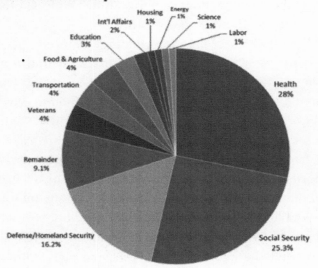

Source: 2018 Office of Management and Budget. The "Remainder" category primarily includes interest on the debt at 9.0% and miscellaneous expenses.

Since the deficit has largely been caused by the combination of spending increases and tax revenue decreases, it seems to make sense to follow the approach used just 20 years ago to balance the budget, and once again combine some spending cuts and some tax revenue increases to balance the budget and stop the increases in the debt balance. At some point in the very near future, we will need to begin reducing the level of our annual deficits. Over time, we will need several years if not decades of budget surpluses to actually pay down some of the accumulated debt, to protect our future economic security from the damage that rising interest rates could represent. That outcome will be possible only if we can establish an effective national pro-growth economic policy that achieves the multiple objectives of driving greater economic GDP growth (target of 3% annual GDP growth or more) and supporting business profit growth via an innovative tax policy that supports raising middle-class incomes via profit sharing.

In addition, continued positive growth will also require investments to provide the world-class infrastructure and the education and training programs needed for an improving workforce to sustain a stronger economy. We cannot build and sustain a world-class economy on the third-class infrastructure we have today. Repairing the existing infrastructure problems is necessary, of course, but won't be sufficient for future growth. Without an investment in designing and beginning to develop an innovative infrastructure that can support the future level of economic activity we are targeting to achieve in the next 20–30 years, we may find our economic growth level is limited simply by the lack of an adequate infrastructure.

For perspective, if we are able to achieve a 3% annual GDP economic growth rate, our level of economic activity would double in the next 24 years. Can our current infrastructure support twice the level of economic activity we have today? Would it be sufficient to just add more highway lanes and more fossil fuel plants to enable us to support that level of economic activity? If not, and a major new infrastructure is needed to be "world class" by 2050 and beyond, how many years will it take to build an expanded and future infrastructure? Probably about 20–25 years, I'd guess. Meaning we had better get started about now with the design stage!

When we prepared for economic growth following World War II, did we just build more two-lane highways? Or did we invest in designing, developing and creating an innovative infrastructure of the future, the interstate highway system, one that would support our economy and quality of life for the next 40–50 years? Where would our economy be today if that innovation had not been seen as a key to future economic growth in the 1950s? Where would we be today if those leaders had failed to set the tax rates to pay for that investment, instead of increasing the debt and passing it on to our generation?

Policy 2—Healthcare

As we did in the previous section, we'll start with key questions relating to policy goals to enable a data-driven analysis of how to achieve better healthcare outcomes, and identify new innovative non-partisan policy concepts or solutions we might employ.

Goal: Improve healthcare access and affordability for all Americans

Questions:

1. Should the Affordable Care Act (ACA) be repealed so we can return to the previous healthcare status?

- Would repeal without replacement be positive for most Americans? Should we consider a full repeal or a partial repeal? What would be the outcome for most Americans?
- Under the "old" healthcare system before ACA, who paid

for emergency room and ambulance services costs for those without insurance?

- Does it make sense that everyone should have access to and be required to have a minimum level of affordable insurance to at least cover these costs? Should every adult have this minimum level of insurance coverage?

- Most issues with the ACA seem to be related to the number of services and coverages being required in ACA programs without matching services and coverages to individual family needs; and the requirement for businesses with more than 50 employees to provide insurance coverage for employees.

  - The lack of individual choice and tailoring program coverages to the needs and choices of individual families results in paying for services that are not used or relevant, thus increasing the costs of coverage for individuals.

  - The lack of national competition also seems to be an issue leading to higher costs. Some states have only one or two provider options, as providers are able to exclude cities and counties with lower profits in preference for a focus on higher profitability locations.

2. Instead of being repealed, should ACA be changed in some key ways? Some changes that might help reduce costs and improve access are:

- To increase the individual coverage choices consumers can select based on their needs and situation, versus requiring a prescribed and limited set of choices;

  - To include a "basic" coverage only for emergency services, and a menu of other coverage options recommended based on personal and family profile data, but selected by individuals;

- To require that every adult citizen pay something toward having access to emergency care;
- To require all insurance providers to offer policies in all states;
  - No "cherry-picking" of states, counties or demographic groups allowed by insurance companies;
- To remove the requirement for small businesses with 50 or more employees to provide coverage for employees;
- Require policies to be issued to individuals, not to companies; companies can provide cash support payments to employees to reduce their insurance costs, but without having a dedicated company plan.
  - This would "level" the playing field between large and small businesses, reduce costs for businesses that offer their own plans today that can be used for employee support payments for their personal insurance plans, and enable all policies to be "portable" for employees and retained with a job change or if retiring before Medicare eligibility age.

3. Or should we develop a new approach to healthcare programs?

(a) Consider a "Medicare for All" approach.

- Pros
  - The main benefit of this option is to reduce overall healthcare system costs by eliminating the profit that insurance companies make, and to simplify the processing of insurance payments between providers, insurance companies and consumers.
  - In addition, this approach could increase the coverage of all citizens by auto-enrolling citizens in the program.
- Cons
  - The current Medicare program only covers 80% of

medical expenses and has no coverage for prescription drugs. Most current Medicare recipients also buy either an additional plan, or a Medicare Supplement or Advantage plan, as well as a prescription drug plan. So, to provide coverage that is comparable to many private insurance plans, there would need to be major changes to the current Medicare program. These changes would obviously increase the costs of a national "Medicare for All" program.

○ Medicare holds down costs by "fixing" lower costs for Medicare-provided services than most providers and hospitals charge patients with private insurance. As a result, not every provider or hospital accepts Medicare patients. What happens to the delivery of services in a "Medicare for All" approach if just one-quarter of those providers who currently don't accept Medicare choose to retire instead of working under Medicare payment limits? Can new doctors expect to repay student loans at Medicare payment levels? Or will the government have to subsidize education and training for doctors completely? What would control those costs and annual cost increases?

○ Are we confident that a government-run healthcare program can be effective in terms of costs and quality of delivery, in the fair and just allocation of limited services versus needs, and minimization of fraud? If we look at the Veterans Administration's healthcare performance as an example of a government-run healthcare program, it would seem that there is some basis for concern with this approach controlling 6% of the US economy and healthcare that impacts the lives of all citizens.

○ What about the nearly 160 million citizens who currently have private health insurance through their employer? Should the preferences for private insurance supported by contributions from an employer of this many citizens be ignored? Is it necessary to ignore those preferences in order to achieve a much better solution for 28 million citizens who are uninsured? There are also an estimated 22 million citizens covered by individual private insurance, and it is likely that a good percentage of those citizens might prefer private insurance to Medicare.

(b) Consider a "public–private" approach, where all policies funded, partially or completely, by a company or organization are required to be individual policies—no policies would be owned by the employee's company—and consumers choose their own benefits based on individual household need and income.

- Pros
  - This approach could reduce costs for businesses who offer their own policies today. Instead of researching and managing some level of employee registration and issues with the company's health insurance policy, companies could simply offer a cash payment benefit to employees to offset the cost of the private policies that employees choose for themselves.
  - This approach could reduce administrative costs within the system as well, since both insurance companies and providers would have many fewer options and contacts to deal with in processing insurance claims, making digital automation much more affordable for both companies and providers.
  - This approach also removes the requirement for small businesses to offer healthcare policies to their employees. This burden would be removed, and small

businesses could better compete with large companies by simply offering a similar cash payment.

- This approach would expand the market for individual policies, from an estimated 22 million today to 180 million. Such an expansion would help to significantly increase competition and efficiencies of scale in the private market, a key to reducing costs.

- With the expansion of the individual private market to an estimated 180 million, companies would be required to offer national policies covering every state and county. They would not be able to "cherry pick" the most affluent counties or states. This ensures that the benefits of competition and access to all policy options would be available in every state and in every region, to every citizen.

- The change from company ownership to individual ownership would ensure "portability" of an existing policy between jobs and remove a major driver of "pre-existing conditions" events.

- This approach would eliminate the conflicts that have occurred when companies want to opt out of offering healthcare benefits in their policies based on their own beliefs, that many employees with different beliefs would like to have.

- This approach would also increase individual citizen choice of benefits and policy elements that best fit their personal and family situation. The signup process would start with a detailed health profile, and the system would propose suggested elements of coverage, benefits and costs for the individual based on their personal situation. Then they would select the options that work best for their needs.

If any recommended options are declined, the citizen would receive information to educate them about the risks of higher costs in the future if they are not covering a potential illness or accident that could be relevant to them. They would confirm receiving and understanding the information and risks, and could download the education for retention.

- For the estimated 28 million currently uninsured, some will likely become private insurance policy holders, as competition drives down the costs from today. For the balance, providing an option to access a public plan option similar (or identical) to Medicare would be provided, to ensure full coverage of all citizens.

- Cons
  - This approach does not offer the same degree of automatic registration for all citizens that a government-run "Medicare for All" would provide. However, as any uninsured citizens access emergency room care, they can be helped to apply for the public option at the emergency site before or after receiving treatment, as appropriate.
  - Some may see the continuation of private company profit in the system as a barrier to achieving lower costs. However, it would be hoped that the country's leaders could evaluate the total costs, the service delivery quality (e.g. the impact on doctors leaving the medical field), accessibility (e.g. wait times for procedures), and the degree of positive health outcomes before selecting a new approach to the nation's healthcare system. While profits may exist, these may be not much higher than the human costs of a government-run system with less innovation and fewer incentives for greater efficiencies.

Policy 3—Investing in Energy and Transportation Infrastructures

Goals: 1. Repair and maintain the existing infrastructures to a B+ grade

Questions:

1. Does the US currently have a "world class" infrastructure?

- The survey of the US transportation infrastructure by the American Society of Civil Engineers in 2017 rated both the energy and transportation infrastructures as a D+. In 2021, the rating had "risen" to a C-. This is hardly the level of quality that equates to the "world class" infrastructure that the USA needs to support a world-class economy and quality of life.

2. What are the barriers to investing in repairing these key infrastructures?

- Neither party, when in control of the Presidency and Congress on their own, has made investing federal resources in repairing and maintaining our national infrastructure a major priority, or in helping the states with the investments for local roads. Nor when government control has been "shared" by the parties has either party been anxious to work with the other.
- In past years, Democrats seem to have focused more on spending on social programs, while Republicans seem to have focused more on tax cuts. Both of these directions have consistently taken priority over spending to repair, maintain or expand our economic infrastructures.
- Especially in energy, progress would require the federal

government to partner with private industry and with the states to repair and maintain national energy systems. With no agreement on the appropriate "formula" for these partnerships, essentially little to nothing is getting done, outside of what states are doing with their own resources.

3. Have we initiated investments in the innovative energy and transportation infrastructure elements that could support future economic growth and quality-of-life improvements over the next 40–50 years? As mentioned earlier, we could fail to reach our annual economic growth target of 3% in the next decade or two if we only focus on repairing the existing infrastructure and don't plan to support the increased level of economic activity we are working to achieve via other policies.

- As mentioned earlier, if we are able to sustain an annual growth rate of just 3% in economic activity, our future level of economic activity would double from the current level in just 24 years. Is our current level and type of energy and transportation infrastructure able to support twice the level of activity we have today?
- What should be the level and type of energy and infrastructure we will need to support economic growth? Should we drill for more oil and build more highway lanes? Or should we envision an innovative approach in both energy and transportation infrastructures that would support growth and quality of life for the next 50 years?

4. What are the risks of continuing to ignore these needs?

- Our energy and transportation infrastructures are the foundations of our economy. If these elements are not at "world class" standards, it is nearly impossible for our economy to be "world class."

- How many years would be required to build an infrastructure to support the level of activity we have today? At least 20 years would seem likely. So if we do not begin a major development effort now, might the lack of an adequate infrastructure strangle our economic growth and result in a declining quality of life?

- For example, the I-75/I-71 bridge between Ohio and Kentucky in Cincinnati is estimated to carry 6% of the total US GDP each year. Our national goal of 3% GDP growth would be pretty impossible to reach if that bridge fails and 6% of our national GDP is limited in its growth. And it is at a substantial risk of failing as of 2021.

5. What actions should the federal government take to address these needs?

- Ultimately, the federal government should take the lead in developing the national blueprint needed for the repairs and ongoing maintenance of these important infrastructures, and make sure that the funding mechanisms are in place to accomplish these goals without adding to the national debt and passing those costs on to future generations.

Goals: 2. Develop and fund an innovative infrastructure approach for the twenty-first century

Questions:

1. Is the existing level of energy and transportation infrastructure adequate to support our target level of economic growth for the balance of the twenty-first century?

- Our country has been at our strongest, from a national security and quality-of-life standpoint, for a majority of citizens when our economic growth has been at 3% or greater.

- However, we have not been able to sustain a 3% average annual GDP growth rate over a ten-year period since the 1990s. Unemployment has declined dramatically since the 2008–2010 recession. But at the average rate of 2.5% GDP growth over the last nine years, average household incomes for the bottom 60% of American households have barely kept up with inflation. Many households have both spouses working, but are living from paycheck to paycheck, saving little for emergencies or retirement.

- We have stated that with a 3% target economic growth rate, the level of economic activity would double in 24 years. It is obvious that the current level and quality of energy and transportation infrastructure can hardly support today's level of economic activity, let alone *double* the level we have today. But, if we do not plan for and invest in the infrastructure needed for that level of economic growth, as we have stated earlier, then an inadequate infrastructure could severely limit our future economic growth rate, with significant impacts on future employment, income, quality of life and even our national security.

2. Does the US have a plan for the energy and transportation infrastructure that will support our target economic GDP growth for the balance of the twenty-first century?

- There does not seem to be a plan for repair of our existing infrastructure, let alone any thinking about the energy and transportation infrastructure needs to support twice the level of economic activity we have today—and one that could sustain our economic growth and quality of life for the next 60 years or more.

- Why is this important? Once again, let's look back at history to hopefully enlighten us. In 1950, the USA was a nation of two-lane state and national highways crisscrossing the country, with lots of traffic lights and intersections. The Administration could see that just building more two-lane roads of the same design wasn't going to support the kind of economic growth they expected to follow World War II.

- As a result, they developed the interstate highway design, laid out north–south and east–west routes with "beltways" around major cities, and invested in the costs of a multi-decade project to complete the construction. Additionally and very importantly, they established the tax rate needed to generate the revenues to pay for the costs as incurred, instead of passing the costs on to our generation in debt. Can you think what our economy and quality of life would have been like over the past 60 years if either (a) there was no new infrastructure and the current infrastructure was neglected and allowed to fall into a D+ to C- level of disrepair; or (b) the costs to build the interstate highway were simply passed on to our generation to either pay off or pay the interest on?

3. What kind of innovative energy and transportation infrastructures might be needed in the future?

- In transportation, we need to ask, what is the equivalent of the interstate highway system relative to two-lane highways that would support a doubling of our economic activity in the next 24 years? Is it just a matter of increasing the number of lanes in our existing highway system? Or should we look to innovative transportation systems that would leverage the new technologies of the twenty-first century?

We can look around the world and see what the countries that are our primary global competitors are investing in, and it's not primarily more asphalt highway lanes—it is high-speed rail driven by electric power, for the rapid and convenient movement of both goods and people. So, as the source of electric power changes over time, the basic transportation infrastructure will not require conversion. They are also investing in electric and hydrogen fuel-cell cars, trucks, buses and streetcars, and even farming equipment. The question for us is, what does a world-class transportation infrastructure look like for the twenty-first century and beyond?

- In energy, the considerations for the future would seem to be twofold: (a) which energy sources can be economically viable for the next 60 years or more, without limited availability or geopolitical issues impacting the supply and economics of the resource; and (b) which energy sources can reduce the amount of carbon and greenhouse gases related to climate change that are released to the atmosphere, and have fewer environmental impacts in producing the energy source?

When we consider the first factor, it seems clear that our current reliance on fossil fuels cannot be permanent, as these resources are not renewable or inexhaustible. Whether it is 60 years or 160 years from now, we will eventually exhaust the supply of fossil fuels. In addition, it is unstable from an economic viability standpoint due to the geopolitical issues related to the concentration of the world's supply of these fuels in the Middle East. Further, while we have achieved increased oil and gas production in the US due to fracking and increased exploration in public lands, do we want these actions to increase over the next 50–60 years?

When we consider the second factor, it seems clear that it has become urgent for the health of the planet that we reduce the amount of carbon and other greenhouse gases that our energy sources release to the environment in use. You don't have to accept the linkage between carbon pollution resulting from human activity and climate change. Just consider that it is likely that 100 years ago, we couldn't see the future problems that would be created by discharging industrial and human waste into our water systems.

But history again holds lessons for us today if we just listen. It has taught us that we can lose the natural resource of clean water unless we protect it from these abuses. Could it be that we have been in a similar mindset with regard to discharging industrial, electrical energy production and transportation wastes into the air, unaware of or uncaring about the long-term consequences of polluting the natural resource of clean air, and the impact on factors like breathing that can result in the long term? Add just the chance that the scientists could be right about climate change, and there would seem to be a pretty strong incentive to change the status quo in this area. After all, without clean water and air, what kind of quality of life would we be leaving to our grandchildren?

Once again, we can look around the world and see that our major global competitors are investing not in more fossil fuel development, but in new renewable and inexhaustible energy sources. Major economic competitor countries in both Asia and Europe have been investing in hydrogen fuel-cell technologies for years. Dubai, a country sitting on one of the world's largest reserves of oil, has purchased one of these units to produce hydrogen for their streetcar system that is powered by hydrogen fuel cells. Do you think they know something about prospering in the twenty-first century that we don't?

These fuel cells combine hydrogen with oxygen in the air to produce electricity and water as the only "exhaust." The advantage over electric-battery vehicles is faster refueling, more similar to gasoline refueling than battery recharging, and faster building of a national refueling infrastructure with less government subsidies required. And when integrated into a solar and wind electrical energy production facility, hydrogen fuel cells become an effective approach for storing excess energy produced on sunny and windy days as hydrogen, and using the hydrogen to generate electricity without sun or wind, providing a truly 24/7/365 renewable and inexhaustible energy system.

In the US, we are beginning to catch up. For example, Millennium Reign Energy (MRE), a small company in Dayton, Ohio, has developed an integrated hydrogen generation and dispensing station that can produce "green hydrogen" by splitting water into hydrogen and oxygen with electricity from solar panels or wind turbines, and fill hydrogen fuel-cell cars similarly to a gas pump. MRE has built and is operating the "Ohio Hydrogen Triangle," with three hydrogen generation and refueling stations in Dayton, Columbus and Portsmouth in Ohio. The company plans to build 27 more stations across the USA, connecting California with New York, and providing the first "Transcontinental Hydrogen Highway" to enable hydrogen fuel-cell vehicles—cars, trucks, buses and tractor-trailer rigs—to travel across the country. The station designs are scalable, in both hydrogen production and refueling capacity and required investment, so they are profitable for private operators from initial adoption to broadscale use, without requiring government subsidies, as the high-capacity electric charging network would require.

4. What causes our current leaders to ignore these real needs to sustain our economy and quality of life into the future?

There probably is no answer to this question with which a majority of Americans from both parties and political ideologies would agree. Here is just one possible answer from my personal perspective:

- I believe the cause might be related to the concept of *purpose*. I believe that the Administrations and congressional leaders of the 1950s, having gone through the challenges that World War II presented to all of us as Americans, still carried a sense of commitment both to country and to service over self, and also gratitude that, in the peace after World War II, they had the chance to look forward to the future.
- Today, if our leaders in both parties are more focused on commitment to their own careers and self-interest, to partisan interests and special-interest donors over the national interest, and have little sense of obligation to the future economic or national security of the country, that would explain the lack of action we see in these areas. It would also explain the focus of one party on short-term issues like tax cuts that benefit only a small part of the country, while putting the long-term future of the country overall at risk. And it would also explain the focus of the other party on providing short-term benefits to several small special-interest groups, while neglecting the needs of the majority segments of the country overall.
- If this is a valid rationale, then it would seem that making new "Citizen Rules" to minimize career self-interest, the impact of donors and money in politics, and the impacts

of partisanship, might be actions that would help develop leaders who come to Congress to serve the nation for a term, work together with their colleagues in both parties to accomplish effective solutions for the country overall, then return to private life as citizens. Today most of our congressional leaders are seeking one political position after another, to win one election after another, or they trade being in Congress for being a congressional lobbyist. Either way, the small group of people who are our political leaders today seem far removed from the realities of everyday American life, and do not seek these offices with a purpose to serve others beyond themselves, their party and their donors.

Policy 4—Investing in a Skilled and Educated Workforce

Goals: 1. Invest in growing the number of technically skilled workers

Questions:

1. Is it in the best interests of the country to invest in supporting the growth of a skilled technical workforce in the key areas needed for economic growth?

In many key skilled areas, there are thousands of skilled technical jobs that would provide a middle-class income going unfilled today across many key industries. Without providing the talent to fill these jobs, our overall target economic growth rate, which is driven by existing and emerging technical industries, will be difficult to sustain.

While the percentages of unemployed Americans overall are at historic low levels, there are still 6 million people unemployed. But there are also 4.4 million Americans who are classified as "involuntary part-time" workers, meaning they are seeking full-time work but are forced to settle for part-time work. There are also 1.6 million unemployed Americans who are not counted as unemployed as they have not looked for work in the past four weeks due to personal reasons. That is a total of 12 million Americans not employed in full-time jobs who would seemingly desire full-time work.

Here's the change that has happened in the past few years in the economy, however. The number of unfilled job openings exceeds the number of unemployed Americans for the first time in decades. There are 7.6 million unfilled jobs at the end of 2019. Around 20% of these are low-skill jobs; 32% of these require high skills; but a full 48% of these unfilled jobs are "middle skill" jobs. These jobs require at least a high-school degree and some level of post-secondary education—either a two-year technical education, or some degree of a trade skill experience. The middle-skill jobs provide a middle-class income opportunity for far less investment in education than a four-year college degree requires.

Investing in a program to help close the "skill gaps" would require additional funding at the local levels across the country, to support additional training at high-school age levels. Rather than coming from additional property taxes, a more equitable and effective approach would be to develop a funding formula based on the training requirements of each technical career path, and develop public–private partnerships with the technical trade unions and companies requiring employees with these skills, to share the training costs across the country. The government share of the training expenses would come from the federal education budget.

2. What are some of the key changes we need to make in order to develop an increased skilled technical workforce?

- In our high schools, we seem to be primarily focused on preparing all students for college. We have many college preparatory courses and programs in almost every high school. The guidance offices in many of our public high schools are filled principally with brochures on colleges and university options, and provide help and support mainly in the college preparation and application processes.

- But there is very little support given to helping students prepare for a career as a skilled technician, which usually involves some technical-school training and apprenticeships. Most of the "blue collar" jobs today require expertise in a technical area such as heating, air conditioning, auto repair, construction, traditional and automated manufacturing, or wind turbine and solar panel installation and service, many of which involve computers and/or digitized equipment. Also, many of these skilled roles can lead to owning small businesses in the future.

- Instead of forcing most students into a college preparatory curriculum in our high schools, we should be identifying those with a preference for these paths and providing them with the same quality of preparation as we provide for those destined for college. We should design our education system for high-school age students to provide multiple paths to middle-class lifestyles, instead of focusing nearly all our resources on the college path only.

- We primarily celebrate those students who take Advanced Placement (AP) courses, who qualify as Merit Scholarship winners, who achieve high scores on college acceptance tests, and who are accepted at prestigious colleges and universities. And our high-school "score cards" primarily reflect these benchmarks.

- We should equally celebrate student accomplishments in

selecting specific paths, qualifying for technical schools, gaining acceptance into apprenticeships, and so on. These paths should be seen as equally important to the individual student, to the community and to the country as any college path.

Goals: 2. Invest in reducing the student loan debt for university and technical skills training

Question: Does it really make good sense to invest government resources to support the costs of both college and technical school education?

Our country needs a skilled technical workforce of adequate numbers with skills matched to fill the positions that can drive our economic growth forward; otherwise, our economic growth will stagnate. If training is not provided to unemployed or displaced workers who have fallen from the ranks of the middle class, we will also experience social welfare problems in addition to the economic ones.

In addition, we need our workforce to be the best educated in the world. Education levels are rising around the world, and we must ensure that the level of education in our workforce not only keeps pace, but keeps exceeding the levels of the other countries with which we compete for development and innovation. With the rising costs of education and a corresponding increase in student debt, we are at risk of not being able to keep pace with other countries where such education is heavily subsidized by government.

We have an example we can follow from the not-too-distant past. In the 1950s and 1960s, following World War II, the country invested in sending over 4 million GIs to college for free, to provide the foundation for an educated workforce to help grow the post-war economy. These costs were included in the federal budget in those years, and the costs were funded by tax rates necessary to generate the revenues to pay for them, without increasing the federal debt by borrowing and passing the debt forward to this current generation. That investment helped generate much of the economic growth that led to the wealth, prosperity and quality of life that the US has enjoyed in the 70 years since the 1950s.

As we saw earlier, our economic growth in this new century has fallen as average middle-class incomes across the country have failed to sustain reasonable growth, while business profits and stock market values have grown to record levels. To help middle-class incomes grow, we need to help grow the number of citizens capable of earning middle-class incomes, by supporting the growth of both skills and education in our workforce. And this is an investment that the private sector should and, I believe, will partner with the public sector to support.

We reviewed the fact earlier that 70% of economic GDP growth is middle-class income and spending. A growing number of middle-class households, with growing incomes, is vital to achieve the level of economic growth that benefits the entire country, and all segments of the economy. If the country's overall pro-growth economic policy does not focus directly and effectively on generating growth in middle-class income and the number of middle-class-income households, it is almost mathematically impossible for economic GDP growth to achieve and sustain the healthy growth we need for both economic and national security.

Further, we have seen that rising levels of student debt are having a negative impact on the starting of households and families by the new generations of graduating students. At the point where the new generation of 20-somethings and 30-somethings should be buying homes, starting families and spending to acquire the items every young family needs, too many of them are unable to do so because of the impact of student loan payments on their spendable incomes.

How should we help? Some political leaders have proposed essentially a "bail out" program to eliminate student loan debt. Some have proposed more government support to offset at least some of the debt burden, either by lowering interest rates charged, or lowering the income-based requirement payment level, or by offering a delay in the start of repayments, or by income tax credits, or some other approach. Still others have proposed initiating a community service requirement in exchange for some student debt relief.

Finally, who should we help? Should we help undergraduates only? Or graduate students as well? Should we help students in technical schools as well as traditional four-year programs? Should we vary the degree of financial help depending on the income or wealth of the student's family? Should we vary the degree of help based on the career path that the education supports or results in after graduation?

Whichever approach to addressing this issue is eventually chosen by voters, any relief from the student loan burden would be a boost to the quality of life for these graduates, and a boost for the economy as well. But the choice of an approach should be made with the same degree of respect for spending public money as was discussed under the budgeting approach section earlier. That is, there should be specific goals for the program stated upfront, in terms of benefit delivered to a specific group for a specific cost and outcome for the country overall. There should be measures in place to let us know if we are achieving the goals or not, and the program should be publicly evaluated at the end of each two-year budget cycle to determine if the results warrant continuing, expanding, or discontinuing the program.

Policy 5— Comprehensive Immigration and Border Security

Goals: 1. Reduce illegal immigrants and drug flows into the United States from all sources

Questions:

1. What are the sources of illegal immigrants into the USA?

- Research estimates that there are about 11.3 million undocumented immigrants living illegally in the US (the statistics relate to the year 2018). An estimated 76% of these undocumented immigrants are from Mexico, Central America and South America; 16% are from Asia; 5% are from Europe and Canada; and 3% are from Africa.
- The majority of these undocumented immigrants, an estimated 62%, have been living in the US longer than ten years; the balance (38%) of the undocumented immigrants have been living in the US less than ten years. Only about 18% have been in the US for five years or less.
- Research on this subject has indicated there are two main sources for the increases in undocumented immigrants in the US. These are: (a) illegal border crossings, and (b) illegal overstays of temporary visas. It may be surprising to note that in the past decade, there have been more illegal overstays of temporary visas than illegal crossings of the border.

  Specifically, an estimated 60% of total undocumented immigrant increases over the past decade involved people who actually arrived in the US by air legally with temporary visas, then failed to leave the US when their visas expired. About 40% of total undocumented immigrant increases involved people who illegally crossed the southern border.

And more than 50% of these illegal crossings happened at legal ports of entry, with people smuggled in vehicles, not making illegal crossings in unfenced areas of the border. So, effective border security actually requires a focus on the data indicating the source of most of these illegal entries, and not focusing billions of dollars of resources on the areas of entry that represent the smallest impact on the illegal resident population growth.

2. What are the levels of legal immigrants that are granted entry into the US?

- Historically, the US has not altered legal immigration levels very frequently. These levels seem to have been driven by ideological fears of social change, and disconnected from the needs of the economy. The last time there was a major change in the level of legal immigrants was essentially in 1965. In the past decade, we have accepted an average of about 513,000 immigrants per year. About 52% are from the western hemisphere, primarily Mexico, Central America and South America; about 32% are from Asian regions; and about 7% each from Europe and Africa.
- In 1986, new categories of temporary entry visas (non-immigrant) were defined:
  - H-2A visa for temporary or seasonal agricultural workers;
  - H-1B visa for highly skilled technical workers;
  - H-2B visa for temporary or seasonal non-agricultural workers.

    There was an average of about 9 million non-immigrant visas in these categories issued over the past decade. About 200,000 per year are H-2A visas for seasonal agricultural workers.

Goals: 2. Set reasonable levels of legal entries for all categories of immigrants, including asylum seekers

Question: Should we balance both a skill-based and family-based immigration policy?

- We have about 1.5 million unfilled low-skill jobs today, many in roles and industries that American citizens are not interested in fulfilling. There are also the 4.4 million part-time jobs currently filled by workers who would rather be training for one of the unfilled middle-class-income jobs. These unfilled, lower-skill job openings would seem to be a good opportunity for admitting temporary immigrant workers, without impacting the job availabilities for Americans.
- We do not seem to have a process for reviewing the unfilled jobs that Americans are not willing or available to fill. It would seem that if many immigrants are illegally entering the US to take advantage of unfilled low-skill jobs, then a process to match legal temporary worker visas to the level of unfilled low-skill jobs would be likely to significantly reduce the number of illegal immigrant crossings. So it would seem to be a clear priority for the country to have an open, objective and data-driven process to adjust these levels annually to meet the true needs of the economy.
- We should be able to allow immigrants who have become naturalized citizens to easily apply for temporary visit visas for immediate family members. If family members seek to apply for temporary residency, then they should be required to follow the same requirements as non-family applicants for temporary residency status, with a preferred priority status.
- The numbers of total temporary worker entries into the

US should be reviewed each year, based on real economic needs that don't jeopardize jobs for existing Americans in the industries where the visas are requested. A similar data-driven review of the numbers of temporary residency entries leading to permanent residency and naturalized citizenship should be carried out each year as well.

- Employers should be required to pay immigrant visa holders the same wages and benefits as they would pay to citizens doing the same work at the same skill level. This would ensure that a preference for citizens would result, since hiring visa employees would involve paying visa fees, some degree of language barrier, and likely the need for more training than would be required for citizen hires.

Goals: 3. Address the existing population of undocumented immigrants via a new Two-Tier Visa Entry and Residency Status Policy

Question: How should we address the existing population of undocumented immigrants?

- The existence of over 11 million undocumented immigrants in the US has created many conflicts in our country and many difficulties for local governments and communities, not to mention the quality of life for these 11 million people and their families.
- President Reagan passed an immigration law in 1986 that granted amnesty to the millions of existing undocumented immigrants in the US at that time. However, the Administration did not take adequate measures to prevent new illegal immigrants from continuing to enter the US, and we are now back in the same situation as then with regard to the millions of undocumented immigrants

in the country today.

- The existence of undocumented immigrants in the US has been allowed to persist because of the inability of the Administration and Congress under either party's majority control to take effective action. It seems some Republican donors favor the existence of low-wage workers "under the radar," who will perform jobs and work for lower wages than native Americans. It seems some Democrat donors favor the existence of minority populations with a high likelihood of eventually becoming Democrat voters.

- Under a Congress focused on serving the national interest instead of partisan interests and self-interest, there could be a solution developed to address the existing population of illegal immigrants and remove this wedge between the parties and their advocates. We could establish a Two-Tier Visa Entry and Residency Policy to address immigrants who are in the US without documentation, and who have not committed any felony or violent behavior charges. Each undocumented immigrant would be required within a six-month period to come forward and apply for one of these two paths to legal status, by declaring their reason for entering the US illegally: (1) they desire just to work as temporary or seasonal workers and then return home; or (2) they seek to relocate permanently to the US.

  ○ The temporary or seasonal worker visa would create a legal status for workers who are needed and who would add a benefit to the country, by entering the US to fill temporary or seasonal jobs in certain industries where Americans are not available or willing to fill those jobs.

    These visas would be for specific dates of less than a year, but could be issued for the same period over several years. The applicants would be sponsored by a specific company or industry, and would not require any language skills or understanding of US laws for approval and entry, beyond the residential limits of a temporary visa. The sponsoring company or industry would need to certify the income to be provided, and the applicant would have to certify a US address and contact details.

○ The temporary residency visa would create a legal status for immigrants who seek entry to the US for the purpose of relocating to the US from their home country. During the temporary residency period established by law, the immigrant would be required to establish an address, obtain and sustain an income, develop basic English competency, be free of any criminal felony or violent criminal record, and perhaps enter a school or job-training facility. At the end of the period of temporary residency, the immigrant must be able to meet requirements in these areas and apply for permanent residency status, or be required to leave the country.

○ The permanent residency visa would create a key step toward naturalized citizenship status, but not a guarantee of naturalized citizenship status until the completion of requirements. The applicant would be required to complete all the steps above, and learn the basic elements of our laws and Constitution, to be a citizen and voter. There would be an established period of time between permanent residency and an application for naturalized citizenship, as discussed below, during which time these higher requirements would need to be met.

For immigrants who have entered the country legally, current law requires a minimum period of five years between permanent residency and application for naturalized citizenship status. This period is reduced to three years if the resident is married to an American citizen. For immigrants who have entered the country illegally and are granted temporary residency status within the six-month period after this policy is implemented, the period between permanent residency and naturalized citizenship application, if they qualify, would be longer, eight years instead of five years, and five years instead of three years if married to an American citizen, for example.

Goals: 4. Enforce the laws against illegal entry and overstaying of visas

Question: Is it important to have secure borders and a controlled legal immigration system?

- Once we have established a new process for setting annual targets for admitting immigrants, as discussed above, and have addressed the existing undocumented immigrants in the US, it should then be appropriate to enforce existing immigration laws prohibiting illegal entry and overstaying of visas.
- People who enter the US illegally would be directed to an immigration center to be processed. They would be given instructions for applying for one of the legal immigrant visas and being added to a list of those desiring entry. If the skills of these individuals matched the needs of unfilled openings for seasonal workers, they would be connected with those opportunities. If there was not a match, and there was not an asylum case, they would be deported with information for applying for an appropriate opportunity for the following season.
- People who overstay visas or who are not processed crossing the border would not be eligible for any public

support of any kind. When their status is discovered, they would be directed to an immigration center to be processed as described above.

As a result of these policies, the existence of a major population of undocumented immigrants and their families in the US should be essentially eliminated over time; the need for seasonal workers hopefully would be matched with temporary immigrant visa holders; the ability to receive new permanent immigrants would be addressed; and the ability to unite families of citizens would be accommodated. And, just as importantly, a major source of divisiveness in our country would be eliminated from our national experience.

Policy 6—Gun Safety, Mass Shootings and Gun Rights

We have experienced an incredible number of mass shootings in our country in the past decade, with a shocking number of deaths and injuries to innocent citizens. These events have occurred in our office buildings, in our schools, our churches, synagogues and mosques, in our movie theatres and in our shopping malls. The victims have involved men, women and children of all ages.

Yet, as of this writing, as a society and as a government we have not agreed upon nor taken any significant action to reduce the impact of these events on our country. I believe we have not been able to bridge the partisan divides on what actions to take because our political leaders jump right to solutions without seeking to get agreement on goals. Diverse groups will find it very difficult to agree to actions if they haven't agreed to the goals those actions should achieve.

So, at the start of this policy discussion, I am going to suggest three goals that any actions taken would need to achieve, if the impact of these events on our country is to be minimized. Without considering yet *how* these goals would be achieved, I ask all readers to consider two questions: (a) If we were able to achieve these three goals, would this result in a significant reduction in the impact of mass shooting events in our country? (b) If we don't achieve all three of these goals, will we be severely limited as a society by the impact that results? I won't tell you as a reader how to answer these, but I suggest strongly that the answers are Yes to both.

Given that discussion, let's now consider what actions would be required to achieve each of those goals.

Goals: 1. Reduce the number of mass shooting events

Question: What actions would be effective in reducing the number of mass shooting events?

- The actions that lead to mass shooting events seem to be a combination of the following:
  - People involved in mass shooting events have been shown to have had a mental or emotional disturbance, resulting often in a history of some violent behavior and/or some association with groups who advocate hate speech and/or violence against certain minority groups.

    It would seem that an effective way of reducing the number of mass shooting events would require a process that would prevent such people from either buying or possessing weapons that could be used in a mass shooting event.
  - But in order to accomplish that outcome, it would seem we'd need to have a few tools to enable these actions:

    (a) We'd need to have access to a national database of people who have been treated for mental or emotional disturbances that could be related to future violent behavior; of people who have exhibited violent behaviors, those convicted, and those charged but not convicted; of people who have associated with groups who have advocated hate speech and/or violence against certain minority groups; or people who have expressed hate speech or the desire or intent to commit violence against minority groups or any other person.

(b) We'd need to have a process for accessing that database easily and quickly for any and every gun purchase or transfer, and record the results of the database check for each specific purchase; a process that would provide a serious penalty to any seller and purchaser who completes a gun or ammunition purchase without first performing the required database check and receiving a "clean record" confirmation prior to the purchase.

(c) And here's one more tool: Since the mental, emotional or violent behavior history of an individual can change after purchasing a gun, we'd need to have a process for periodic review of past purchasers and gun owners with the database to see if the individual's record has changed to the point where starting the legal "due process" removal of access to guns might be appropriate to protect the public from a possible mass shooting event.

(d) And finally, we'd need to have a process for handling concerning information about an individual's mental or emotional state; about their association with groups engaging in hate speech or advocating violence against minorities or others; or about their observed violent or other concerning behaviors. Such a process could be referred to as a

"Red Flag Law," which would trigger a legal "due process" review that could lead to the removal of access to guns if deemed appropriate.

The key is, no citizen should be denied the right to purchase or own a gun without due process that would confirm facts indicating behaviors that qualify under the law for denying gun ownership rights.

- It is often argued that it is not guns that kill people, it is people that kill people. The mental and emotional state of some people who have acquired guns and then became involved in mass shootings is certainly an important part of the problem. However, if the above elements are not included in a comprehensive background-check database that is updated daily, and/or if the database cannot be easily and quickly accessed in all gun or ammunition purchase and transfer events, then the legal requirement of background checks would be ineffective in minimizing the potential incidences of mass shootings.

Goals: 2. Reduce the number of deaths and injuries when mass shooting events occur

Question: What actions would reduce the number of deaths and injuries in mass shooting events?

- No matter how effective the process is for checking on the mental and emotional state of gun purchasers and owners, it is unlikely that this process would enable us to identify every potential mass shooter before taking action. So, when a mass shooting event does occur, we want the number of deaths and injuries that result to be as low as possible.
- The Dayton mass shooting event in August of 2019

showed clearly that the type of weapon involved in a mass shooting event can have a significant impact on the number of deaths and injuries. In that event, the time from the shooter's first bullet until he was taken down by the police who responded to the event was 32 seconds. In that time, the shooter was able to kill 9 people and injure 17 others, a total of 26 casualties. This number of casualties resulted from 42 shots being fired in 32 seconds.

Even if there is a "good guy with a gun" at the site of the shooting, it is unlikely that a shooter can be neutralized any faster than 30 seconds. If a shooter is armed with a weapon with a firing rate of more than a round a second, the chance that casualties can be limited to fewer than 20–25 total, and deaths to fewer than 8–10, is extremely low. If minimizing the number of total casualties and deaths in mass shooting events is an important national and societal goal, then it would seem that some limit on the firing rate of weapons and magazine capacity available to the general public should be part of the solution.

- A rational, data-based approach to addressing the issue of limiting public access to a category of weapons is important if as a society we are to succeed in making policy that will have a positive impact on the number of deaths and injuries in mass shooting events. Proposing policy to limit the public's access to "assault" or "military" weapons is language that will surely guarantee an emotionally charged division on the policy, undermining any chance of agreement to a policy that could have a meaningful impact on the deaths and injuries from mass shootings.

- As a society, it would seem to be unreasonable to base public safety on our ability to find every potentially disturbed person before they are able to purchase or otherwise acquire a weapon from what is publicly available. So it would seem that there are going to be some of these mass shooting events happening over time despite our best efforts. But hopefully we can significantly reduce the frequency and severity of these events with the actions above.

Goals: 3. Reduce the number of gun deaths in crime and gang activities

Question: What actions would reduce the number of gun deaths in crime and gang activities?

- This question is almost never raised in any political discussion or major news analyst segments on the issue of deaths by mass shootings in the US. Yet, it is a large portion of the total number of deaths and injuries from mass shootings each year.

   So a comprehensive solution to the total issue should eventually include exploring how to reduce the number of deaths and injuries in mass shootings that result from crime and gang activities. The first goal we discussed above would have only a limited impact at best on the ability of criminals and gang members to obtain guns. This is because, of course, most criminals and gang members probably don't obtain guns via public gun sellers.

- However, the second goal would likely have some measurable impact on the number of deaths and injuries from mass shootings related to crime and gang activities. If rapid-fire weapons and large-capacity magazines become less available from US sources, a portion can of course be made up from foreign sources. However, this would certainly make it more difficult to obtain these items, a situation which would result from some number of criminals and gang members not being successful in obtaining the high firing-rate weapons. So it is probable that some reduction in deaths and injuries would result in these events from achieving Goal 2 above.

Policy 7 — Ensure and Protect Voting Integrity and Voting Rights

Goals: 1. Provide oversight for congressional district alignments to prevent gerrymandering

Question: Is any level of drawing voting-district boundaries by one party to achieve a voting advantage over another party considered constitutional?

- The Constitution defines the details and processes of voting for Congress. Article 1, Section 4, of the Constitution states that "The Times, Places and Manner of holding Elections for Senators and Representatives, shall be prescribed in each State by the Legislature thereof; but the Congress may at any time by Law make or alter such Regulations, except as to the Places of chusing Senators." So this section of the Constitution seems to indicate that Congress may pass a law to make or change any of the details and processes of voting for Congress in the states, except for the places of choosing Senators (the spelling of "chusing" is what was in practice in the 1780s).
- For many years, the boundaries of some individual state voting-district alignment maps have been drawn to provide an advantage for the majority party in the state legislature over the minority party, and to limit the impact of the votes of minority groups. When these district maps have been reviewed in the past by the courts, the judges have indicated that they were generally unable to determine if this practice was constitutional or not. Amendments to the Constitution have been passed to

211

prohibit the denial of voting rights on the basis of race or sex, but no Amendments have yet been written to prohibit the denial of or disadvantage for voting on the basis of party voting history.

It appears that the creation of an unfair voting advantage for one party over another was not envisioned in the Constitution. But it also appears that neither party in Congress wanted to change those processes when used by the states. This may be because both parties have benefited from this practice in states where they are the majority party and thus in total control of the process of drawing voting-district boundaries.

- In light of these points, it is interesting to note that the word "party" does not appear anywhere in the Constitution. Party was and should not today be a consideration in any aspect of our government structure or key processes, such as the election of Senators and Representatives. It would seem obvious to conclude that if voting-district boundaries were drawn only by one party, and if party voting history of citizens was shown to be used in the process or if unusual district boundaries resulted in a voting advantage for one party over another, then these boundaries would result in denying fair and objective election outcomes to voters of one party and providing unfair advantages to voters of the other party. As such, these boundaries would seem to be in conflict with the right to equal voter representation under the law, which is guaranteed under the Constitution.

To address a question that judges and justices have been unable to answer to date, what then is the level of the influence of party membership or voting history in the practice of drawing district boundaries for congressional elections by a state? Isn't it clear that *any* level of using party membership or voting history in drawing congressional voting districts should be unconstitutional? If judges and justices can't agree, perhaps it should be the Congress that acts, as the Constitution seems to allow. But when partisan self-interest leads Congress not to act, it then falls to the people to petition Congress and then the state legislatures to pass a Constitutional Amendment clearly forbidding the use of *any* level of partisan data in drawing voting-district lines. However, such an effort could be readily resisted by incumbent partisan elected officials of both parties. Since neither the courts nor Congress have been unwilling or unable to act due to partisan influences, the new Citizen Rules are designed to define such requirements.

Goals: 2. Establish requirements for truthful campaign and issue messaging

Question: Do you believe most political campaign and issue advocacy messages are truthful?

- Anytime we discuss any limitations on free speech, we know we must be aware of the protections provided to speech by the Constitution, and the very limited constraints on speech that would be allowed under the Constitution.

  Let's look at some background information. Most people may not be aware that there is a federal law that places a restriction on "commercial speech." The standard for commercial speech that the Federal Trade Commission is charged to enforce is stated on the FTC's website: "The FTC requires that all claims be true, non-misleading, and substantiated at the time they are made. The FTC's post-market review of advertising claims and application of tailored remedies in advertising cases curb deception without overly restricting truthful commercial speech, thus promoting the goals embodied in the First Amendment."

- So, coming back to the question, do you believe most political campaign and issue advocacy messages can meet the FTC standard of being "true, non-misleading, and substantiated at the time they are made"? Or do you find that most of the messages in a campaign or advocating for or against a key issue or policy action are factually incorrect or, at best, misleading in the way they present information?

- Is this a problem for our democracy? Does false or misleading messaging in a campaign have the potential to unfairly influence the perceptions, preferences and voting choices of citizens? If we are concerned enough about how false or misleading messages in business can influence consumers' choices of products and brands, how can we not be concerned that false or misleading messaging in politics can influence voters' choices of candidates or support for issues? It would seem that the unfair influence of untrue or false campaign messaging on choosing our elected officials, to whom we have given great powers, is a much greater source of concern to our society than the unfair influence on choosing a detergent or toothpaste.

- If this is a valid concern, then might it make sense to require the same standard for political messages, to be "truthful, non-misleading, and substantiated at the time they are made"?

The key element that should make political messaging truthful is the requirement that statements have to be substantiated. When the truthfulness of commercial speech is challenged, the advertiser is required to show the research or other data that substantiates the basis of the message. If there is not a basis to support the message, then the advertiser must change or remove the messaging.

It would seem a similar requirement could be employed with political speech. Political messages about candidates or issues must be able to have a fact-based source to support the content and context of the message. Promises of a policy benefit must be supportable in an objective review, if not supported clearly in the message itself. As stated previously, the responsibility for providing facts to validate messages rests with the candidate or distributor of the message.

As stated on the FTC website, "available evidence suggests, however, that the general benefits of an enforcement approach that encourages dissemination of truthful information, while vigorously attacking misleading claims when they occur, produces benefits for consumers." A greater benefit for the citizens as well as the country would likely result from a program to enforce the truthfulness of political messaging in candidate and issue advocacy campaigns.

Goals: 3. Ensure the security and accuracy of voting records

Question: How do we ensure the security of voter records from outside cyberattack, and how do we guarantee the accuracy of voting records and processes to minimize voter fraud?

- First, let's consider the security question goal. Obviously, all voting record databases and systems to record votes on election days need to have the highest degree of cyber security protection possible. Although the states are legally responsible for and in control of their own election process, the federal government has the resources to access the highest-performing security protection possible for data and operating systems, including the secure transmission of voter information between states. In addition, the federal government can help defray the costs not only for each state, but for the combined national costs as well.

Of course, if any of the states resist this "support" from the federal government in this critical area of importance to the country, the Congress could choose to enact federal law to define the "manner" in which election data should be protected (under Article 1, Section 4, of the Constitution as discussed earlier).

- Second, let's consider the goal of enhancing the accuracy of voter registration records. In many states, the voter registration records are regularly reviewed to update the voting lists for non-voters. However, in many states, the actions that are taken are simply to try and connect with non-voters to confirm that they are still located in the area. If these contacts are not responded to, then the citizen is purged from the voting rolls with no further due process.

In some states where this practice takes place, thousands of voters have had their names removed from the voting rolls by mistake. Instead of depriving a citizen of their voting rights without a confirmation of their status, might it make more sense to require states to confirm that the citizen has either left the area or died before removing them from the voting rolls? Isn't the right to vote an important enough right guaranteed by the Constitution that a clear confirmation of the citizen's status should be required before depriving them of their right to vote?

As a potentially better process to be followed when registered voters don't vote in an election, perhaps the records of non-voters should be checked against death records to see if non-voters should be deleted from the records. If there is no participation in voting for several elections, then other records should be accessed to contact them and to confirm they are still in the area—records such as auto registration, driver's license renewals, filing of state income tax returns, and so on, and including a request for other states to check for a duplicate registration, before simply removing a citizen from the voting rolls for non-voting.

- Finally, as in the case we discussed of requiring a due process step before depriving a citizen of their Second Amendment rights, shouldn't a similar due process step be required before depriving any citizen of their right to vote, as elimination from voting rolls essentially does?

Goals: 4. Ensure fair and convenient access to voting processes for all citizens in all states

Question: What does equality of access to voter registration and voting for all citizens require?

- Let's consider what the goal of equality of access to voter registration and voting for all citizens might require in implementation. Citizens in lower socio-economic groups or who are limited in mobility may have more difficulty getting to registration sites, sites where voter photo IDs are produced, or to precinct locations during voting hours. Citizens who work in hourly jobs or who work multiple jobs may not be able to access these offices during normal business hours on any day. Citizens in these groups may not have personal transportation to these offices, but may have to take public transportation, even if available, that could require hours each way. Depending on where voting precincts are located across the state, and how they are staffed, some citizens may have no more than a few minutes' wait to vote, while in other precincts the wait may be hours long.

In order to fulfill the principle of equality of access for all citizens, these differences across the citizen population in a city, county, or state should be considered in the implementation of voter registration and voting plans and laws. No state should incorporate into law a plan for registration or voting access policies that ignores these issues and thus results in wide inequities in the ease of access for voters of different socio-economic or health situations.

- Many if not all of these inequities can be addressed by several voting practices that have proven to result in higher voter participation rates with no discernable level of voter fraud. Such policies as liberal vote-by-mail systems, including the sending of vote-by-mail applications to the homes of registered voters, or even the sending of technically secure and individual traceable blank ballots to voters' homes, have been proven to be capable of increasing voter participation without any discernable level of fraud. An increase in early voting days with extended hours, voting access on weekends, and using voter and demographic data, as well as data on previous voter numbers and waiting times at precinct locations in previous elections, can be used to provide more equality in terms of convenient access for all citizens.

Finally, new technologies offer the opportunity for new registration and voting systems in the immediate future. Many cell phones now provide fingerprint identification for the security of access to the phone, and could be used to provide remote access to registration and voting ballots for voting processes. The federal government should provide the lead in exploring these new technologies and then in funding the adoption in the states, moving us closer to equality in the convenience of voter registration and voting access that will lead to high levels of voter participation with an equally high level of security against voter fraud in our elections.

Question: Is voter participation being suppressed in some states, cities and counties by making it very difficult for voters in some precincts to cast votes on election days?

There have been numerous reports in recent elections of state, city or county election officials unfairly allocating voting equipment in locations across the precinct, or by precinct. This has resulted in the closing of some precincts in areas where citizens have a very difficult time traveling to a distant precinct. Also, without extended early voting and hours, many citizens who cannot take time off work to vote have difficulty getting to a precinct outside of working hours.

When states, cities, or counties have great discrepancies in the travel distance and time, and the waiting time to vote across a region, the Federal Election Commission should have the authority to either require changes to the allocation of equipment and poll workers to equalize the voting experience, or extend early voting days, as appropriate. In addition, regions with habitual patterns of unfair voting experiences should be required to enhance their vote-by-mail processes, with ballots linked by computer codes to each voter.

Policy 8—Religious Practices and Non-Discrimination

Goal: Resolve conflict in religious practice rights and non-discrimination in public commerce

Question: Does the right of one citizen to practice their religious beliefs extend to discriminating against another citizen in public commerce situations?

There have been several high-profile cases where the rights of one citizen to practice their religious beliefs have come into conflict with the prohibitions against discrimination in public commerce. One of the most notable types of case involves retail establishment owners who do not agree with the right of LGBTQ citizens to marry and otherwise be treated like every other citizen, due to their beliefs that gay relationships are considered serious sins in their religions.

One key question that comes out of this situation is, what does a citizen involved in public commerce or service do if their religious beliefs state clearly that people engaging in gay relationships are committing serious sin, and the legality of gay marriage directly violates the teachings of their religion that marriage is a sacrament only between one man and one woman? What if they honestly believe that serving such people would be utilizing their talents, their skills, their "earthly treasure" to support people engaged in actions they cannot tolerate religiously? Do they follow civil law or religious law?

In our democracy, each citizen is guaranteed many rights under our Constitution related to freedom and individual liberty. These rights are at the core of what we value and cherish as Americans. In regard to religious freedom, and the right to exercise religious beliefs freely, that right is guaranteed in the First Amendment to the Constitution, the first of the Bill of Rights.

But our Founders, in their wisdom, were aware that in a diverse community where everyone is guaranteed a set of freedoms and liberties, it is possible that the exercise of one citizen's rights can come into conflict with the rights of another. We've seen that in the increased bans on smoking in public areas, restaurants, theatres, offices, and so on. Initially, this was seen as a conflict between the rights of smokers to exercise their right to smoke and the rights of non-smokers to enjoy a smoke-free environment. Once secondhand smoke was clearly linked to cancer and other serious health conditions, then the rights of non-smokers to enjoy environments free of unhealthy situations was almost universally considered to be the more "important" right to prevail.

To address this situation in the Constitution, there is also the Ninth Amendment in the Bill of Rights. This Amendment states that these rights articulated in the Constitution and Amendments "shall not be construed to deny or disparage others retained by the people." This has been interpreted to mean, in simpler words, that the granting or practice of one citizen's rights should not be able to deny other rights of other citizens. This Amendment does not define a process for resolving the conflicts of rights in such situations. But as in most instances, the Constitution is not a document that defines the processes or "rules" to implement the intention of the Constitution. Those processes or rules are left to Congress, the Administration, and the courts to define.

In addition, there is the Fourteenth Amendment, which states in part that "no State shall make or enforce any law which shall abridge the privileges or immunities of citizens...nor deny to any person...the equal protection of the laws." This has been interpreted, in part, to reinforce the Ninth Amendment concept that laws written to implement a right under the Constitution cannot abridge the rights or privileges of citizens, nor deny to any person the equal protection of the laws. Again, the processes or rules to implement this Amendment are left to Congress, the Administration, and the courts to define. These processes and rules to implement these rights may change over time, but the guiding principles for the processes and rules themselves, as defined in these Amendments to the Constitution, do not change over time.

Given this background, then, let's return to our example of the religious beliefs about gay relationships and the exercise of these beliefs in the commercial sectors of our country. Is it a reasonable extension of the First Amendment protections against the "free exercise" of a religious belief into the public commercial roles that someone may choose to follow to make a living?

Is there a potential for such an extension to lead to the claim that religious beliefs extend to not wishing to serve other segments of the public? Might some business owners seek to claim that their private religious beliefs prevent them from serving women, or people of certain racial or ethnic groups? Wouldn't such an action fall into the area of denying the "natural" rights of these other groups of American citizens to equal protection against discrimination in the areas of commerce and services offered to the public?

A commercial business license is issued by the state, not any church, and this requires businesses holding a license to comply with *civil* laws, not religious or secular beliefs. Under the principle of the separation of church and state, and the principle of religious diversity and acceptance of *all* religions in our country, we expect citizens who choose to apply for a business license to agree to this separation. If secular commercial laws violate the personal religious beliefs of any business owner, perhaps that business owner should avoid a career in that business?

Another way to think about this issue might be to ask if there can be any reason to justify the denial of any citizen's right to fully participate in commercial services offered to the public — to all citizens making up the general public. Would we be living the words in our Declaration of Independence that "all men (persons) are created equal, and are endowed by their Creator with certain inalienable rights. And among these are life, liberty and the pursuit of happiness," if any portion of our citizens did not have the full exercise of their rights as citizens in fully and freely accessing all public and commercial services? Can it be considered constitutional if any portion of our citizens are denied the rights to shop where everyone else shops, or to be served as every other citizen is served, for any reason related to their natural makeup?

No citizen's practice of their religion within a church or other religious building or property, within their home or their own property, or in appropriate places in the public square, can be limited by civil law. But doesn't the license to operate a business and offer products or services to the public represent an obligation to serve all citizens without discrimination? Isn't that what the Declaration of Independence and the Constitution guarantee to all citizens in commerce? Or in our democracy, do business owners have the right to choose not to serve some citizens because of their natural makeup? Of course, business owners have the right to choose not to serve some citizens based on the dress code of the establishment, or because of their behavior. But being gay is not a behavior that is a choice, nor is it a behavior that violates the accepted standards of dress or other behavior that might disturb other customers or affect their health.

Now let's consider briefly the other side to this issue. The alternative point of view would seem to enable any business owner to discriminate in their business against any group of citizens they choose, and they can justify this action based on the claim of a religious belief. One might claim a belief that African American citizens were not created to be equal to white Americans; one might claim a belief that Americans of Jewish faith have the blood of Jesus Christ on them, as quoted in the Bible, and therefore cannot be served by them in their business; very traditional Muslims might believe their religion requires women to be in public only with a male family member and that they cannot be served if they are alone in public. Does that seem like America?

Of course, not all citizens will agree with the summary above of the appropriate way to address the conflict of rights in this case. But I hope most might consider that the summary above is a reasonable and objective application of the principles of our democracy and might be worth considering on their own.

* * *

In the next chapter, we will discuss how we might actually implement the changes we discussed in the previous chapters — how we might actually implement Citizen Rules to replace the current rules defined by our elected officials that have led to much of the divisiveness in our politics and lack of focus on the needs of the country over most of the past 40 years.

Chapter 6

Summary and Details of the Specific Amendments to Be Proposed

In Chapter 3, we discussed the causes of the divisiveness and failure to serve the nation's interest that exist in our politics today.

To review, there are three major factors that seem to be at work today causing congressional members to focus on loyalty to partisan interests and, by doing so, fail to truly serving the nation:

1. Career self-interest. As our elected officials seek to make careers out of serving in Congress, most of their priorities seem to focus on the actions and behaviors that will perpetuate their own careers, meaning their own re-elections. Most members of Congress spend about 40% of the time they are in Washington working to raise funds and votes for their next re-election campaign, rather than working on issues to benefit the country or their constituents.

2. Partisan interest. In order to rise to positions of leadership and increased responsibility in Congress, elected officials must be willing to follow the directions of party leaders when it comes to supporting party positions on proposed legislation. This means supporting all party colleagues in whatever positions they advocate, not criticizing the actions or behavior of party colleagues, and following party leaders in criticizing the actions and behaviors of members from the other party. It also means blindly supporting the President of their own party, failing to be a true "check and balance," but then criticizing any President of the other party.

3. Donor interest. In order to raise the money needed for re-election activities, elected officials must spend about 40% of their time in Washington out of their office making fundraising calls, and spending a major part of their office time meeting with donors, special-interest groups, and lobbyists. These people become very important to their re-election and thus the long-term career of elected officials, but often their interests run counter to large segments of the country overall, and their constituencies.

Our purpose in this book is to discuss what potential changes would enable our country to overcome these influences in our elected leaders — that list of the new Citizen Rules that "We the People" would like our leaders to follow in governing — and then to discuss how these changes might actually be implemented in our political system of government. Here once again is a summary of that list of changes we introduced earlier that are designed to overcome these negative influences in our current political environment:

Listing the Changes We'd Like to See Happen — Citizen Rules

1. Setting term limits, compensation, and health and retirement benefits for members of Congress and senior Administration officials
2. Defining new rules for the legislative processes to limit partisanship; confirming primacy of Citizen Rules in the Constitution over procedural rules enacted by members of Congress
3. Defining timing requirements for Senate votes on treaties and presidential appointments; limiting the duration of acting presidential appointments; limiting absolute presidential reprieves and pardons
4. Strengthening congressional oversight of executive

implementation; strengthening the independence of Inspectors General and key executive departments in the Administration

5. Defining rules for budgeting, taxing and spending processes—balance, timing, accountability, transparency, effectiveness

6. Prohibiting Congress members from paid lobbying roles after serving in Congress

7. Prohibiting laws exempting Congress from laws enacted on citizens

8. Changing the allocation and certification of Electoral College votes in presidential elections

9. Limiting the terms of Supreme Court justices and federal court judges

10. Ensuring fair and equitable access to registration and voting for all citizens, and elections free from fraud

11. Defining rules for campaign financing—donation limits and disclosure requirements

12. Defining rules for truthful messaging and timing of campaign advertising

13. Providing an independent council to oversee voting-district alignments after census

14. Defining rules for ethical behaviors and financial conflict of interest, and for handling non-salary personal income for President, Vice President, and all senior elected and appointed officials

15. Defining a non-partisan judicial process for impeachment and actions considered as impeachable offenses

16. Establishing a program of required national service for all citizens between the ages of 18 and 29

Most of the changes we've reviewed are central to the purpose of getting Congress to serve the nation, and to unite the nation behind bipartisan governing, instead of dividing the nation with partisan governing. Achieving this goal will require that the changes we propose would be effective in minimizing or even eliminating all three of the interests that compete with the public or national interest: career, partisan and donor interests.

These changes in fact are integrated. No single one of them would likely be effective alone. It is the combination of all these changes enacted together that will provide the greatest impact on the effects of career self-interest, partisan interest and donor interest, and replacing these influences with a commitment by congressional members to follow the Constitution and their oath of office to serve the national interest. We've also discussed how implementing these changes will require approving Amendments to the Constitution, in order to have them take effect without Supreme Court oversight, and to ensure they have lasting impact without being easily overturned or negated in law by a subsequent partisan and self-focused Congress.

Some readers may be wondering at this point, why are these proposed changes needed — these Citizen Rules — to the existing rules of how Congress operates that have been written by our elected officials over the past many decades? Why doesn't our Constitution address these issues? Let me suggest three reasons why this situation may not have been addressed by the Founders in writing our Constitution:

- In Article 1, Section 5 of the Constitution, it states that "Each House may determine the Rules of its Proceedings…" As written, our Constitution gives the members of Congress the power to determine their own rules for the process of governing. The Constitution itself focuses on defining the "structure" and "division of power" for the first government based on the principle of self-governance — a government "of the people, by the people, and for the people" — in the history of the world. As a result, our Constitution makes no effort to define the "rules" of how

Congress should govern.

- Realizing that this was the first experiment in the world in creating a citizen-governed republic, it is possible that the Founders believed they could not foresee in the drafting of the Constitution how best to define these rules and processes. Perhaps they believed these process rules were best left to the Congress members themselves to discover the most effective ways to govern. It could also be that the Founders simply had great faith in the quality and character of the people who would be chosen by the citizens to represent them and govern them, and equal faith that the citizens enjoying this new freedom and responsibility would not tolerate members of Congress who proved to put their own interests, partisan or special interests above the interests of the people they served.

- It should be easy to understand that at the time the Constitution was written, our Founders could not foresee the extent to which the influences of money, partisanship, and donor power, nor the development of a career legislative culture, would rise after 240 years to threaten the very republic they established. Since these interests now seem to have negated the focus of Congress on working together to serve the national interest first above all else, it now falls to "We the People" to come together, without partisan, regional or demographic bias, to define the Citizen Rules for how we want Congress to operate, in order to best serve the citizens, and the nation overall.

First, in previous chapters we discussed how these rules need to be designed and approved as Amendments to the Constitution to ensure that a new set of elected leaders in Congress would support the nation's interests instead of their own careers, their donors' interests or their party's interests. I think of this not as a rejection of or even a major change to the key elements of the existing Constitution, but as "constitutional reformation," the repair of and restoring of our Constitutional Republic, via an updating of the rules of governing, based on 240 years of learning. There is no change to the principles or elements of governmental structure that our Founding Fathers designed.

In fact, the "Citizen Rules" changes would actually strengthen many of the core principles and elements of the Constitution, such as the system of checks and balances between the branches of government, and an unbiased, judicial process for impeachment, and a more bipartisan, democratic process for proposing and passing legislation. The changes being proposed simply add a few "Citizen Rules" to the Constitution, which were not included in the existing Constitution, but very well might have been, had our Founding Fathers had the benefit of 240 years of seeing the congressional rules made by many of our past elected leaders.

To implement these "Citizen Rules," the changes have been organized in groups that combine similar topics that could be addressed by changes in specific sections of the Constitution. Let's look at an overview of how the changes above would be enacted via proposed Amendments to the Constitution. The goal is to incorporate the "Citizen Rules" as an integral part of the Constitution defining the rules and procedures for how Congress operates.

Just as the first ten Amendments were grouped together into a single bill, the Bill of Rights, the "Citizen Rules" would be grouped together into a single bill called "The Bill of Public Service and Accountability." The bill, which is highlighted below, includes all the Amendments and a Preamble patterned after the language that our Founders wrote, to provide a clear statement of purpose that defines the overall objective that these proposed Amendments to the Constitution are intended to provide.

The Suggested Approach — Proposing Six Amendments to the Constitution in One Bill:
The "Bill of Public Service and Accountability"

Preamble:

We, the People of the United States, in order to recommit the operation of the Congress to serve the interests of the nation and its citizens over personal, party, or special interests, to provide more openness and full transparency in congressional legislative and budgeting processes, to promote collaborative bipartisan policy development and accountability in the exercise of these responsibilities, and to ensure the integrity of federal elections, do hereby present the following Amendments to the Constitution of the United States.

We the People propose the following Amendments to the Constitution of the United States, which shall be valid to all intents and purposes as part of the Constitution. Supported by millions of citizens, We the People further require that these Amendments be voted upon together as written for approval with a single yes or no vote for the entire bill, by a majority of state representatives in a "limited" constitutional convention to be called for by two-thirds of the several states (34 of 50), when petitioned by the people in each state. These Amendments would take effect when ratified by the legislatures of three-fourths of the several states (38 of the 50) within seven years after the date of its submission for ratification to the states.

1. Amendment XXVIII (28) — to Article 1, Sections 2, 3, 5 and 6

- Changes to term limits, compensation, and health and retirement benefits for Congress and other government executives

- Defining a non-partisan impeachment process based on judicial rules rather than House and Senate rules; defining actions considered as impeachable offenses
- Primacy of Citizen Rules in the Constitution over congressional rules enacted by members in each House

2. Amendment XXIX (29) — to Article 1, Section 7, and Article 2, Section 2

- Changes to the legislative processes
- Limiting the duration of acting presidential appointments
- Defining timing requirements for Senate voting on treaties and presidential appointments

3. Amendment XXX (30) — to Article 1, Section 8

- Requirements for a balanced budget and greater transparency and accountability in the congressional budgeting, spending and taxing processes
- Requirements for effectiveness in program spending and for program solvency for Social Security and Medicare/Medicaid
- Strengthening the independence of key executive departments and of the Inspectors General role for oversight of legislation implementation and ethical requirements
- Prohibiting congressional members from lobbying activities after serving
- Prohibiting any bill exempting Congress from laws passed for citizens

4. Amendment XXXI (31) — to Article 2, Section 1, and Article 3, Section 1, and Amendment 20, new Section 3

- Changes to the allocation and certification of states' Electoral College votes in presidential elections, and certification of the national vote totals by Congress
- Providing term limits for Supreme Court justices and federal judges, while providing for reappointment for additional terms
- Requirements for handling personal non-salary income for President, Vice President, and senior elected and appointed officials

5. Amendment XXXII (32) — new Article 4

- Setting contributions limits and reporting requirements for federal candidates, campaigns, parties, PACs and issue action groups, for individuals, companies and all organizations
- Setting requirements for truthful campaign messaging from all sources, and time limits on distributing election campaign messages
- Providing non-partisan oversight of congressional voting-district boundaries; ensuring fair and equitable access to registration and voting for all citizens, and elections free from fraud
- Providing clearer ethics and conflicts-of-interest standards for all Congress and Administration officials, including the President and Vice President

6. Amendment XXXIII (33) — new Article 5

- Requirement for all citizens between the ages of 18 to 29 to complete a paid public service program role for at least two years

Details of Amendments

The specific Amendment language proposed in the Bill of Public Service and Accountability is provided in the Appendix to this book. Listed below are additional details for each of the Amendments to discuss how the changes we've discussed would be implemented, and how these Citizen Rules would define key operational processes for Congress, and thus become an integral part of the Constitution.

Detailed Summary

Here is a detailed summary of the key elements of the proposed **Bill of Public Service and Accountability** as six Amendments to the US Constitution:

1. Amendment XXVIII (28) — to Article 1, Sections 2, 3, 5 and 6 of the Constitution

- Changes to compensation, term limits, and health and retirement benefits for Congress and other government executives
  - Congressional terms — Congress will be limited to one term; a four-year term for the House of Representatives, one-half elected every two years, and a six-year term for Senators, one-third elected every two years.
  - Compensation — Remove the ability of Congress to set their own salary levels; salaries of Congress are tied to the US military pay scale; salaries of politically appointed Administration and federal employees indexed to Congress salary levels.
  - Health benefits — Remove the ability of Congress to set their own healthcare program; healthcare programs for Congress and politically appointed Administration and federal employees will be tied to the same program options available to average citizens.

- ◦ Retirement benefits—No special retirement benefits for Congress; members participate in individual IRAs and 401(k)s as most Americans do; after serving one term, each congressional member receives a relocation allowance to return to private life.
- Restrictions for Congress members after serving one term
  - ◦ No Congress member may serve more than one term in any office, nor run for another office while serving.
  - ◦ No Congress member may be employed as or receive compensation as a paid lobbyist to Congress or any Administration official or staff members after serving in Congress.
- Restrictions to Congress in determining the rules of its proceedings
  - ◦ Congress shall follow the Citizen Rules defined in various articles of the Constitution for certain of its proceedings.
  - ◦ Congress may determine the rules for other proceedings not specifically defined in the Constitution.
- Defining a non-partisan impeachment process based on judicial rules rather than House and Senate rules
  - ◦ Specifies the non-partisan rules and judicial process for the House in investigating questions of potential actions by officials to determine a relevant basis for confirming that an impeachable offense has been committed by a sitting official, and that an impeachment vote requires only that a preponderance of the information gathered indicates that the accused official committed the action charged.
  - ◦ Defines the non-partisan trial process in the Senate for determining a finding of guilt beyond a reasonable doubt, following the established judicial rules for a trial. Confirms that officials who committed an impeachable offense and were impeached by the House

for an offense while serving are still subject to trial by the Senate and barring from holding any future office if convicted after leaving office.

○ Establishes a three-justice panel to preside over impeachment trials of the President. The senior member shall be the Chief Justice of the Supreme Court; the other two members shall be senior Associate Justices of the Supreme Court, neither appointed by the current President, one appointed by a different President of each of the two major parties.

○ Defines the authority of the presiding three-justice panel to oversee the impeachment trial procedures in the Senate. Their authority includes determining the application of the rules of evidence and witnesses relevant to the impeachment offense during the trial, approving the issuing of subpoenas, resolving any claims of executive privilege in the issuing of subpoenas for documents and the testimony of witnesses, and resolving objections to evidence and statements presented and made during the impeachment trial.

2. Amendment XXIX (29) — to Article 1, Section 7, and Article 2, Section 2 of the Constitution

- Define rules by which Congress proposes and passes laws
  ○ Eliminate the practice of combining bills on multiple, unrelated issues into one single voting item; require each item to be voted on in a separate bill.
  ○ Reduce the power of the majority party leadership and committee process to keep bills from coming to the floor for a vote; require that any bill co-signed by 10% of the members of either chamber be brought to the floor for a vote within 20 session days after introduction, allowing for normal committee review

and markup.

- To allow for the reading of bills before voting, require that bills brought to the floor for a vote must be voted on no earlier than three session days after being called for a vote; debate, amendments and voting must be completed no later than six session days after being called for a vote.

- Define limits of duration for acting presidential appointments
  - Limit the duration of acting positions named by the President to 60 days to fill the vacancy of a congressionally approved appointee and the nomination of a formal replacement for Senate confirmation.

- Define the timing requirement for the Senate to confirm a presidential appointment
  - Require the Senate confirmation process for presidential appointments to be completed within 60 session days of a presidential nomination.

3. Amendment XXX (30) — to Article 1, Section 8 of the Constitution

- Requiring greater transparency and accountability in the congressional budgeting, spending and taxing processes
  - Require that the Congress pass a balanced budget at least ten session days before the start of each fiscal year, except in the event of a declaration of war or national emergency declared by the President and agreed by Congress; Congress loses pay permanently if not passed on time for each day late.
  - Require that all programs that spend public money have a clear statement of specific benefits to be provided by the program, the population to receive

the benefits, the outcomes expected as a result of the program over time, the efficiency with which the program will achieve the expected outcome, and the source of funding.

- Establishing stronger protections for the independence of key executive departments
  - While traditionally all presidential appointees in the executive departments of the Administration serve at the pleasure of the President, for over 200 years there has been respect for a "firewall" between the President and the operation of certain key Administration departments. These include the justice and the military departments, and more recently, the national security agencies and the Internal Revenue Service under the Department of the Treasury.

    As a nation, we have realized that if the President were to directly interfere in the investigative decisions of the Justice Department, we could lose the principle of "fair justice applied impartially and without bias to all citizens." There is too great an opportunity for corrupt action from the President to stop investigations against his interests, family, or friends, and to start investigations against political opponents or the companies that support them or that they represent. A similar concern exists with the operation of the Internal Revenue Service and the private information they hold on citizens, and the decisions they make to investigate citizens' financial activities.

    Similarly, as a country we expect the professionals in the major national security agencies to have some degree of independence in the conduct of their roles, so they are free to present unbiased information, analysis, and insight to the President.

    Thus, key positions within the executive branch

will be provided with an extra degree of independence in the conduct of their positions. Specifically, once appointed and confirmed by the Senate, their reason for removal and/or reassignment shall be investigated by the Senate, and shall only be carried out with the advice and consent of the full Senate. These positions are:

- The Attorney General of the United States, the Directors of the FBI and CIA, and all appointed US Attorneys;
- The senior military officers who serve as chairman and members of the Joint Chiefs of Staff, and the senior command officers of each of the military services branches;
- The Directors of National Intelligence and the National Security Agency;
- The Treasurer of the United States and Commissioner of the Internal Revenue Service.

• Establishing stronger protections for the role of Inspectors General in each Administration department, with authority to do the following:
  ◦ Given recent actions by the President and a Supreme Court decision to favor the independence of the executive from too much oversight of presidential actions by Congress, the "Citizen Rules" would strengthen the role of oversight and investigative authority for the implementation of congressional legislation by Inspectors General. This is important to ensure the effective and efficient spending of public funds approved by Congress to implement policies and programs, and for compliance with laws on conflict of interest, abuse of positional authority, and all applicable laws.
  ◦ Provide at least annual reports to the Congress,

the President and the public on the effectiveness of Administration departments in implementing legislation, and results versus expected outcomes for programs that involve the spending of public funds.

○ Limit the removal or reassignment of Inspectors General to issues of unbiased job performance, and ethical, moral, or legal causes, which may be recommended by either the Senate or the President. If removal is recommended by the Senate, the approval of a majority of the Senate shall be required, with the provision of 5% of the majority coming from the minority party. If recommended by the President, the approval of a majority of the Senate shall also be required.

○ Provide similar protections for the independence of key executive departments specified above from interference by the President for reasons of personal or political benefit. Similar to the limits on the removal or reassignment of Inspectors General defined above, provide the same requirement for Senate confirmation for the removal or reassignment of the directors and secretaries of those specified executive departments.

• Changes to the rules by which Congress proposes spending and tax bills to provide more public transparency and accountability for government revenues, spending and deficit growth

○ Require each new Congress elected every two years to pass a balanced budget for the two-year period following the election no later than ten session days before the start of the first fiscal-year cycle, except when a state of war or national emergency has been declared by a majority of both Houses of Congress and signed by the President.

○ Provide that congressional members receive no pay if

the budget is not balanced and passed on time for each fiscal year, until the requirement is met; such pay to be forfeited permanently. Staff and third-party vendors to Congress shall not forfeit pay during a period of no approved budget.

- ○ Require that any new spending bills not accounted for in the original balanced budget be combined with specific cost reductions or new taxes to maintain a balanced budget.
- ○ Require that Congress not increase the national debt, but act to pay down the existing debt in each fiscal-year budget cycle, except when a state of war or national emergency has been declared by a majority of both Houses of Congress and signed by the President.
- ○ Require that Medicare, Medicaid and Social Security programs be funded by separate taxes to maintain fiscal solvency, and to be managed and reported separately from the national budget.
- ○ Require that funds collected for Medicare, Medicaid and Social Security from separate program taxes shall not be used by Congress for any other purpose, except when a state of war or national emergency has been declared by a majority of Congress and signed by the President.
- • Provide that any new spending approved after the adoption of a fiscal-year balanced budget must be offset by new tax revenues or reductions in other planned spending.
  - ○ Provide that all bills that spend public money must include: the specific purpose and benefit each provides; which groups are supported; the expected outcome; and the goals or measures to determine whether successful.
- • Provide that members of Congress cannot exempt

themselves, as individuals or as an organization, from the requirements of any laws enacted on citizens or organizations in the USA.

- Provide that members who have completed any term of service in the Congress may not engage in direct paid lobbying to anyone in government.

4. Amendment XXXI (31) — to Article 2, Section 1, Article 3, and Article 4 of the Constitution

- Revising the Electoral College process
  - Require that in presidential elections, all states allocate Electoral College votes on the basis of the share of the popular vote in each state awarded to each candidate.
  - Require that state election officials complete and announce the popular vote results in each precinct, county, and the state overall, the proportion of the popular vote won by each candidate, and the proportional allocation of the state's Electoral College votes to each candidate, as soon as possible after the election. All outside reviews, recounts and challenges shall be completed within six weeks of the election.
  - The final popular and Electoral College vote totals shall be reviewed and certified by the Secretary of State and Governor in each state, no later than six weeks after the election, by the second week in December. A certificate of Electoral College votes awarded to each candidate will be completed by the Governor and presented to the Congress, no later than nine weeks after the election, by the first week in January. The Congress shall meet in the first week in January to receive the certificate of Electoral College votes awarded to each candidate, to be opened, counted, and the national

totals of popular and Electoral College votes certified, without authority to challenge, change or reject the state's certified totals.

- Providing for term limits for Supreme Court justices and federal judges, while providing for renomination to additional ten-year terms
  - Set term limits for Supreme Court justices and federal judges at ten years. Allow for renomination and reconfirmation at the completion of each term to an additional ten-year term.
  - Prohibit nominations of justices and judges by a President during the 120 days before the national election date in a presidential election year.
- Setting requirements to end the gerrymandering of state congressional voting districts
  - There shall be a citizen-led, independent, unbiased, bipartisan Federal Election Oversight Board to ensure that voting-district lines in each individual state represent a fair, objective and non-partisan representation of the state's regional population, with approximately equal number of citizens per district, without regard to racial, ethnic or partisan demographics, and a minimal division of existing city and county boundaries.
  - Board members shall be appointed by the Federal Election Commission, and shall consist of citizens who are not serving and have never served as elected or appointed officials or political party officials at the federal or state level, who come from different regions of the country, and who shall volunteer for consideration to serve. They shall serve for a single term of six years, with an equal number of members from each major political party.
  - The Federal Election Oversight Board shall have the

authority to review voting-district maps from all states, and require states to revise and draw new congressional voting-district lines at any time following a census year and at least one year prior to a state-wide or national election. The Board's requirements for an individual state to redraw voting-district lines may be challenged by the state in federal court.

- Setting requirements to ensure fair and equitable access to voting for all citizens, and elections that are free from fraud

  ∘ In addition to the authority to review the states' congressional voting-district maps, the Federal Election Oversight Board shall have the authority to review state laws and results in the areas of fair and equitable registration and voting access for all citizens. If the results from elections indicate the lack of equitable results in these areas across the state, or if new laws are judged to erode equitable access in these areas, the Board shall require the states to revise the laws and/or the operational siting, staffing, or hours of service for registration and voting locations. If any state disagrees with these rulings, it may challenge them in federal court.

  ∘ The Federal Election Oversight Board shall also have the authority to review the states' results in investigating and documenting any evidence of voter fraud in elections, and the laws or actions taken by the state to minimize voter fraud. The Board shall require that state laws designed to minimize voter fraud are based on evidence or facts of voter fraud levels and causes, and that the laws or actions relate to the specific levels and causes determined by voter fraud investigations.

5. Amendment XXXII (32)—insert new Article 4 of the Constitution

- Defining rules for campaign financing—donation limits and disclosure requirements
  - ○ This Amendment will clearly specify that "money is not speech." It will require and authorize Congress to pass Federal Election Laws to set specific limits on the level of contributions, in terms of money or gifts of value, from each individual citizen allowed each calendar year to all candidates, parties, political action committee (PACs) and issue action groups, based on an amount a citizen with average income could reasonably afford.
  - ○ The Amendment will further require that all contributions to every candidate, party, and issue action group be publicly reported, and the individual donors identified for all contributions received. It will prohibit anonymous contributions to any political group, campaign, candidate, inauguration committee, political action committee or non-profit issue action group that engages in political messaging activities.
  - ○ The Amendment will require Congress to limit contributions from companies, unions and all organizations, including PACs and issue action groups, to any political group, campaign, candidate, PAC or non-profit issue action group that engages in political messaging activities, to the same amount as the limit to an individual. Separate political messaging actions by these groups are not limited by these requirements, nor are other voluntary actions other than monetary or message distribution actions in support of candidates, parties or issues limited by these requirements.
  - ○ The Amendment will require that this legislation

245

empower the existing Federal Election Commission with the authority to require reports on all federal election campaign donations and donors as required by the new Federal Election Laws under this Amendment. Also empower the Commission with authority to issue subpoenas for information not forthcoming from organizations making or receiving donations, and the authority to initiate federal court proceedings for violations of the requirements defined in this Amendment.

- Setting requirements for the fairness of federal elections' defining of truthful messaging requirements for political messages
  - Require Congress to empower the Federal Election Commission with authority to appoint a non-partisan, independent, unbiased Federal Election Message Oversight Board with the authority to conduct proactive reviews of all political messages about candidates, candidate positions and legislative issues. This Board would have the authority to require changes to or removal of messages in any public channels that are found to contain false or misleading statements, videos or graphic elements.
  - Require all such reviews by the Federal Election Message Oversight Board to be publicized, including the details of the review, the findings, the required actions of the distributor, and the response by the distributor.
  - Require that this legislation empower the existing Federal Election Commission with the authority to require reports on all federal election campaign donations and donors as required by the new Federal Election Laws under this Amendment. Also empower the Commission with authority to issue subpoenas

for information not forthcoming from organizations making or receiving donations, and the authority to initiate federal court proceedings for violations of the requirements defined in this Amendment. Also provide for message originators or distributors to request reviews by federal courts of disagreements over the Board's rulings.

○ Board members shall consist of citizens who are not serving and have never served as elected or appointed officials or political party officials at the federal or state level, who come from different regions of the country, and who shall volunteer for consideration to serve. They shall be appointed by the members of the Federal Election Commission. Board members shall serve for a single term of six years, with an equal number of members from each major political party.

• Defining clearer requirements for ethics and conflict-of-interest standards for all Congress and Administration officials

○ When filing as a candidate for elected federal office or when nominated for an appointed position in the Administration or federal government, require that all candidates release ten years of tax returns, in addition to other required financial disclosures. Candidates who fail to release tax returns would not be allowed to run for federal office or to be considered for appointment.

○ Before taking the oath of office, require that all candidates for elected federal offices and all nominees for appointed positions in the Administration or federal government place all investments in businesses, property, partnerships, and so on, and the ownership of any business, in a blind trust administered by an objective third party for the duration of their service.

6. Amendment XXIII (33) — insert new Article 5 of the Constitution; renumber existing Articles 4–7 as Articles 6–9

- Establishing a new program of required national service
  - ○ In order to strengthen the sense of national service as an element of citizenship in our society, this Amendment requires all citizens to complete two years in a national service role, to be started no earlier than their eighteenth birthday and completed no later than their thirtieth birthday.
  - ○ Congress will establish a National Service Program Board to oversee the identification of roles that qualify as a national service role, and will provide the funding for the appropriate levels of citizen interest in the various roles. The Board will create and manage a program to maintain the records of national service completion for all young citizens.
  - ○ Board members shall consist of citizens who are not serving and have never served as elected or appointed officials or political party officials at the federal or state level, who come from different regions of the country, who reflect the diversity of the country, and who shall volunteer for consideration to serve. They shall be appointed by the President and confirmed by the Senate. Board members shall serve for a single term of six years, with an equal number of members from each major political party.

Reviewing Benefits and Risks of the Key Changes That the "Citizen Rules" Amendments Represent

It will hopefully be clear that these six Amendments, when taken together, will accomplish the objectives that are stated in the bill's Preamble:

(1) To restore the focus on the national interest over the negative influences of the three interests that compete with or supersede a priority focus on the national interest;

(2) To provide for more complete transparency in the legislative and budgeting processes;

(3) To provide for more collaborative bipartisan policy development and accountability in the exercise of these responsibilities; and

(4) To ensure the fairness, equality of access and integrity of federal elections.

It is also hopefully clear how these six Amendments are integrated in working together to accomplish the objectives. If one Amendment or one of the 16 changes represented by the Amendments were to be removed from the Bill of Public Service and Accountability, the remaining changes would be significantly weakened in their ability to accomplish the purposes, the desired outcomes, stated in the Preamble.

In the discussion which follows, we'll review how the elements of the proposed Amendments would deliver the outcomes identified in the Preamble to the Bill of Public Service and Accountability. Many of the details of the changes were discussed in Chapter 4. Here we will discuss some of the key benefits and risks of these changes.

1. Eliminating career self-interest

- **Benefits.** By instituting the limit of a single term for Congress, we eliminate the influence of the focus of building a career in national political office, that can lead to a member putting his or her career interest above the national interest or the interest of the public. It is the focus on re-election and building a political career in national political office that can lead to the partisan loyalty required to support a political career. As a result, an elected official almost out of necessity must put their own career self-interest above the national interest or the obligation to serve the public and the nation. These influences very often have a controlling impact on how elected officials act with regard to avoiding collaboration with the other party and governing only to their party's base voters.

In addition, this term-limit provision eliminates the need for any member of Congress to spend time while in office raising funds and seeking support for the next election. Running for election while holding any office is prohibited by the Amendment. Thus, the 40% of time on average that members spend on these re-election activities today can be used to work on programs and legislation to benefit the country and its citizens. They would have time to read and research issues with legislation, and to work with members of the other party, before having to vote upon it.

Finally, this Amendment also eliminates the ability of members of Congress to establish their own compensation levels, health benefits and retirement plans. It also eliminates the all too frequently used "revolving door" between members holding elected office and then serving as paid lobbyists, to influence their former colleagues and their staffs for the benefit of clients seeking special favors or support for legislation for their own benefits.

Taken all together, this Amendment will hopefully mean that the people who will seek elected offices will be motivated by the same sense of service to country that drives thousands of our fellow citizens who volunteer every year to serve the country in the military, and then return to their "normal" lives as citizens when their period of service ends. This change would go a long way to removing or eliminating the sense of the "governing elite" and the "career politicians" that utilize partisanship and donor loyalty to stay in office by winning election after election, that we seem to have in Congress today.

- **Risks.** I have presented this material to several classes in Institutes of Learning in Retirement programs at three local universities. While nearly all attendees favor term limits, the concept of a single term always raises the most concerns. While everyone acknowledges the benefits of elected officials doing all the fundraising and seeking of voter support before they are in office, and of not running for the next election while in office, many attendees are understandably concerned about the loss of experience and expertise in our members of Congress.

  Here are some of the most common concerns with a single term limit expressed in these classes:
  - Proposing laws and bills is complicated and can take a couple of years for a new member just to learn the issues and the processes.
  - Without having experienced elected officials, the staffs will be able to mislead or exert control over the actions of elected officials who won't understand the processes or issues as well as the staffs do.

    These concerns are fully reasonable. These are some of the risks that could result from enacting the single-term limit. But consider the following facts:
  - If the expertise of long-serving elected officials is so very important to the quality of the laws and bills that are proposed, how is that working for us today? Could the quality of our laws and bills possibly be of much lower quality from the standpoint of serving the country, providing effective solutions to major problems, or in failing to unite the country, than we

have seen from an "experienced" Congress over the past several decades?

Consider how many bills have been written by a small number of elected officials, most often senior party leaders, and then presented to the House or Senate with just a day or two to read the bill, with very little or no time to debate, before the bill is brought up for a vote. Might the quality of bills and laws be better if there were more time for elected officials to spend on reading and researching bills and laws, including more debate among the members once proposed, before they are brought up for a vote? And if more members of the House and Senate are able to propose ideas, and to work with their colleagues, not just the senior party members, might we get better ideas than under the current processes?

○ Much of the detailed work on laws and bills is currently done by staffs, but the focus and direction of the staff work is led by the elected officials. That is unlikely to change even with elected officials serving single four-year or six-year terms.

Consider that after a year of education and training on nuclear engineering and reactor operations, a young junior naval officer in his/her early twenties is placed "in charge" of very sophisticated systems in one of the many technically complex department functions on a nuclear-powered submarine. While not the most knowledgeable or experienced person in the department, they are almost uniformly effective as the leader of the people in the department, without being misled or having inappropriate control exerted over them by others.

The true leader in any organization does not need to be the most knowledgeable or the most experienced person to be effective in leading an organization. In fact, the most effective leaders know they don't know everything, that the experience and knowledge of others is respected and necessary, and they seek input from others who have knowledge and expertise they themselves lack, and use that input in their decision-making for more effective outcomes.

- As mentioned previously, studies and reports have indicated that most elected officials spend about 40% of the time they are in Washington working on their own re-election instead of working on laws and bills that might benefit the country. And of course, Congress is only in session, and elected officials in Washington, for only about 145 days out of 260 normal workdays in a typical year. If up to 40% of these days are spent focused on re-election, meeting with major donors and party leaders, might that mean our average official spends fewer than 90 days out of a full year in Washington working on legislative issues for the country?

Might there be a better quality of legislation happening if *all* of the 145 days were spent working on the country's issues, rather than losing 40% of the days to campaigning, fundraising and focusing on the issues important to donors and special-interest groups? Also, with the extra focus on addressing issues rather than campaigning, might there be a greater opportunity to discuss and collaborate with others in developing better legislation, even including colleagues from the other party? Might that represent a greater advantage for the governing of the country than the experience gained in serving multiple terms, each under the influences of partisanship and donor interests instead of the national interest?

So the key question in regard to the potential risk of this change may be as follows: Where is the greater risk to the quality of future congressional operations and legislation? Is it with the proposed change to a one-term limit, or is it in continuing the adverse influences of career self-interest and focus on re-election that we have today?

2. Minimizing partisan interest

- **Benefits.** By removing the focus on running for re-elections, the influence of the national or state party's control over the re-election support for currently serving officials would be significantly reduced. All of the party's support for the election of congressional members would take place *before* the election and *before* taking the oath of office if elected. Since no congressional member would be running for re-election while serving, the influence of needing to "toe the party line" to maintain support for their re-election and avoid having the party support an alternative candidate during the party primary would not exist.

How real is this concern today in the behavior of existing elected officials? Recall former Senator Jeff Flake's statements and actions during the hearings for Supreme Court Justice Brett Kavanaugh, after his announcement that he would not seek re-election in 2018. Before joining the party-line vote in the Senate Judiciary Committee, Jeff Blake stated that he could not vote for confirmation until there was an FBI investigation of the sexual assault charges from Justice Kavanaugh's youth. When asked if he would have taken that principled stand if he was running for re-election, he stated clearly there was no way he would have opposed the party's position in the Committee.

The other influence that both political parties exert over their members while in office relates to the party's control over the assignment of elected officials to committee positions. That influence is stronger when congressional members are seeking to move up in the party hierarchy during a career, and when the party leaders have strong control over the party hierarchy due to their own seniority in their positions. When all members are serving a single term, the most senior members would be the third of the Senators who have served four years and are serving their last two years, and the half of the Representatives who have served two years and are serving their last two years. It is hoped that in this environment, senior positions in party leadership and committee positions would be much more likely to be based on expertise and experience, and less on straight partisanship and seniority, without the leverage of career incentives.

- **Risks.** It could effectively be argued that there would be no really obvious risk to better governing for the country if the partisanship influences were minimized. While there will always be activists in both parties who will seek absolute control via majorities so they can define the direction of policies without the need to consider the concerns or interests of members of the other party, this wonderfully diverse country will never be united by the ideologies or policies of just one party.

  ○ One of the larger risks to our democratic republic is the continuation of rampant partisanship in those who govern. The word "party" is not found anywhere in the Constitution; and no one takes an oath of loyalty to a party when elected — they take an oath of loyalty to the Constitution and the country. That should mean that every elected official in every party should govern by representing all the citizens in their district or state, and in the country overall as one of our only 535 national leaders, whether those citizens voted for them or not.

Achieving that outcome will require that elected officials of both parties work together to understand how to address the needs and concerns of citizens with needs and concerns different from those of their own party's base voters. Minimizing the influences of career self-interest and partisanship might give us the best path toward that "more perfect union," the key purpose of our Constitution as stated in the Preamble. There's certainly little chance, given the current level of partisanship in Congress, that congressional leaders of either party will ever move the Congress or our country in that direction.

3. Defining an unbiased judicial impeachment and trial process

There is confusion in the constitutional requirements for how the impeachment and trial processes should be implemented. In Article 1, Sections 2 and 3, the Constitution states that "the House shall have the sole power of Impeachment," which is the power to bring a charge of an impeachable offense; and that "the Senate shall have the sole power to try all Impeachments," which is the power to determine the guilt or innocence of a charged offense. Article 1, Section 3 states further that "when the President of the US is tried, the Chief Justice shall preside."

No other description of the rules, the processes for how to bring a charge of impeachment to trial, or how to conduct a trial, is provided in the Constitution. Then in Article 1, Section 5, the Constitution states that each House (Senate and House of Representatives) may determine the rules of its proceedings.

There is the source of confusion, and the conflict. Did the

Founders fail to provide more specific descriptions in Article 1 for the processes to bring a charge of impeachment to trial and how to conduct a trial, because these processes were already established in the definitions of judicial proceedings? Could it be that they expected normal "charging" and investigation procedures to be followed by the House, and the normal procedures for conducting a "trial" under the normal powers of a "presiding judge," to be followed in the case of impeachments in the Senate? If so, then perhaps they determined that detailed descriptions in the Constitution would be unnecessary and could not easily change as these normal judicial procedures might change over time?

Or did the Founders fail to provide specific descriptions of the impeachment processes in Article 1, Sections 2 and 3, because they intended for each House to define its own procedures for impeachments, as provided for in Article 1, Section 5? That is apparently what current elected officials believe.

The country has recently witnessed what the impeachment and trial processes look like, twice in just over a year, when the sitting elected officials have chosen the latter interpretation for impeachment and trial processes. Instead of adhering to well-established judicial processes and procedures, under the leadership of our elected officials the House impeachment and Senate trial processes became very politicized; the processes seemed to be subject to corruption by partisanship, and bore little resemblance to the fairness and objective lack of bias that an established judicial process would hopefully provide.

Did you watch the 100 members of the Senate stand, raise their right hands, and take an oath to do "impartial justice" in the impeachment trial proceedings? Did you watch them each sign the "oath book" confirming their commitment to do "impartial justice"? And then many of them would leave the Senate floor and tell their favorite media reporters, from either Fox or MSNBC, that the President would be acquitted or found guilty before the trial even began? Is that what "impartial justice" should look like?

The purpose of this element of the Amendments is to clarify that the process and procedures for impeachment and trial should not be a political process but a judicial one. Impeachment is a political event, because it concerns potentially removing an official from an elected or appointed political office. But the process can still be more of a judicial than a purely partisan one. This approach would be more consistent with the language in Sections 2 and 3, and is most likely to ensure a much higher level of fairness and objectivity in bringing this most serious of charges against an elected or appointed official, especially a President, by the House, and in resolving the guilt or innocence in a trial by the Senate. It also clarifies that these requirements specifically supersede the statements in Section 5 that each House has the authority to make rules for its own proceedings, and exempts impeachment and trial proceedings from being defined by the elected officials in each House. In addition, the Amendment also specifies that a sitting official who commits an impeachable offense and is impeached by the House while serving is subject to a trial by the Senate and barring from holding any future office, even if the official leaves office before the trial begins.

- **Benefits.** With the changes defined in this element of the Amendment, there would be clarity as to how to follow the processes of bringing an unbiased impeachment charge forward from the House and conducting a fair, unbiased and, importantly, *non-political* and *non-partisan* trial in the Senate.

  The change includes confirmation that when the Constitution requires a "trial" in the Senate, it means that the process in the Senate should reflect the normal existing procedures of a judicial trial process, and should not be overridden by the political and partisan interests of the members of the Senate. It also includes confirmation that when the Constitution states that the trial should be "presided" over by the Chief Justice, it means that the normal authorities and powers of a presiding judge in a trial should also rest with the Chief Justice in an impeachment trial of the President. His or her decisions as the presiding judge should not be overridden by the political and partisan interests of the members of the Senate, who are intended to sit in impartial judgment based on the evidence presented during the impeachment trial.

In addition, the change would prevent a recurrence of the recently witnessed confusion as to whether the Senate has the constitutional authority to try an official who committed an impeachable offense and was impeached by the House while serving, but had left office before being tried by the Senate. This Amendment specifies that if an impeachable offense occurs while serving in office, and the official is impeached by the House while serving, they are subject to trial by the Senate even if they have left office before the trial begins, whether by resignation or losing an election.

Finally, these changes also replace the Chief Justice as the sole presiding judge in an impeachment trial of a President with a three-justice panel, with the Chief Justice as the senior member. The makeup of this panel would add a level of objectivity and fairness to the decisions regarding admission of relevant evidence and documents, and resolving questions of executive privilege, that the presiding judge panel has the authority to make.

- **Risks.** With as much objectivity and lack of bias as humanly possible, I have not been able to see any real risks with these changes. They are not intended to change the requirements of Article 1, Sections 2 and 3, but to clarify the "implied" requirements of the language of these sections. By clarifying that these new requirements supersede the authority granted to elected officials in both Houses in Article 1, Section 5 to make the rules for their own proceedings, and that neither the House nor the Senate can override the normal judicial processes and procedures used for investigations, bringing charges, and conducting trials, there appears to be no risk in ensuring greater confidence in the objectivity and lack of bias or partisanship in the impeachment charge and trial processes.

4. Minimizing donor interest

- **Benefits.** The extent of money in politics coming from major donors and special-interest groups is a major issue that distorts the principles of our democratic republic. Elected officials should focus primarily on addressing the interests and concerns of most citizens. But the money that donors, lobbyists, and special-interest groups contribute to campaign funds often skews the time and attention of elected officials. The focus on addressing the interests of partisan donors also minimizes the incentives of elected officials to work together across party lines to develop policies that can address the needs of a majority of citizens.

When contributions to campaigns from all sources are limited to the same levels as individual citizens, the incentive will be to serve the public instead of serving the interests of donors and special-interest groups. This would restore the balance intended in the principle of "one citizen, one vote"; large amounts of money can result in great imbalance. Votes should count more than dollars, but this is hardly the case in today's political environment.

In addition to limiting the level of donations, donor interest can be further minimized and collaborative governing increased, by limiting the time spent on campaigns. Currently, as soon as an election ends, it seems the campaign for the next election begins. This situation undermines the effectiveness of collaborative governing in the continuing heat of campaign rhetoric and vitriol, increases the total campaign funds needed to be spent and raised, and undermines the attention and the interest of citizens in the issues, through years of mostly consistent and negative campaign messages.

- **Risks.** The only risk in reducing the level of money in politics is that the amount of available funds for spending on campaign advertising might be reduced, making it potentially more difficult for candidate messages to reach voters in elections. Although in recent years, the ability of individual citizens to donate online to political candidates and issue campaigns has enabled political parties and candidates to broaden the audience of donors and still raise hundreds of millions of dollars, at average donations below $50.

In addition, less spending on campaign advertising would probably lead to a concentration of messaging in the months before the election instead of all year, and result in a shift to less expensive internet and digital channels to reach voters directly. Both these changes would likely be appreciated by most voters, who often feel inundated by the many campaign ads and messages that fill TV and radio airtime and email inboxes, seemingly starting right after one election ends until the next election. Much of this spending is likely not effective in impacting voter choices too far in advance of the election timing. Many polls indicate that a large percentage of voters remain undecided until near the election itself, especially if debates between the candidates happen near the end of the campaign. I'm sure the average voter can gain all the information needed to be an educated and informed voter in much less time than is spent today on campaigning.

5. Providing for more openness and transparency in the legislative and budgeting processes

- **Benefits.** As we've stated earlier, the Constitution is essentially a structure document for our government, not a document that defines the processes for how government should operate. The Constitution left the authority to make the rules for governing to the elected officials. But over the past several decades, elected officials have shown that they are not making rules to benefit the national interest; they have made rules primarily to benefit their careers and their party's power.

   It is now time for We the People to define the "Citizen Rules" for how we want our elected officials in Congress to operate in governing, and to add them to the Constitution. As Constitutional Amendments, these "Citizen Rules" could not be overridden by existing elected officials who would likely see them as undermining their career self-interest, or their partisan or donor interests. They also cannot be overridden by the Supreme Court, which has become increasingly an extension of the partisan divisiveness in our country today, instead of being a check against partisan and other non-democratic influences by justices supposedly insulated from these influences by their lifetime appointments. If and when these "Citizen Rules" are ratified by the states to become part of the Constitution, the Supreme Court would hopefully become supporters, if not enforcers, of these rules.

What follows is a brief discussion of the key elements of the Amendments in the area of greater transparency and accountability in both the general legislative processes and specifically in the budgeting, taxing and spending processes. The proposed changes in brief:

- Require Congress to pass a balanced budget each fiscal year. The only exception is if both the Senate and the House declare a formal state of war or a national emergency that is signed by the President. It also requires that the balanced budget be finalized and approved by Congress and signed by the President at least ten session days *before* the start of the fiscal year; and provides that Congress receive no pay if they fail to meet this time requirement until the budget is passed and signed by the President, and that their lost pay be forfeited without restoration after the budget is passed.

- Require that all programs that spend public money have a clear objective for the benefit to be delivered, the specific population to receive the benefits, the efficiency of delivering the benefit, and the measures that define success, specified as part of the proposed program by fiscal year. It also requires that the outcomes achieved by each program be reported to Congress and the public at the end of each fiscal year, prior to continuing, renewing, or expanding the program into a new fiscal year.

- Require that in the course of each fiscal-year budget and operational cycle, Congress will not increase the overall debt and will in fact act to pay down existing debt, except when a state of war or national emergency has been formally declared. Further, any new spending bills proposed during the fiscal-year budget cycle, not accounted for in the fiscal-year budget, must be offset with specific cost reductions or new revenues to maintain a balanced budget.

○ Require that funds collected for specific programs such as Medicare, Medicaid and Social Security shall not be used by the Congress for any other purpose, except when a state of war or national emergency has been formally declared. The program expenses shall be funded from revenues provided by program taxes without running deficits.

These elements are designed to ensure that the budgeting, spending, and taxing processes are managed in a fiscally responsible and transparent way. The total debt level in our country represents a ticking time bomb putting our economic and national security at risk. With interest rates on the debt at historically low levels, the interest payments each year now take up about 7%–8% of the total budget. Should interest rates rise from the current historically low levels, the level of the current debt could take up 15%–20%, or more, of the budget. This could add a new level of spending equal to the current defense and homeland security budget, taking total spending to a level that might jeopardize our ability to fund necessary programs or to sustain a tax rate to support strong economic growth. Balancing the budget in "normal" economic times is the first step to arresting the rise in our overall debt and gaining control of our economic and national security future.

○ Openness and transparency in the development of all legislation, while minimizing the influences of partisanship and seniority, would be achieved by these specific "Citizen Rules" that are included in the Amendments. The proposed changes in brief:

- Reduce the power of individual party leaders in the House and Senate to block legislation from coming to the floor for review, debate and voting;
- Increase openness by eliminating the practice of combining multiple bills of no relevance to each other for a vote, so that the individual member accountability on whether or not they would vote for each bill would be totally clear;
- Establish specific time requirements for bringing proposed legislation to the floor, including the requirement for time to read and review legislation before a vote;
- Eliminate the exemption of the Congress, as an organization or as individual members, from the requirements of any law they impose by legislation on organizations and normal citizens.

- **Risks.** While these more detailed requirements on how the legislative process should operate are quite different from the processes in place today, and should result in better legislative outcomes, there are obviously potential downsides.

  - It is possible that elected officials may find the specified time requirements difficult to work within. But these requirements do not impact the time taken to develop legislative proposals, of course, so the quality of proposed legislation should not be impacted by these requirements. Only once legislative proposals have completed development would the time requirements which specify a prompt process for reviewing and discussing the legislation in committee and on the floor of the Senate or House become controlling. This encourages the Congress to be effective and efficient in how it processes proposed legislation from presentation through discussion and debate and on

265

to a vote, either up or down, by the entire Senate or House.

6. Providing for more collaborative bipartisan policy development and accountability

The Amendments provide that legislative proposals can be passed by a simple majority in both the House and Senate, but the majority must include at least 5% from the minority party or parties. This requirement is designed to encourage a more collaborative bipartisan approach to policy development, and to prevent either party from approving legislation on a partisan-only vote.

One of the outcomes of having a very diverse country is that policies that would address the concerns of the country overall require more than just the ideological approaches of more than one party. No single party's policies will address the needs of urban and rural; highly educated and less educated; office and manufacturing plant; old, young, and in between; and rich, poor and middle class. Each party has an evolved ideology about governing that is designed to appeal primarily to a subsegment of the country. Neither party collaborates with the other very often to develop policy solutions that would work for most of the country.

While the competition of diverse ideas for addressing our key problems should be a strength of our democratic republic, in today's environment of rampant, winner-take-all partisan politics, citizens are forced to make an "or" choice between one option or the other, based on their own life experience and concerns. The ideal outcome would be an "and" choice, where the advocates of diverse approaches come together, respecting and valuing the ideas of the other, and work together to develop a win-win policy versus a win-lose policy—where 40%–49% of the citizens will always lose, regardless of which party is in power.

When each party governs only to their base, a large segment of the country is essentially not represented. As discussed earlier, most of our elections have been decided by narrow margins: 51%–49% to as much as 59%–41% in a very rare "landslide." So governing with a partisan focus on only one party's base essentially ignores the needs of between 41% and 49% of the country. This drives the parties to a winner-takes-all mentality that increases the divisiveness in the country, building a fear of and a distaste for the other, and encourages an attitude that any tactic is fair in an effort to "win at all costs." As Senator Mitch McConnell famously stated, in our current environment, "winners govern and losers go home"; that is not a description of how a democratic republic should govern. This more aptly describes a winner-takes-all society where only the majority party's interests are the basis of governing.

Let's consider an additional point about "one party" legislation and almost "blind" party loyalty becoming too often the standard for major legislative bills with a significant impact on the whole country. Are there examples in the world where we can find governments where one party dominates and "makes all the rules," and where party loyalty is not only a major factor in governing, but is often the primary factor of political life and death?

In the Preface, we looked at examples of one-party governments in existence today, including the undemocratic regimes in Russia and China, and authoritarian regimes in the Middle East, as societies where the concerns of any other views than the majority party are ignored or crushed, and any minority party or group has no rights at all. In history, we looked at Nazi Germany. Germany was a democracy at the time Hitler's party rose to a position as the majority party. Once in power, loyalty to the Nazi party became synonymous with loyalty to the country, the "Fatherland," and it was essentially "treason against the state" to disagree with the party or the Nazi party leaders.

In all these cases, the rights of a diverse minority in these societies ceased to exist, and as these societies became dominated by one political party, they ceased to be free societies. Are we so arrogant that we believe such an outcome could never happen in America, even as we seem to edge ever closer to the state of one-party governing?

Many polls of the American people indicate that the ideologies and approaches to governing and addressing our key national priorities of either party alone will never unite our wonderfully diverse country. Only by working together in collaboration, not competition, can our elected leaders truly serve the national interest in governing.

- **Benefits.** The benefits to the country would be:
  - Reducing one-party governing by eliminating the passage of laws and bills that don't have the input and support from at least a limited number of members from the other party or parties. Since neither party has rarely held a 60% preference of the country's voters, one-party governing is ignoring the interests of at least 40% of the country. One of the key principles of a democratic republic should be that after an election, the elected officials of both or all parties work together to serve the needs of *all* voters in their districts or states, not just those who are in their party, who donated to them, or who voted for them.
  - As stated earlier, the best ideas on governing have and will come from the collaboration of both parties in the development of laws and policies. Much as diversity of thinking makes a business more competitive and successful in achieving outcomes, leveraging our diversity of political thought in legislation development will almost certainly lead to more effective governing.
  - Since the 40% of time now spent on running for re-

election would be eliminated, there is more time for members to work together on legislation, to have open discussion, debates, to explore more innovative "third alternative" solutions to key problems, and then to hold votes up or down on more legislative ideas.

- **Risks.** While there are risks in these changes, as there are risks in any change of the status quo, I ask that readers consider if there are other approaches that could achieve the stated purpose of greater national unity through increased bipartisan collaboration in governing.

  ○ One of the major risks is that the minority party or parties would be more empowered to block all action on bills proposed by the majority party. And of course, that could certainly happen as an outcome, leading to total gridlock instead of the partial or occasional gridlock we often see today. Such a choice of action by the minority would be entirely against the oath of office elected officials take to serve the nation, and would violate the reasons why they were elected to Congress by their fellow citizens.

  ○ The good news is, any member or party choosing this outcome would be replaced by new candidates in the very next election. But because the elected officials would not have the influence of career self-interest, nor partisanship or donors while serving, it is more likely that they would only raise their hands to serve if they had the spirit and intent to give four or six years of service to the country. It is unlikely that such officials, once in office, would waste their limited service time in just blocking all action and failing to address any of the nation's issues.

7. Defining a specific timeline for the Senate in exercising their "advice and consent" role

The Constitution requires that when the President makes treaties or nominates senior members of the Administration, ambassadors, federal judges and Supreme Court justices, the Senate shall provide advice and consent.

You may recall from a previous discussion, that when President Obama nominated Neil Gorsuch to fill a vacant Supreme Court justice position in January of an election year, the Senate Majority Leader decided that the Senate would not hold interviews with the nominee or hold a vote of the Senate to confirm him during an election year. This action ignored the requirement of the Constitution for "the Senate" to provide advice and consent. The language in the Constitution states that the President "shall nominate, and by and with the Advice and Consent of the Senate, shall appoint...Judges of the Supreme Court." This language does not give the Senate Majority Leader, a position not even mentioned in the Constitution, the power to withhold a vote of the Senate to provide advice and consent. The Senate does not have to approve an appointment, but it has a constitutional duty to perform the "advice and consent" role by taking a vote of the full Senate.

This was an unfortunate example of our elected officials defining rules for the operation of Congress in order to provide a partisan benefit that actually violated a specific requirement of the Constitution.

This element of the Amendment formally defines "advice and consent" as requiring a vote of the full Senate to approve or reject a treaty or presidential nomination. Further, this element requires that such vote be taken by the full Senate within 60 session days of a nomination, or the Senate members will permanently forfeit all pay for each day the vote is delayed. Finally, this element requires that no nominations requiring the advice and consent of the Senate be made by the President within 120 days of the next presidential election.

- **Benefits.** This element of the Amendment will provide clarity around how the process of nomination and appointment by the President and the advice and consent of the Senate shall take place. Without adding such specificity as provided in this element of the Amendment, it is possible that future elected officials might, for partisan political reasons, fail to execute their constitutional duties again.

- **Risks.** The risks with this element of the Amendment would be that a President and Senate, in the last 125 days of their current terms in office, would still have the ability to nominate and appoint a federal judge or Supreme Court justice who will serve a ten-year term. Additionally, there is a risk that a vacancy in a key position might remain vacant for as long as six months.

  While neither of these outcomes is desirable, these risks are less than what we experienced in 2016, with a full-year vacancy on the Supreme Court, and in 2020, with a Supreme Court appointment confirmed just eight days before a presidential election. In addition, the risk of not specifying time requirements would be that the decision on whether to make or approve appointments in the final year of current terms would be left to elected officials to make such determinations, likely based primarily on partisan influences. It is considered more desirable to have a specific, objective timetable defined as part of this Amendment to the Constitution than to leave the timing to partisan influences.

8. Ensuring fairness and honesty in election messaging and equality of voter access to registration and voting

- Eliminating gerrymandering of districts

    The Amendments provide for the establishment of a non-partisan Federal Election Oversight Board, consisting of ordinary citizens, not past or present elected officials or those serving as party officials. This Board would be empowered to review congressional district alignments to ensure the absence of partisan or demographic advantage for either political party, or any discrimination against any racial, religious, ethnic, party affiliation or other minority group.

    Within their authority, this Board would be empowered to require that changes be made by states to district alignments judged to be biased and unfair. The states would have the ability to challenge the requirements for changes from the Board in federal court if they disagreed with the Board's judgment. Citizen groups within states would also have the ability to appeal directly to the Board to request reviews, shortcutting the current arduous process of citizen groups collecting thousands of signatures for an appeal to the legislature or a ballot initiative. The states should be notified of any changes required by the Board at least one year before any election.

- Eliminating any state limits on voter registration and voting access laws or situations that do not apply equally and justly to all citizens

    This Board would also have the authority to require that changes be made to any state voter registration or voting access laws or operations that do not apply equally and justly to all citizens. The Board would also have the authority to require that changes to voting laws or operations be justified by factual evidence of significant voter fraud, and that the proposed changes effectively address the identified evidence. The states would have the ability to challenge the requirements from the Board in court if they disagree with the Board's judgment. The states should be notified of any changes required by the Board at least one year before any election.

- Ensuring that campaign messaging is truthful and honest

The Amendments also provide for the establishment of a Federal Election Message Oversight Board with the authority to review campaign messaging for truthfulness. The first Amendment provides for the protection of all speech, especially political speech, but it does not provide for the protection of false speech, untruths, or lies that could impact an election unfairly. In the era of technology-enabled "fake news," the fairness of our elections is at significant risk if there is no restriction on distributing false or misleading messages about candidates and issues. Our democracy cannot survive without citizen confidence in the truth of political advertising and messages. And citizens will never be able to choose candidates who offer effective solutions to problems if elected officials seek to provide proposals without real facts and truthful information.

Most citizens would probably agree that the negative impacts of false messages or "fake news" on the integrity and fairness in our elections should be eliminated. The key question of who or what authority will be the arbiter of truth is always the key concern, of course. The test of truthful political advertising and messaging is actually quite simple: Statements made about a candidate, party, or proposed piece of legislation must be able to be supported by facts. If the speaker, writer or distributor of messages cannot provide facts to support any statement they make, it would be required to be taken down or changed. Statements of opinion must still be reasonably consistent with facts. Projections of outcomes in the future of potential actions also must be consistent with some relevant fact or experience in history, not merely the result of a baseless rumor or theory.

The Federal Election Message Oversight Board would publish all decisions taken with regard to challenging or validating any campaign advertising or messaging. If a campaign or candidate resisted the decision of the Board, the Board would turn the issue over to the FTC to enforce.

The principle is that the speaker or writer has the obligation to make truthful statements, and when asked, must present the evidence or facts that support the truthfulness of the statement. The distributing platform has the responsibility to request that support, and deny access if the support either is not provided or is judged to be insufficient to support the message.

These are essentially the same procedures that have been in place for decades to enforce the requirements that all commercial advertising and messaging should meet the standards of being "truthful and not misleading" by the non-partisan National Advertising Review Board. Why are these standards allowed to be enforced for commercial advertising, if they might be a restriction on the free speech of businesses? Perhaps it is because fraudulent or false speech was never intended to be protected by the First Amendment?

But more to the point, the impact of fraudulent commercial advertising puts consumers at risk of making purchase decisions based on false information, and thus being defrauded. And it gives an unfair and undeserved advantage to the company using the false advertising and messaging against its competitors, and puts at risk the investments and innovations of a potentially better product or service.

So the question is, which decisions are more important to the country? Which laundry detergent a consumer chooses, or which elected official voters choose to be one of the 535 national leaders of our country, or the President? Does it make sense that we allow elections to be conducted with no regard as to the truthfulness of advertising and messages distributed to voters concerning the personal backgrounds, professional history, or stands on issues of importance to the country? Shouldn't we require that messages about candidates and issues, from whatever source, be based on facts? Or, if false messages can be used in election campaigns, then might undeserving candidates derive an unfair advantage over a potentially better and more deserving candidate? And might the country choose ineffective solutions based on incorrect or untruthful data about the problems or the expected outcomes?

If most citizens understand that many Supreme Court judgments have confirmed that there is clear precedent indicating that our rights as defined in the Constitution are not absolute rights, and that there is no intention for these rights to supersede or excuse behavior that otherwise would be criminal or damaging to the integrity of our commercial or democratic processes, then there shouldn't be a concern that this element of the Amendments violates any important aspect of our democratic principles or way of life.

- **Benefits.** These elements of the Amendment will eliminate three key areas where partisan interests have undermined the integrity and equality of access for registration and voting access for all voters. The unfair influence of donor contributions leading to dollars counting more than votes in the influence of policy and the access to candidates or elected officials; the unfair gerrymandering of voting-district alignments; and the corrupting influence of false and misleading campaign messages, have all undermined the ideal of unbiased elections based on true and transparent messages and the objective choices of the voters. If allowed to continue to influence elections without reform, they will continue to put our democracy at risk.

- **Risks.** The major risk to the implementation of these oversight roles will be that the Federal Election Commission and the two non-partisan oversight boards will not be staffed by true non-partisan and unbiased citizens. The selection of the members of the two new oversight boards by the Federal Election Commission and not the President or the Congress will hopefully help minimize the risk that partisan biases might render these oversight boards ineffective or biased in their actions.

9. Replacing lifetime appointments for federal judges and Supreme Court justices

Lifetime appointments for the highest levels in the judicial branch of our government were deemed important to the Founders in writing the Constitution, to insulate the judicial branch of government from the influences of partisanship. Rising to their positions by appointment and confirmation instead of election, the hope was that justices would not be subject to the partisan influences of campaigning and elections to attain or sustain them in their positions.

However, over the past several decades, we have seen Presidents and the Senate majority from both parties inject a significant level of partisanship into the selection and confirmation of federal judges and Supreme Court justices.

Unfortunately for our country, the result is that the judicial branch today has become nearly as partisan as the other two branches of government. Lifetime appointments can be made and confirmed by one party when they have won the Presidency and have a majority in the Senate—even if these majorities are very small majorities—meaning again that the needs and concerns of almost 50% of the country might be ignored for the lifetime of a partisan appointment.

- **Benefits.** The proposed Amendments are designed to minimize the potential partisan influences of lifetime appointments in the judicial branch by providing the following changes:
    - As discussed earlier, the influence of partisanship in Congress would be minimized by limiting members to a single term without the prospect of running for re-election while serving; and by ensuring a measure of bipartisan support for all Senate confirmations, by requiring that votes for all laws, bills and confirmation of appointments be approved by a majority that must include at least 5% of the majority from the minority party or parties.
    - In addition, the Amendments propose limiting the terms for federal judges and Supreme Court justices to ten years, with the prospect of being renominated by a different President and reconfirmed by a completely different Senate at the end of each ten-year term. Lifetime terms are still possible under this amendment for judges and justices whose decisions consistently reveal a non-partisan balance, and are renominated and reconfirmed for multiple ten-year terms. The ten-year limit also enables a President and a Senate to choose not to extend the terms of very elderly judges and justices.

- **Risks.** As stated with earlier proposals, there is always a risk, in making a change, that the desired and intended outcome may not be realized due to unforeseen issues. In this case, as in some of the others discussed earlier, the benefit of eliminating the problem of partisan influence that has emerged under the current system, and does not seem possible to be eliminated or minimized by other actions, makes the risk of not changing much greater than the risk of making the proposed change. Readers are encouraged to consider whether the proposed changes are likely to result in a better situation for the country than what we have today, or are likely to have in the future without making these changes.
  - The major risk, therefore, is that the changes in the proposed Amendment may not reduce the divisive influence of judicial partisanship in our country. But it is hard to consider that these changes could result in the influence of partisanship being greater than it is today. Shouldn't we take a chance on reducing the influence of partisanship in our judicial branch, and restoring the kind of objective judicial oversight our Founders intended?

10. Requiring that Electoral College votes for President be allocated proportionally to candidates based on the percentage of the popular vote in each state

The Electoral College was created as part of the original Constitution in 1789. The Electoral College system for presidential elections was designed as a compromise between two factions in the Constitutional Convention, one that favored electing the President and Vice President by Congress and one that favored electing the President and Vice President by the popular vote of citizens. There were also concerns that the former approach would create conflicts with the separation of powers, and the latter approach would overwhelm the minority influences of smaller states.

The Electoral College was a compromise to ensure that large majorities in a few big states would not overwhelm the needs, concerns and preferences of a smaller number of citizens in many less-populated states in the election of the President and Vice President by popular vote. The Founders sought to preserve a major objective they held to be important in the new representative democratic republic, that the "tyranny" of the majority should not overwhelm the rights of the minority. After living under the tyranny of the elite classes in European monarchies, they carried this concern in developing the new government.

In addition, the electors, the members of the Electoral College, were to be chosen by the state legislatures, and they would vote for President and Vice President, without the influence of the popular vote. State laws have since been passed to require their appointed Electors to cast votes for the candidate who won the majority of the state's popular vote for President and Vice President.

As discussed earlier, in the past 16 years and the last five presidential elections, we have seen a candidate win the majority of the national popular vote but lose the majority of the national Electoral College vote. That circumstance being repeated twice in a short period of time has led several politicians and partisan interest groups to begin arguing that, in our democracy, the Electoral College process seems to result in denying or even negating the will of the majority of citizens. They further argue that the presidential candidate who wins the majority of the popular national vote of all citizens should be declared the winner of the election. However, this seems to be a short-sighted and, quite frankly, obvious partisan approach to the issue. The Electoral College and its purpose of minimizing the dominance of large states over small states is judged to be too important an element of how our Founders intended our representative democratic republic to operate, to simply remove it entirely from the Constitution.

However, there is a real shortcoming with the Electoral College. The current system of allocating all the Electoral College votes of one state entirely to the winner of the state's popular vote introduces an undesirable winner-takes-all aspect to the process. This exaggerates the partisan divisions in the country and the governing to one party's base, which is what is needed to win Electoral College votes in the states where a majority of the voters tend to support their party.

There is an additional reason why this is a problem that needs to be addressed. Does it seem fair or consistent with representative government principles that the candidate who wins 50.1% of the popular votes should receive 100% of the Electoral College votes that determine the state's preference for a presidential candidate? This seems to ignore the will and preferences for a presidential candidate of perhaps as much as 40%–49% of the state's citizens, while majorities as small as 50.1% of the popular vote cancel out the preferences of the minority. What that leads to today is that in presidential elections, each major party focuses mostly on the "swing" states where both parties have a chance to win the state's Electoral College votes, while both parties also avoid allocating limited campaign time and money to those states where their party has historically done poorly and is judged unlikely to win Electoral College votes.

To remedy that aspect of the current system, the proposed Amendment would replace the current winner-takes-all allocation of Electoral College votes present in almost all states. This change would require that in all states, the Electoral College votes in a presidential election should be allocated on a proportional basis to the percentage of the state's popular vote won by each candidate.

- **Benefits.** The key benefit of this element of the Amendments is to minimize one of the winner-takes-all aspects of today's political environment, while maintaining the important aspect of protecting minority voices in our elections that the Electoral College was intended to provide.
  - With this change, candidates for President would have a much greater incentive to campaign in all states, and thus develop a better understanding of the needs and concerns of citizens in all states. Even in states where a candidate would be unlikely to win the majority of the popular vote, they could earn a number of Electoral College votes based on the percentage of the popular vote they receive.
  - As a result, Presidents and their Administrations would perhaps be more likely to work with both parties in developing policies and programs in governing, with the incentive of maximizing the popular vote in each state in the next election.
- **Risks.** In all honesty, there does not appear to be a risk to the principles or the operation of our representative democratic republic from this change. However, there is always the risk that impacts could result from this change that we are unable to foresee—much as our Founders could not foresee how some of the elements of the original Constitution would be impacted by 240 years of changes in the political and societal environments. That unknown potential risk seems to be much smaller than the known risks of maintaining the current allocation system, or of abandoning the Electoral College completely in favor of electing the President and Vice President by the national popular vote.

11. Defining the processes for converting the popular votes in each state for President and Vice President to Electoral College votes and certifying the vote in Congress

Once the election for President and Vice President has been completed in the states, the election officials in each precinct and county will report results of the popular vote to the state election officials who will compile the state's total popular vote, and the Electoral College votes will be awarded to each candidate on the basis of the proportion of the state's popular vote won by each candidate. Any recounts and investigations of potential irregularities or fraud should be immediately begun, to be concluded in the six weeks before the Secretary of State and Governor of each state are required to certify the election results, by mid-December.

Following official state certification in mid-December, the formal certificates of both the popular and the Electoral College votes awarded for President and Vice President should be delivered to the Congress. Congress will meet in early January as currently required by the Constitution to open the state's certificates and formally count the national totals. The Congress shall have no authority to question, object to, or reject any official certificates from the states in this process. In the event of a tie in the Electoral College votes, or that no candidate achieves a majority of the Electoral College votes, then the Congress shall refer to the national popular vote count, and the candidates with the largest number of popular votes shall be declared the President and Vice President. The current step of having the House of Representatives decide the President and Vice President by a political vote, sure to be partisan, would be eliminated.

- **Benefits.** The key benefit of this proposal is to protect the final certification process of the Electoral College vote from being challenged politically, either by partisan state legislatures or by the Congress, and either totally discounted or replaced by votes in the Senate, or having the House of Representatives choose the President and Vice President instead of the citizens. This section of the Amendment also removes the naming of electors by the state legislatures after the popular vote, and the actual voting of these electors in the Electoral College. It also clearly states that all challenges to election results must be investigated and resolved in the six weeks following the election, and that the final certification of the Electoral College votes in each state is by the Secretary of State and Governor, not the state legislature, and the authority of Congress is limited *only* to opening and counting the certified vote totals from the states.

These steps will clearly exclude any objections to or rejections of the popular votes of the citizens via a political process in Congress. The certification of the national Electoral College vote for President would now be based on a direct mathematical calculation of the percentage of the state's popular vote won by each candidate, with no partisan political action overriding the vote of the citizens.

- **Risks.** In all objectivity, I can see no risks to this section of the Amendment. The original process in the Constitution was written in the days of paper ballots and mail by horseback. With the use of computers with paper backup, and computer calculations of the popular votes and the translation to Electoral College votes proportionately in each state, the need for electors or congressional review of the validity of certified counts is just not necessary for accuracy and fairness. And the elimination of any political influences in the state legislatures' or in Congress's roles in the final certification of results cannot be seen as anything but a benefit to our democratic principles and values.

12. Establishing limits on contributions to federal candidates and issue advocacy groups and the period of public campaigns

A decision by the Supreme Court several years ago, the case known as "Citizens United," essentially equated the limiting of monetary spending on political or campaign ads by companies and organizations, and donations to political campaigns and candidates, with unlawful constraints on free speech. The decision determined that under the First Amendment, money spent on political messages cannot be limited any more than political speech can be limited. The decision cites the important role that free speech plays in the political and electoral processes in our country, a role that cannot be limited by congressional action.

This decision has led to an explosion of the amounts of money being contributed to candidates and campaigns, skewing and distorting the influence of large donors over many more individual citizens and their smaller donations. This environment would seem to be at odds with the principle of "one citizen, one vote" that is at the core of our democratic values.

However, the Supreme Court in historical decisions has indicated that no "right" enumerated in the Constitution is an absolute right, and any of these rights can be limited for a small number of reasons. Thus, this element of the Amendments focuses on the principle that the level of spending on speech and contributions to candidates can overwhelm the issue of "one citizen, one vote." More money being spent by companies and wealthy individuals than the average citizen can afford creates more access to and influence on candidates and issues, not due to the logic of the argument but simply on the basis of the money spent or contributed to promote the argument.

As a result of no policy being able to level this imbalance under the existing Constitution, this Amendment makes the clear statement that, under the proposed "Citizen Rules," We the People believe and affirm that unlimited money imbalances create unfair influences in political speech that result in political influence more determined by dollars than by votes, and therefore can be limited. Further, companies and organizations, not being citizens or having a vote, should not have a greater influence on political processes than an individual citizen, and thus should not be able to contribute more money to candidates or issue-advocacy campaigns than an individual citizen.

Research clearly indicates that most citizens believe there is too much money in politics; believe that money does influence access to candidates and elected officials and the policies they support; and believe that campaigns are too long and send out many more messages than are helpful for educating citizens on issues, and may in fact deter citizens from paying attention until near election day.

The specific requirements included in this Amendment are as follows. Congress is required and authorized to pass new Federal Election Laws that will accomplish the following goals:

- Set specific limits on the total amount of money or gifts that an individual citizen can contribute in a calendar year on a total basis to all candidates, political parties, or issue advocacy groups, and require full and quarterly public disclosure of all contributions received by all candidates, all political parties and all groups accepting contributions and spending money on campaign or political messages. These limits should be set to a level that would be reasonable for the average citizen to afford.

- Limit all contributions on an aggregated basis in each

election year, from companies or organizations, including special-interest groups, labor unions, and any other organization, to the same level of aggregated contribution limits as individual citizens, in making contributions to any candidate, political party, or special-interest or issue advocacy group.

- Require full public disclosure and full public accounting of all contributions received and made by organizations, and of total messaging spending and delivery channels by all companies, organizations (public and private), special-interest groups, labor unions, PACs and political issue groups.

- Instruct the Federal Election Commission to establish an independent, unbiased, non-partisan Federal Election Oversight Board with the authority to review all reports of election contributions and spending reports from all candidates, parties, PACs and political issue action groups. Instruct Congress to implement federal election law concerning contribution limits and reporting requirements.

- Require that campaign spending by, from and about candidates by all sources begins no earlier than January 3 in a federal election year for candidates for national office (Congress, President and Vice President).

- Clarify that there is no limit to the amount of volunteer hours a citizen can contribute to a candidate's or an issue advocacy group's activities. Companies, organizations, businesses, PACs and issue advocacy groups have no limit on messaging sent directly to their employees, stakeholders, and members or volunteers who expressly "opt in" to receive their messages.

- **Benefits.** These elements of the Amendments will essentially overturn the "Citizens United" Supreme

Court decision, which essentially gave a "green light" to unlimited amounts of money flowing to candidates and their campaigns. That decision also allows political action groups and public issue advocacy groups (PACs) to collect money from individuals, companies and organizations without attribution, and when they contribute to candidates or political parties, only the name of the group is required to be publicly announced, not the names of the individuals, companies or organizations that contributed to the group. The environment that exists following that decision at least invites, if not facilitates, many levels of unfair influence on candidates to pursue certain policies.

○ While all elected officials regularly declare that large contributions do not impact their positions on policies, this declaration violates common sense and the observations of the majority of citizens. Most citizens believe that significant access and influence follows large contributions.

○ Companies and organizations may of course distribute information and messages of their own positions on candidates and legislative issues within their organization to stakeholders, members, customers and suppliers. When they do so, they must publicly disclose all individual citizen contributions and must publicly account for total messaging spending and delivery channels, including separate public and regular accounting of their contributions to individual candidates, political parties, PACs or issue advocacy groups.

○ When campaign dollars are limited and the period of campaign messaging spending is also limited, it is likely that citizens will pay more attention to candidates' backgrounds and policy positions during the election year.

- **Risks.** There is a risk that this might limit campaign funding levels so that there may not be sufficient money contributed by individuals to support sufficient messaging levels to ensure the electorate is knowledgeable about the candidates and their positions. However, as stated above, concentrating messages into the year of the election may likely increase voter attention, and fewer messages may minimize the "eyes glazing over" syndrome that can come from the high level of messaging received now over a long period of time before the election.

In recent elections, most campaigns have shifted a great percentage of spending and message delivery to the targeted media delivery channels in preference to the more traditional but expensive national media TV channels. This shift has been enabled by the large amounts of individual voter information that both major parties and most candidates have collected from previous election campaigns. And in recent years, the funds contributed to campaigns by individual donors have been quite large and sufficient to support impactful messaging levels.

12. Establishing new requirements for elected officials to minimize conflicts of interest and strengthen ethical conduct

The current requirements for the standards of behavior for elected officials with regard to conflict of interest and ethical behavior have been developed by the elected officials themselves. While these requirements are fairly limited in scope, there have been numerous and frequent violations in Congress with little or no accountability or consequences. Moreover, neither of the two major parties seems willing to ever call out and hold accountable members of their own party for whatever violations occur. There is probably not a more important area where Citizen Rules are now needed.

Here are the key elements of the Amendment in this area that apply to all members of Congress, to the President, Vice President and all senior members of the executive branch, the Administration, or congressional or committee staffs:

- Prohibit any official in the stated organizations from serving as a paid lobbyist in dealing with any members of an Administration, congressional members, or congressional or committee staffs after serving a term in Congress or for any period in the Administration.
- Require that all elected officials in the stated organizations release ten years of federal and state tax returns when filing as candidates for federal elections. Require that all politically appointed officials in the stated organizations file ten years of federal and state tax returns at the announcement of their nominations.
- Require that all elected and politically appointed officials in the stated organizations place all personal investments, ownership in any business, and all other equity assets in a third-party blind trust, not supervised by family or business partners, after winning an election or securing a confirmation of their appointment to office, before taking the oath of office.
- While serving in office, elected and politically appointed officials are required to publicly release each year their tax returns, and blind-trust asset, income and transaction statements, so that any potential benefit from serving the public would be available for public review.

- **Benefits.** The benefit of this element of the Amendments would be to specify actions to minimize the opportunity that elected officials could use their positions of public trust to benefit themselves financially.
    - The prohibition against paid lobbying roles by elected

and appointed senior officials following their service will help stop the undue influence that former elected officials have over current elected officials and their staffs and committees, that they can leverage in highly paid positions funded by lobbying firms, corporations, and issue advocacy groups. Those elected officials who choose not to pursue a career in elected office seem to choose a more highly paid career in leveraging their contacts and relationships for the benefit of major corporations and issue advocacy groups. This new career opportunity is often made possible by the same group of lobbyists who have made large campaign contributions to the members while in office. Such a relationship is fraught with opportunities for conflicts of interest between the officials and lobbyists, putting the interests of donors above the interests of serving their constituencies.

- The requirement for publicly releasing tax returns at the time of filing as a candidate for federal elections, or when nominated for a senior Administration or judicial position, is designed to ensure that information about the candidate's finances and sources of income and expenses—areas that might be potential sources of conflict of interest for a candidate seeking an important position via election or appointment—is available for public review and congressional review during confirmation hearings. It is important to have transparency into this aspect of a candidate's background for the public and Congress to be able to make an informed decision with regard to the connections and potential influences on candidates for senior positions within our government.

- The requirement for placing investment assets into a blind trust is designed to ensure that any decisions public officials make once in office will not be influenced by profiting personally. In recent times, there have been several public officials who have profited personally from decisions made in overseeing industries where they held investments. Others have passed on confidential information received in their position to family or friends for their financial benefit. These violations of the public trust would be significantly more difficult and less frequent without the ability to realize a short-term personal financial benefit.

- ○ The annual public release of tax returns and blind-trust assets, income, and transactions each year would provide an ongoing check on the potential conflicts of interest or misuse of their public office while serving.
- **Risks.** The major risk in this element of the Amendments is that people with many assets to disclose and to place in a blind trust managed by a neutral third party may be reluctant to volunteer for a period of public service, either as a candidate for elected office or as a member of an Administration. Such people often have talents and experience that could potentially benefit the country, if there is no intent to use public office to enhance their own personal finances. So this requirement might discourage some citizens from agreeing to serve the country, even for a limited term in office of four years or six years. But without these requirements, the public and Congress would have no ability to effectively determine potential conflicts of interest before and during the period of serving the country.

13. Establishing requirements for public service obligations for all citizens

We have dedicated much space in this book to defining the

"Citizen Rules" designed to help restore a commitment in our elected and politically appointed officials to serving the country over serving a party, donors, or their own career interests. But the lack of commitment of too many citizens to put the interests of the country above their personal beliefs and needs or their party affiliations also needs restoration. At the time our Constitution was drafted, there was no conflict with the commitment of individual citizens to the interest of the country. Many sacrificed personal wealth and fortunes, and indeed their lives, in service to the country.

At this "Turning Point" in our history, in order to fully "Repair and Restore Our Constitutional Republic" and to become again that "One Indivisible Nation," we must also dedicate some discussion to how we might renew the average citizen's commitment to service to the country. It could be argued that one of the elements that made the Greatest Generation so great was that nearly everyone in that generation, both men and women, spent some number of years in selfless service to the country. Many served in combat in World War II, including women, and many more served at home by taking on production roles for necessary equipment and materials, and by sacrificing their own comforts. And when the war was over, they came home and built the greatest economy in the history of the world, even accepting a high personal top tax rate, as high as 91% from 1949 to 1963. This funding enabled the government to pay for much of the war debt, the building of new national infrastructures, the sending of over 4 million GIs to college for free, and investing in rebuilding the economies of our World War II allies and our enemies, to build a more secure and peaceful world.

Fast-forward some 70 years and a couple of generations removed from that period. It seems today that most citizens are neither required to nor do they seem willing to sacrifice any aspect of their personal comforts for the benefit of others, or to put their loyalty to a party or a President beneath the need to serve the country. In the midst of a global pandemic, the necessity to wear masks to limit the spread of a deadly virus as a national public health imperative is rejected by perhaps one-third of our citizens as an unlawful and unwarranted infringement on their personal liberties.

But our liberties are not free; their existence and protection have always required sacrifice and service from citizens. It is perhaps the experience of spending time in the service of the country or the community, not only putting the needs of the country or others above our own needs but doing so working alongside other citizens who are different from ourselves, which builds the strongest sense of citizenship and respect for the needs of others with a different life experience than our own. Those elements of citizenship are not only a critical need in our elected and appointed leaders; they are also needed within our citizenry.

This last Amendment would require that all citizens spend at least two years in a national or community service role, beginning after their eighteenth birthday and completing their service before reaching their thirtieth birthday. That means they must choose to start an identified national or community service role no later than their twenty-eighth birthday, or they would be assigned to an appropriate role. That range of ages means that some will choose to serve right after high school, some after a trade school and/or apprenticeship, some after college, some after graduate school, and some after becoming a doctor or lawyer, or completing a doctorate degree program.

The range of roles would include but not be limited to the many positions in the military; to police, fire or first-responder positions; to teachers and/or medical professionals in under-served areas; or to several other roles that would fill needs in our country and communities. There would be no exemptions or waivers for this required service, except for obviously limiting physical, mental, emotional, or other medically certified conditions.

- **Benefits.** There are benefits for both the individual and the country:
    - ○ For the individual, whether they choose to begin service at 18 or at 28, they will gain personal and professional skills and experience that will help make them more effective and successful later in life. In addition, following whatever service role they choose, they will emerge with a greater understanding of another part of our society than that part from which they were raised. And finally, they will gain an understanding of what it means to serve others, the importance of service to our country, and the satisfaction that comes to the individual. This experience will reinforce the core value of interdependence that is uniquely American, that was expressed by our Founders in the last sentence to the Declaration of Independence, written before we were a country:

        "And for the support of this Declaration, with a firm reliance on the protection of divine Providence, we mutually pledge to each other our Lives, our Fortunes and our sacred Honor."

Today, our country is largely divided by "tribal" partisan ideologies, which is putting the future of our democracy at risk. As citizens, we are not fulfilling the pledge we teach our children to make to our flag—that we are "one nation…indivisible" by our actions and our politics. And we are certainly a long, long way from the unity, respect, and caring about our fellow citizens that is reflected in the last sentence of the Declaration of Independence.

But among the portion of our citizens who have served

in the military or other similar service roles, most have lived periods of service and sacrifice, and learned to respect and care about the others on their team as much as or perhaps even more than themselves, without regard to party, religion, race, gender, or sexual orientation. Ensuring that most citizens have that experience can only be exceptionally valuable to our future.

- **Risks.** With every attempt to be objective and unbiased, I do not foresee a major risk to either individuals or to our country from this element of the Amendments. Perhaps there is a risk that some people will have difficult experiences, and of course, the quality of the leaders individuals may encounter during their service will be as varied as the types of people in our country. Quite frankly, those are common life experiences in all lives and careers, and learning to deal effectively with them is a beneficial experience. But without such a commitment to national service in our future generations, it is difficult to see that simply changing the focus of our elected leaders, should these Amendments be implemented, will be sufficient to unite our citizens and fully reverse the "tribal" partisan divisiveness that exists today. I hope most readers would agree that, whatever risks there may be, they are worth taking in order to achieve this benefit in future generations.

In the next chapter, we will discuss how these changes to the Constitution can be implemented.

Chapter 7

How Do These Changes to the Constitution Get Enacted?

In chapters 4 and 6, we reviewed 16 overall areas of change to the existing rules for how Congress operates—what we called the new "Citizen Rules." As a reminder, here is the list of changes we have discussed:

1. Setting term limits, compensation, and health and retirement benefits for members of Congress and senior Administration officials

2. Defining new rules for the legislative processes to limit partisanship; confirming primacy of Citizen Rules in the Constitution over procedural rules enacted by members of Congress

3. Defining timing requirements for Senate votes on treaties and presidential appointments; limiting the duration of acting presidential appointments; limiting absolute presidential reprieves and pardons

4. Strengthening congressional oversight of executive implementation; strengthening the independence of Inspectors General and key executive departments in the Administration

5. Defining rules for budgeting, taxing and spending pro-cesses—balance, timing, accountability, transparency, effectiveness

6. Prohibiting Congress members from lobbying after serving in Congress

7. Prohibiting laws exempting Congress from laws enacted on citizens

8. Changing the allocation and certification of Electoral

College votes in presidential elections

9. Limiting the terms of Supreme Court justices and federal court judges

10. Ensuring fair and equitable access to registration and voting for all citizens, and elections free from fraud

11. Defining rules for campaign financing—donation limits and disclosure requirements

12. Defining rules for truthful messaging and timing of campaign advertising

13. Providing an independent council to oversee voting-district alignments after census

14. Defining rules for ethical behaviors and financial conflict of interest, and for handling non-salary personal income for President, Vice President, and all senior elected and appointed officials

15. Defining a non-partisan judicial process for impeachment and actions considered as impeachable offenses

16. Establishing a program of required national service for all citizens between the ages of 18 and 29

Under each of these 16 areas, we have described the specific changes to the current rules under which Congress and/or the Administration operates to meet the improved outcomes we seek to achieve in each area. These changes have been combined in six Amendments to the Constitution to be called "The Bill of Public Service and Accountability," as described in detail in the preceding chapter. The result of ratifying these Amendments as proposed would be to replace many of the existing procedural rules made mostly by elected members of Congress, some of the powers granted to the President in the Constitution, and some of the precedents set by the Supreme Court's interpretations of the Constitution in individual cases, with new "Citizen Rules," to be included within the Constitution itself.

Question: **How Can the Amendments and the "Citizen Rules" Best Be Implemented?**
There are only three ways to implement the Amendments to the Constitution and enable the "Citizen Rules" to take effect that we have defined in Chapter 4:

1. Citizens petition Congress to pass new laws and rules.

- For the rules that are defined by Congress, and not by the courts' interpretations of the Constitution, Congress could draft new rules and laws to enact the "Citizen Rules" requirements. But the Supreme Court may overturn some of them, such as those that limit campaign contributions, campaign periods, and the truthfulness of campaign messaging. And any new laws or rules enacted by one Congress can be overturned and replaced by the succeeding Congress just two years later.

2. Citizens petition Congress to draft Amendments to the Constitution to implement the new rules.

- Congress can draft Constitutional Amendments to establish the requirements of the "Citizen Rules" (requires two-thirds of both Houses to agree) and send them to the states for ratification (requires three-fourths of states to ratify to take effect).

3. Citizens petition the states to request Congress to call for a "limited" constitutional convention to approve the new Citizen Rules in the Bill of Public Service and Accountability as Amendments to the Constitution.

- States can pass legislation to request that Congress call for a "limited" constitutional convention (requires two-thirds of states to make the request); the convention representatives would review and approve the Amendments (by majority vote), and send them back to the states for ratification (requires three-fourths of states to ratify to take effect).

Action 1: Petitioning Congress to pass new laws and rules

- This action would require the sitting members of Congress who are benefiting from the current rules, a large percentage of whom are seeking to make a career out of serving in Congress, to be willing to eliminate their existing career path, much of the power and control, and many of the benefits, they currently enjoy.

- However, even if we could expect over half of both Houses to agree to these actions, the next Congress could simply decide to change the rules again after the next election. This approach is not only unlikely to ever happen through the initiative of existing members of Congress, influenced as they are by career self-interest, and partisan and donor influences; it is also unlikely that it would be sustained over time. Thus, this approach is probably not worth the considerable time and energy that would be required to implement it.

Action 2: Petitioning Congress to draft Amendments to the Constitution

- This action would also require the sitting members of Congress to be willing to amend the Constitution to permanently eliminate their existing career path, much of the power and control, and many of the benefits, they currently enjoy.

- This approach would require that two-thirds of the sitting members of Congress in both Houses would agree to take this action. Given that this level of agreement would likely require nearly all the members of the party in majority control to agree to these actions that would limit the power of majority control of congressional processes, this approach is also pretty unlikely.

Action 3: Petitioning the states to request that Congress call for a "limited" constitutional convention

- This approach would require a significant effort behind a state-by-state approach, with the goal of having two-thirds of the states pass the identical resolution petitioning the Congress to call a "limited" constitutional convention, for the *sole* purpose of reviewing and approving the six Amendments which define the "Citizen Rules" and including them as part of the Constitution, with no authority during the convention for representatives to propose other amendments, and no authority to edit, add to, or delete any of the Amendments in the Bill of Public Service and Accountability.
- A constitutional convention has not been held since the original convention that drafted our existing Constitution was called by the first Congress, meeting under the Articles of Confederation, which was the first attempt at self-governing following the victory in the Revolutionary War.
- A "limited" constitutional convention means that the scope of the changes to the Constitution that are authorized by the states to be considered for approval would be "limited" only to those changes defined for consideration in the petition from the states to the Congress. Those changes to be considered by the convention would be limited to the changes defined in the package of the six Amendments

in the Bill of Public Service and Accountability, which if approved and confirmed by the states, would enact the "Citizen Rules" suggested in this document. The specific language of the proposed six Amendments to the Constitution is provided in the Appendix. No other topics, no changes or additions, no separate votes on the individual Amendments, or any other amendments, could be considered in this "limited" convention.

- It should be acknowledged that a "limited" constitutional convention has never been tried at any time in our history. In Article V of the Constitution, the language states only that: "The Congress, whenever two thirds of both Houses shall deem it necessary, shall propose Amendments to this Constitution, or, on the Application of the Legislatures of two thirds of the several States, shall call a Convention for proposing Amendments..." A "limited" convention is thus not specifically defined as a permitted approach to amending the Constitution, but neither is it specifically excluded.

- While Article V states that the Convention's purpose is "proposing Amendments," it is silent on the subject of whether the "Application of the Legislatures of two-thirds (⅔) of the several states" can, in the language of the Application or Petition to Congress, specify limits on the scope of the areas where Amendments can be proposed by the Convention. The Convention is not "proposing" Amendments from a blank sheet of paper, but would meet to agree to "propose" that the six Amendments in the Bill of Public Service and Accountability be sent to the states for ratification. It is almost a surety that people and organizations impacted by the changes, specifically including congressional members themselves, would certainly challenge the constitutionality of this approach.

- However, the Tenth Amendment to the Constitution, the last item in the Bill of Rights, states that: "The powers not delegated to the United States by the Constitution, nor prohibited by it to the States, are reserved to the States respectively, or to the people." So it would seem that since Article V of the Constitution does not prohibit the states from calling for a "limited" constitutional convention, the right to do so under the Tenth Amendment would therefore be reserved to the states, or to the people.

- Thus if two-thirds of the states pass legislation with the exact same language indicating it is the desire of the people and, as their representatives, the desire of the state legislatures, to limit the scope of what is proposed by the Convention being petitioned, there would seem to be sufficient constitutional support for such an action. In such an event, it is difficult to imagine that the Supreme Court would conclude that the will of the people, as expressed in the petition from the states, should not be honored and is in fact unconstitutional. And though not a sure thing, and admittedly lacking precedent, it seems that this citizen-led approach to changing our country for the better is worth making the effort.

Summary of the Process for Approval via Limited Constitutional Convention

1. Public review and input—the "online" People's Convention

- The process will begin with a "virtual" online Constitutional Convention of the People. A final version of the six Amendments in the Bill of Public Service and Accountability, and the draft of the petition that the state legislatures would be asked to pass and send to the Congress, would be posted at an online site for public review and online voting by citizens. A website address has been purchased for this first step: www.citizenrules. org (Author's Note: This site is not yet active.) Revenues from the sales of this book will be invested in building this website, providing the online voting software program and voter database capability, marketing the website and its purpose to the public, and publicly reporting the results of citizen participation and preferences.

- Citizens will be encouraged to visit the website and read either a summary of or the exact language of the proposed six Amendments in the Bill of Public Service and Accountability, and the exact language of the state legislature petition. Visitors will be asked to record a vote, up or down, for the package of the six Amendments, just as the states and the representatives at the "limited" constitutional convention will be asked to do. We would ask that they provide their name, contact information, party affiliation (if any), and zip code, so we can make sure that there are not multiple votes from a single citizen, and to provide a validation for the number of votes by state, congressional district and party.

- The goal for total citizen involvement is to obtain a total number of votes of at least 100,000 citizens from each of the 50 states, a total of 5,000,000 votes. The goal for the percentage of "Approve" votes is at least 70%. If both of these goals are not reached, there will be no Step 2. The Bill of Public Service and Accountability must be supported by a large, broad base of American citizens from both parties, or it should not go forward. Once these goals are reached, we will proceed to Step 2, petitioning Congress via the state legislatures in each of the 50 states to call for a "limited" constitutional convention.

2. Petitioning of legislatures in each state to petition Congress

- After reaching the two goals for citizen involvement and approval described above, we will establish a national non-profit organization to work in each state to pass the legislation to petition Congress to call for a "limited" constitutional convention to consider only the six proposed Amendments detailed in the Bill of Public Service and Accountability as a package, with no additions, changes or deletions, and with no other changes to the Constitution to be considered. Each state would use identical language in drafting legislation to define the purpose of and call on Congress to convene the "limited" constitutional convention.

- Support for the legislation would be based on strong state and national support from the people, the citizens, in each state, using data collected from the website. The petition would provide the language to be used in the petition legislation, with the purpose of establishing the defined set of "Citizen Rules" approved by the people for the operation of Congress in serving the People, and to unite the country behind leaders who, under these rules, would be more likely to put country over self, party, and special-interest donor interest.

3. Congress must call the limited constitutional convention if two-thirds of the states (34 states out of 50) pass identical legislation requesting Congress to do so.

- When we reach the level of two-thirds of the states (34 states) passing the legislation petitioning Congress to call for the limited constitutional convention, if not sooner in the process, it could be expected that opponents will challenge the concept of a "limited" constitutional convention in court, as discussed earlier.

- This challenge might delay the completion of this step for months, especially if the challenge makes its way to the Supreme Court. But as discussed, while there is no precedent, there appears to be sufficient constitutional support for such an action.

4. Limited constitutional convention representatives will review and vote either yes or no to adopt the Amendments in the Bill of Public Service and Accountability.

- When at least two-thirds of the state legislatures, a total of 34, pass identical language in the formal petition to Congress to call the "limited" constitutional convention, the convention must be scheduled by Congress. Each state will choose its own delegation, but in voting, each state shall have only one vote in approving or rejecting the full package of six Amendments detailed in the Bill of Public Service and Accountability.
- The proposed Amendment language will be reviewed and the merits discussed by the convention delegates. A simple Up or Down, Yes or No, Approve or Disapprove, vote will be taken. If approved by a majority of the state delegations, each delegation counting as one vote, the six Amendments will be considered adopted by the convention, and will be sent back to the state legislatures for consideration and ratification.

5. The six Amendments must be ratified as a package by three-fourths of the state legislatures (38 of 50) to take effect.

- The last step in the process involves a debate and vote to ratify the Bill of Public Service and Accountability and the package of six Amendments, in each of the 50 state legislatures. The non-profit organization that will be established to shepherd the Amendments and petitions to Congress in each of the individual states will now advocate for the people in encouraging the state legislatures to ratify the Bill of Public Service and Accountability and all six Amendments.

6. Following ratification by three-fourths of the states, the provisions of the "Citizen Rules" would be incorporated into the Constitution and implemented as appropriate.

- The new "Citizen Rules" for the operation of Congress should take effect as soon as the Bill of Public Service and Accountability is approved by the thirty-eighth state legislature. The timing of the implementation for each Amendment within the Bill of Public Service and Accountability is detailed in the Appendix.

  Briefly, the new "Citizen Rules" for budgeting and spending processes should take effect at the start of the next fiscal year following ratification by the thirty-eight states. The new "Citizen Rules" for electing members of Congress to one term should begin with the next federal election cycle. It will take four years to complete the conversion of the existing House members, but no changes to the election cycles of the existing Senate members are required, beyond prohibiting sitting Senators from running for re-election, and limiting newly elected Senators to one-term status. The new conflict-of-interest requirements in the "Citizen Rules" should begin with the next calendar year for the annual reporting requirements, and with the first federal election cycle following ratification for the campaigns of new members of Congress, and with any new Administration officials appointed after the Bill of

Public Service and Accountability is formally ratified.

In the final chapter, we will discuss what we as individual citizens can do to help make the changes in the six Amendments in the Bill of Public Service and Accountability become reality.

Chapter 8

What Can We Do as Individual Citizens to Help Make the Changes We'd Like to See Become Reality?

Lastly, we'll look at specific actions that we as citizens need to take to contribute effectively in our collective decisions about choosing leaders and policies that reflect the needs and concerns of the country; to favor candidates who collaborate effectively with representatives of the other party; and to disfavor candidates who seem unwilling to collaborate or unable to accept change.

1. How Can Citizens Support Changes in Congress by Our Actions and Choices?

Do we as voters support only those elected officials in one party? Is the party we favor always right, and the other party always wrong? Are we contributing to the competitive "or" choices that partisanship and divisiveness provides, or are we encouraging collaborative "and" choices that bipartisanship can provide? Do we even consider people in the other party equal in status as "true Americans" and fellow citizens with ourselves?

If any of these questions are relevant to our attitudes and beliefs today, here are some suggestions for replacing our existing attitudes and beliefs:

- Start by trying to understand both sides of key issues. It is likely that in this large and wonderfully diverse country, it is hard for any one of us, or any one party, to fully understand the needs and concerns of citizens with a totally different life experience than ourselves. But it does not mean that those needs and concerns are any less valid or important to the effective governing of our country.

- Start caring about understanding and respecting the needs and concerns of others, and the ideas of others, who think differently than you do. Work to become a citizen who believes fully that the value of *interdependence* enshrined in that last sentence of the Declaration of Independence is a key value that all Americans, and especially our elected leaders, should embrace.

- Look for and encourage elected representatives who are committed to collaborating and compromising on the solutions to key issues. Let them know that while we hope they will work to represent our values, needs, and concerns included in key legislation, we do *not* want them to stand rigidly only on our needs and concerns, our values, our beliefs, our party, our region. Let them know that you believe that any legislation developed and passed by only one party, however beneficial for ourselves, may not be beneficial for the country overall.

- Start caring about finding solutions that work for both sides, based on facts and objective analysis of the causes of key issues. Work to understand *how* a candidate's proposed solutions would be implemented, and if their approaches are based on facts and proven success from history; or are they based on fears, unfounded theories, or ideologies? Do their proposed solutions seem likely to benefit the country overall, and are the desired outcomes they promise likely to be achieved? Isn't this an important element in having policies that will move the country forward with less divisiveness, and help unite the country once again?

- Encourage our representatives to seek "win-win" solutions that would address the needs of both parties. Understand that the kind of win-lose solutions and winner-takes-all approaches both parties typically implement under today's rules will not make us a stronger, more secure country. In fact, they are not really consistent with the principles and values of a truly representative democratic republic and the interdependent society that we have discussed.

- Consider that this country is "owned" by *all* citizens, that we all have equal rights in it and have an equal share in the responsibility that it should endure. It is the citizens who are responsible for the state of our Constitutional Republic, our democracy, and for its future. Because we choose our leaders, in a democracy, as it has been famously stated, "people get the government they deserve." Our leaders will only behave and act as the citizens allow them.

- Recommit as individual citizens to live the meaning of what it is to be "one nation...indivisible." You've probably repeated that pledge hundreds of times in your life, and taught it to your children. Are we as a country truly committed to living the words in this pledge? If this is not a true description of what we believe in our country today, let us each commit to act this way in our individual citizenship roles and in our daily lives.

- Consider that in order to truly improve our country by changing the operation of Congress, we as citizens must choose to change ourselves as well. Our Constitution is only a strong protector of our freedoms *if* we citizens are committed to holding our elected leaders and ourselves accountable for following the principles and values of the Constitution in their and in our behaviors.

- Consider what it means to love our country. Can we truly love our country if we individually despise nearly half our countrymen, our fellow citizens, and care nothing for their different life experiences, and their different needs and concerns that reflect those different experiences?

2. Changing the Citizen Mindset — Your Role

- Consider ignoring and not sharing divisive posts on your social media sites; provide facts instead of demeaning comments; be respectful and accommodating to the points of views of others, even if they aren't respectful people.

- Consider the impact of win-lose politics to our governing, elections, communities... Can you become a citizen who respects the needs, concerns, and viewpoints of others? Do you want "win-win" policies? Are you willing to support representatives who care about putting the interests of the county above your, and their, party?

- Get involved in understanding the real needs and concerns of the country overall, as expressed in the policy ideas from *both* parties. Be committed to *vote*, and learn the positions of all candidates before voting. Find out not only *what* they want to accomplish, what policy or benefit they are promising; most importantly, find out *how* they plan to accomplish their promises. Speak up about the need for "win-win" approaches with others.

- Write letters to your Representatives, Senators and the President — you can easily access everyone by email on their websites. But with the dominant use of email today, mailed letters and phone calls often have greater impact. Make your voice heard, advocating for "win-win" solutions. Show your elected leaders that you know the data, the facts, and history, and that you understand their plans.

- Be willing to be uncomfortable in groups — listen to others, then encourage others to think about the outcomes of win-lose policies and the facts or thinking behind policies and outcomes. Let people know you want representatives who put the needs of most Americans ahead of party, regional, or donor needs and issues. Ask great questions about whether one party's ideas represent the needs and concerns of all Americans. Ask if the system is working for most Americans, and if not, ask how they would change the system. There is no need for, and little value in, lecturing others about your beliefs, unless asked. The most effective way to influence the thinking of another person is by listening and asking great questions, not making great statements.

3. Why Should You Be Involved and Support the Changes?

The key questions to consider are:

- Are you happy with the divisiveness in our country and between our political parties, and the inability of Congress to develop governing policies that address the needs of the country overall versus the needs of just one party's base? Is our country being led effectively? Are we successfully addressing the major problems in our country today with effective solutions? Are we on the "right track" or the "wrong track"?

  If you are not fully happy with the state of our governing democracy, do you agree it is the obligation of all citizens to get involved to make changes? Will simply voting under the existing rules for how Congress operates going to be effective in making the changes that are needed?

- The actions needed to enact these Citizen Rules and the Amendments in the Bill of Public Service and Accountability have no precedence in our history. The path forward is certainly not an easy or certain one, nor one that is without risk. But when has any major challenge to our country been easy or certain to confront?

  The question for me is, how can we choose not to try?

Have we seen any other actions being proposed that will turn our country from the current path that our politics are on? If we don't make the changes we have outlined, will the divisiveness caused by career self-interest, partisanship and donor influences just lose impact with the passage of time?

Might this time be like the days before our entry into World War II? At that time, it was the state of the free world that was at risk. Our grandparents stepped forward to be the generation that was not willing to risk losing other free societies around the world. Many citizens were reluctant to act while the war raged in Europe initially, but it was the attack on Pearl Harbor that sparked our country into action.

Might the current situation of the attacks on our democratic institutions by Russia and others, and the heightened levels of partisanship and divisiveness in both our leaders and our citizens, be the events that spark this generation into action? Might the events of January 6, 2021 be that spark? We might have only a narrow window of time to change the "rules" by which Congress operates and our campaigns are conducted, to preserve our Constitutional Republic.

Let us commit to work together to enact this "constitutional renewal" that can hopefully strengthen our country for the next 240 years or more.

Please help to build a grassroots organization to implement the changes that would enable us to "Repair and Restore Our Constitutional Republic" by reducing the impacts of partisan and special interests, and move us toward that vision of being "One Indivisible Nation" more completely. If we do not accept this as our purpose, who will? If we do not commit to this purpose now, when will it happen?

My Final Thoughts

Let me close the book as I opened it, with the sharing of my personal concerns: I will repeat my belief that the biggest threat to our country's strength, security and future progress is not who is elected President, or which party is in the majority in Congress. The strength and security of our country does not depend, or should not depend, on loyalty to any individual candidate, elected leader or party. If the concept of party was deemed important to our future, would not the Framers have included the concept of party in the Constitution itself? Doesn't the absence of party in the Constitution indicate that the Framers did not view the concept of party as critical to the future of our Constitutional Republic?

I believe the biggest threat to our country lies in the rise of loyalty to one party and one leader over loyalty to country and the rule of law, and the acceptance of partisanship and divisiveness in our country today that exists in the minds and hearts of most of our elected leaders and in far too many of our citizens.

I would like to suggest again that we as citizens need to recognize and value, above all else, the importance of national unity to our country that the Founding Fathers passed on to us. Our Founding Documents have underscored the importance of *interdependence* to the strength of our country and the security of our individual liberties. As a result, all Americans are encouraged to recommit themselves to the continuation of those values in the coming months and years.

The strength of our country as a democratic republic does not rest solely on the existence of the freedoms we enjoy today. It also depends on the unity of a diverse people coming together, as in the Pledge of Allegiance we teach to our children, to be "one nation...indivisible." I doubt that many of us would feel that we are living that pledge in our politics today—and I wonder if we are really committed today, as citizens and as a country, to do what it takes to achieve that purpose.

In the almost 240 years since the Revolutionary War ended and the Treaty of Paris was signed, where Great Britain formally recognized the sovereignty of the United States, there have been many other democracies established in the world, where citizens also govern themselves and enjoy many of the same personal freedoms we enjoy in our country. So freedom itself is not what makes America so uniquely great. No other democracy has the ethnic, cultural and religious diversity of America, nor has any other democracy unified these diverse groups in their histories. It is the unity of our wonderfully diverse country that makes and has made America great.

But today, we find that our diversity is being used to undermine the strength of our country from within. Diversity is our historic strength, but divisiveness is our current weakness. The strength and security of our country in the future depends on the choices we will make as a free people in the next few years.

In order to revive our strength and minimize our weakness, we need to end the winner-takes-all aspect to governing that leads to a win-at-all-costs competition between the parties; and not just in elections but in the governing processes between elections. Our politics have become a blood-sport competition between the two major parties, where some 40% of Americans lose, no matter which party wins. In our democratic republic, leaders are elected by a majority of voters but are expected to govern as the representatives of all Americans, including those who didn't vote for them. Governing should not be about passing policies that appeal only to the base of one party. Unfortunately, that is not what has been happening recently.

I believe that our future strength and security as a free country depends, as it always has, on the willingness of our citizens to sometimes make a sacrifice for, and serve, the country. It is often said that America is the "home of the free, because of the brave," and that in America, "freedom is not free." Today, I believe that service to country requires that those citizens who believe in and love the principles upon which our country was founded, and want to see a recommitment to those principles in our politics and political processes, must become publicly involved as ordinary citizens in activities that can change the current path of our country. I don't believe we can look to or wait for our elected officials to lead change first.

In working to accomplish this goal, I'm not sure that our existing political parties are assets. As currently operating, they may in fact be two of our largest obstacles. As discussed in Chapter 1, our first two Presidents warned us of the risk of political parties to our system of government "of, by, and for the People" with words that were written and spoken over 220 years ago:

There is nothing which I dread as much as a division of the republic into two great parties, each arranged under its leader, and concerting measures in opposition to each other. This, in my humble apprehension, is to be dreaded as the largest political evil under our Constitution.
—John Adams, letter to Jonathan Jackson, October 2, 1789

I asked earlier if that statement by John Adams seems to foreshadow actions we are experiencing today, such as the gerrymandering of political districts to give a structural advantage in elections to one party over the other—which both parties have done. Seven years later, in his farewell speech after serving as our first President and then voluntarily stepping down to establish the first peaceful transition of power in a government in history, George Washington echoed the fears of his Vice President:

However [political parties] may now and then answer political ends, they are likely in the course of time and things, to become potent engines, by which cunning, ambitious, and unprincipled men will be enabled to subvert the power of the people and to usurp for themselves the reins of government, destroying afterwards the very engines which have lifted them to unjust dominion.

—George Washington, Farewell Address, September 19, 1796

I am not suggesting that any party is better than any other. I believe that one of the major causes of the divisiveness in our country and government today is the polarization of the leaders in both parties driven by career self-interest, partisan interests, and special-interest groups and donors, instead of working together to advance the national interests and the country overall.

Candidates speak during election cycles of "reaching across the aisle," "coming together," "uniting the country," or "working together." But most often, this really means that the majority expects the minority to support their policies and positions. When compromise does occur, it often happens only by trading concessions among the parties' partisan or special interests, often at the expense of the national interest. A common example is Democrats getting increased government spending for social programs in exchange for Republicans getting tax cuts, with the result of an increase in the national debt that future Americans will have to repay.

Have you ever heard a candidate who professes in an election campaign to "work across the aisle" or "unite the country" ever describe *how* they will act to accomplish those goals? Has anyone who has made that promise in a campaign been able to deliver on it consistently during their time in office?

I have stated often in this book that the only way to unite the country is to recommit ourselves to respecting

317

and accommodating differences between the parties in the development of our policies and programs. As has been stated before, data indicates that neither party by itself reflects the concerns of more than about 40% of the country. So one party's ideology or policies alone will never reflect the needs and interests of most of the citizens in our diverse country.

After winning an election, if the majority party focuses on developing national policies only on the needs and interests of its base, without seeking to accommodate the needs and concerns of citizens who did not vote for them, is that good government? Is that the vision that our Founding Fathers had for our democratic republic?

The only way we can minimize political divisiveness and develop effective policies that reflect the needs and concerns of most of the country is for the parties to work together in a collaborative process to develop win-win policies, instead of the win-lose approach that exists today. If our elected leaders worked together in a win-win approach to national policies, wouldn't it be likely that we would have more effective policies than those that come only from one party's ideas? Might this also result in a political culture where it matters less which party is in the majority or holds the Presidency, than the collaborative development of policies that work best for the country overall?

I'd like to recall once again the final sentence in the Declaration of Independence:

And for the support of this Declaration, with a firm reliance on the protection of Divine Providence, we mutually pledge to each other our Lives, our Fortunes and our sacred Honor.

There would be no United States of America today if the leaders of the 13 colonies had not come together, respecting and accommodating the diverse concerns of the very different regions of the country, and accepting the risks to their lives, their fortunes and their honor to declare independence.

There were slave states and free states; there were southern states and northern states; and there were states with agricultural economies and those with industrial, manufacturing, and trading economies. Yet, the representatives of these diverse states came together in the debate and vote to declare independence, to speak and share their own principles and concerns, but not standing so firmly on them that they refused to accommodate other points of view than their own. The vote for independence would not require just 7 out of the 13 colonies to vote for the declaration; the vote had to be unanimous—it had to be 13–0. The representatives recognized that the new nation would only be strong if they found a way to satisfy all the diverse interests. After agreeing unanimously to declare independence, they "mutually pledged to each other their lives, their fortunes and their sacred Honor." The Founders believed that the strength of the independence of the new nation would depend on the strength of the nation's *interdependence*, even before we were a nation. It has been true since before our founding, and it is just as true today, isn't it?

Following victory in the Revolutionary War, the newly free and independent states initially favored a loose confederation of states, choosing to prioritize the sovereignty of individual states over a strong central government. Our first governing document was the Articles of Confederation, which gave only very limited powers to the central government. The development of any "national" policy would require agreement between the individual states, which is where the important policy decision-making authority resided. This of course was a difficult and time-consuming process, especially given the slow pace of communications in those days.

Adopted in 1777 and ratified in 1781, this approach was quickly found to result in a very weak country. By 1787, a constitutional convention had been convened by the states to replace these Articles with a national constitution, to provide for a "more perfect union" as stated in the Preamble, the statement of purpose for the Constitution itself. The Constitution we have today was written that year and was approved by the states in 1789.

Everyone who graduates from high school likely knows of the quote by President John F. Kennedy in his inaugural address:

Ask not what your country can do for you; ask what you can do for your country.

That quote has guided my own sense of what it means to be a citizen in our country, of the sacrifices of so many citizens before me who bequeathed this great country to my generation and future generations, if today we embrace it. It embodies the idea that citizenship requires service to country, not to self, nor to party, nor to special interests, nor to any individual leader.

But there is another quote by President Kennedy that is perhaps even more relevant to the situation we now face in our politics:

For, in a democracy, every citizen, regardless of their interest in politics, "holds office"; every one of us is in a position of responsibility; and, in the final analysis, the kind of government we get depends upon how we fulfill those responsibilities. We, the people, are the boss, and we will get the kind of political leadership, be it good or bad, that we demand and deserve.

If the national polls are right, and 65%–70% of the public today believes the country is "on the wrong track," then we as citizens need to look to ourselves as being the major enabling force in determining which "track" we are on. Today, most often, the majority of us citizens, as voters, have punished those candidates and elected officials in office who have collaborated with their colleagues in the other party, and compromised any element of a partisan position to accommodate differences with the other party. These outcomes negatively impact our elected officials' ability to truly address national needs and interests, and not just the interests of their party's base or their special-interest donors.

So, to fulfill our role as citizens in minimizing partisanship and uniting the country, we actually need to vote *against* any of our candidates or elected officials who do not respect the differences that exist in our country, and aren't willing to work with representatives of the other party to accommodate the interests of both parties and their constituencies. Isn't that what is required to reflect the concept of serving the nation in President Kennedy's quotes, and to reflect the concept of caring for the lives and fortunes of our fellow citizens that is reflected in the last sentence of the Declaration of Independence?

The direction of our country is truly in our collective hands as citizens. The Declaration of Independence states the principle that "governments derive their just powers from the consent of the governed." Are we, by accepting and even participating in the divisiveness in our country today, tacitly giving our consent to be governed this way? Or are we the generation that will choose to change these trends, to essentially withdraw our consent for the current way we are governed, and to secure for our country, as President Lincoln declared in the Gettysburg Address delivered near the end of the Civil War, "a new birth of freedom — and that government of the people, by the people, for the people, shall not perish from the earth"?

Regarding the changes needed to "Repair and Restore Our Constitutional Republic," I believe the key questions for this generation of citizens and leaders are, in short, "If not us, who? If not now, when?"

Appendix

Part 1: Full Text of the Bill of Public Service and Accountability

Preamble

We, the People of the United States, in order to recommit the operation of the Congress and Administration to serve the interests of the nation and its citizens over personal career, party, or special interests, to provide more openness and full transparency in congressional legislative and budgeting processes, to promote collaborative bipartisan policy development and accountability in the exercise of these responsibilities, and to ensure equity in voter access and the integrity of federal elections, do hereby present the following Amendments to the Constitution of the United States.

These Amendments shall be valid to all intents and purposes as integral parts of the Constitution. Supported by millions of citizens, We the People further require that this Bill of Public Service and Accountability and the six Amendments herein be voted upon together as written, with a single yes or no vote to approve the proposal of these six Amendments together in their entirety, by a majority of state representatives in a "limited" constitutional convention, to be called for by two-thirds of the several states (34 of 50), when petitioned by the people in each state. When approved for proposal to the nation by a majority of states in the "limited" constitutional convention, these Amendments would take effect when ratified by the legislatures of three-fourths of the several states (38 of the 50).

Amendment XXVIII—to Article 1, Sections 2, 3, 5, and 6, and Article 2, Section 4 of the Constitution

To detail changes involving the total number and length of terms of Congress; the compensation, and health and retirement benefits for members of Congress and politically appointed officials in the Administration and other government positions; to specify unbiased judicial processes and procedures for impeachment; and to clarify the primacy of the new "Citizen Rules" for proceedings in the House and Senate, as defined in these Amendments, over the other rules Congress may make for their proceedings as provided for in Article 1, Section 5.

- **Article 1, Section 2, new first paragraph (replacing the existing first paragraph):**

The House of Representatives shall be composed of members, half of whom shall be chosen every second year by the people of the several states. The total number of elected terms of each Representative shall be limited to one (1) total term of four (4) years. The electors in each state shall have the qualifications requisite for electors of the most numerous branch of the state legislature, and shall have reached their thirtieth birthday. Upon ratification of this Amendment, existing House members shall be divided as equally as may be into two classes. The seats of the Representatives of the first class shall be vacated without re-election following the upcoming federal election, and of the second class shall be vacated without re-election at the next federal election afterwards, so that one half may be chosen every second year. No sitting House member shall run for election to any other office while serving.

- **Article 1, Section 2, new fifth, sixth, and seventh paragraphs:**

The House of Representatives shall choose their Speaker and

other officers; and shall have the sole power of impeachment, which shall be limited to offenses committed by sitting officials and for which the bipartisan House Impeachment Committee has been empaneled during their period of active service.

When sitting for the purpose of impeachment, the House shall empanel a bipartisan Impeachment Committee, chaired by a member of the majority party, to investigate, in closed session, questions of impeachable behavior or actions, to determine if there is a relevant basis for the finding that an impeachable offense has been committed by a specific elected or Administration official, federal judge or Supreme Court justice. During the conduct of an impeachment investigation, no members of Congress or their staffs shall discuss among themselves, with any member of the Administration, or comment publicly on the proceedings of the investigation. The bipartisan Impeachment Committee shall have the investigative authority to subpoena witnesses and documents from all other branches of government relevant to the impeachable offense under investigation, and shall employ normal judicial investigative procedures and protections for individual civil rights. If objections due to executive privilege or confidentiality are raised by any other branch of government during an Impeachment Committee proceeding, at least three (3) justices of the Supreme Court, one of whom shall be the Chief Justice and the other two (2) nominated by previous Presidents of each party, shall convene immediately in special session to adjudicate the relevance of any objections and resolve the objections in a timely manner.

At the completion of the Impeachment Committee's investigation, if a majority of the Impeachment Committee's members agree that a preponderance of the evidence indicates that an impeachable offense has been committed and the charged official likely has committed the offense, then Articles of Impeachment shall be prepared and transmitted to the full House. If a majority of the full House, of which at least 5% shall be from the minority party or parties, finds that a preponderance of the evidence presented by the Impeachment Committee indicates that an action constituting an impeachable offense has been committed and the charged official likely has committed the offense, the Articles of Impeachment shall be transmitted to the Senate for trial.

- **Article 1, Section 3, new second paragraph (replacing the existing second paragraph):**

The total number of elected terms of each Senator shall be limited to one (1) total term of six (6) years. The existing three (3) classes of Senators standing for re-election every two (2) years shall be maintained following the enactment of this Amendment. In the next three (3) election cycles, if any of the one-third (⅓) of Senators in each section shall have completed at least one (1) term of six (6) years, they shall vacate their seats without re-election and new Senators shall be elected to their seats. The new Senators elected in each cycle will serve one (1) term of six (6) years. Thereafter, no Senator shall serve more than one (1) term of six (6) years. No sitting Senator shall run for election to any other office while serving.

- **Article 1, Section 3, new sixth, seventh, eighth, ninth and tenth paragraphs (replacing the existing sixth paragraph):**

The Senate shall have the sole power to try all impeachments. All impeachment investigations begun in accordance with Article 1, Section 2 and approved as Articles of Impeachment by the majority of the full House shall be tried by the Senate, even if the official is no longer serving in office.

When sitting for that purpose, the Senators shall be on oath or affirmation to "do unbiased justice based solely on the evidence submitted during the trial to determine guilt or innocence beyond a reasonable doubt." Beginning with the conduct of an impeachment offense by the Impeachment Committee in the House, and continuing until the completion of the Senate trial, no members of Congress or the Administration or their staffs shall comment publicly on the proceedings of the investigation, nor shall any member of the House or Senate discuss any aspects of the trial among themselves, with any member of the Administration, nor with any other Senator, nor the House managers, nor the defense attorneys. Senators who violate this oath shall be removed from participating in the trial and shall not vote at the conclusion of the trial.

When the President of the United States is tried, there shall be a three (3) justice panel to preside over the trial, led by the Chief Justice of the Supreme Court as the senior member. The other two (2) members shall be senior Associate Justices of the Supreme Court, neither appointed by the President being tried, one appointed by a previous President of each of the two major parties.

The rules for the conduct of an impeachment trial in the Senate shall follow the prevailing rules for trials in the judicial system, to include the rules for admitting relevant evidence and witness testimony. Consistent with their primary role as jurors under oath to do "impartial justice," the Senators shall have no role in defining the trial procedures or raise any questions or objections during the trial. The presiding three-justice panel shall have full authority to rule on questions and objections between the parties on the issues of admission of evidence and witnesses relevant to the impeachment charges, to authorize the issuing of subpoenas and the enforcement of compliance with subpoenas, and to resolve any claims of executive privilege in issuing subpoenas for and in the admission of any and all documents and the testimony of any and all witnesses.

Judgment in cases of impeachment shall not extend further than to removal from office, and/or disqualification to hold and enjoy any office of honor, trust or profit under the United States; but the party convicted shall nevertheless be liable and subject to indictment, trial, judgment and punishment, according to law.

- **Article 1, Section 5, new second paragraph (replacing the existing second paragraph):**

Each House will follow the rules for its proceedings as defined in the Constitution, as amended by the Bill of Public Service and Accountability, Amendments XXVIII through XXII, and defined therein as the "Citizen Rules." The rules determined by the members of each House shall not infringe on or supersede the Citizen Rules for the specific proceedings as defined and required in these constitutional Articles and Amendments. Rules of the proceedings for each House not otherwise defined by the Citizen Rules in these Articles and Amendments may be determined by each House. Each House may punish its members for disorderly behavior and, with the concurrence of two thirds (⅔), expel a member.

- **Article 1, Section 6, new paragraphs (replacing the existing first paragraph):**

The Senators and Representatives shall receive a compensation for their services, to be ascertained as defined in this Section, and paid out of the Treasury of the United

States. The compensation and healthcare benefits paid during periods of elected service, and retirement or pension benefits of the members of Congress following service, shall be determined as follows:

- The annual compensation of all members of Congress shall be fixed as the compensation levels approved for the base pay for the Flag Officer ranks of the United States military. Specifically, the compensation of each member of Congress shall be fixed as the same compensation of an O-9 officer with 20 years of service. Compensation for members of Congress shall not increase with additional years of service as is the case in the military pay scale. These compensation levels shall only increase consistent with any adjustments made to all military pay levels.

- The compensation for the Speaker of the House and the President Pro Tempore of the Senate shall be fixed as the compensation levels approved for the base pay of an O-10 officer of 20 years of service. These compensation levels shall only increase consistent with any adjustments made to all military pay levels. There shall be no separate compensation provided for the majority or minority leaders or any other position for any political party in the Senate or House of Representatives. All members of the House and Senate except for these two leadership positions as identified in this Amendment shall be compensated equally.

- Congress shall set the pay scales of all politically appointed executive and government officials to be no greater than the O-9 military pay level for the most senior politically appointed executive official positions and Cabinet officials, except that Congress shall set the pay levels of the President and the Vice President by separate law. Any change in this compensation passed by Congress shall not take effect during the term of the existing President and Vice President.

- The Congress and politically appointed senior executive and senior government officials shall not be entitled to any special or government-provided healthcare benefits. They shall purchase healthcare from their salaries via the same options that are available to citizens in the United States.
- There shall be no separate or special retirement benefits for members of Congress who shall be elected following the enactment of these Amendments. Members may receive a matching retirement account contribution as a percentage of salary at a level comparable to average citizen programs each year. Each member of Congress who serves four or six years shall be entitled to a Separation Allowance after completion of their service for their return to private life. This allowance shall be equal to one (1) year of salary.

(Author's Note regarding Amendment XXVIII: The compensation for O-10/20 years is $192,864—compared to the current salary of $225,000 for the Speaker and $193,000 for the President Pro Tempore of the Senate. The compensation for O-9/20 years is $168,684, compared to the current salary of $173,000 for members of Congress.)

- **Article 2, Section 4, new second paragraph**

High crimes and misdemeanors shall include, but not be limited to, any and all acts that violate the public trust, in that the public trust requires that powers of high office shall not be used for any corrupt purpose or personal benefit, but solely for the benefit of the country, in a manner consistent with the oath of office and the requirements and limits of the Constitution.

Amendment XXIX—to Article 1, Section 7, and Article 2, Section 2 of the Constitution

To detail changes to and new rules for the legislative process, and providing advice and consent on presidential appointments.

- **Article 1, Section 7, insert new paragraph two, three, and four (between the existing first and second paragraphs):**

All bills introduced by members in either the House or the Senate and presented for a vote by all members shall be written to focus on a single issue. No bills shall be introduced and presented for a vote that include more than one issue in a single bill.

All bills co-signed by a minimum of 10% of the members in either the House or the Senate shall be brought to the floor for debate and vote by the full chamber within 20 session days after being introduced. All committee and subcommittee reviews and recommendations to the full chamber shall be completed within this period. A vote in each chamber shall not take place before three session days after being introduced in each chamber, and a vote must be completed in each chamber no later than six session days after being introduced. Bills so proposed shall not be prevented from a vote on this timetable by the Speaker of the House, President Pro Tempore or Senate Majority Leader, or any House or Senate senior official, or any House or Senate committee.

All bills voted on in either the House or the Senate shall be considered as passed by that chamber if a majority of that chamber votes in favor of the bill, provided that the majority of members voting in favor shall include a minimum of 5% of the approving members from the minority party or parties.

No bills shall be considered to be passed by either chamber if only approved by the majority party.

- **Article 1, Section 7, insert new paragraph (after the existing final paragraph):**

Any bill passed by both the House and the Senate, if objected to by the President and returned for reconsideration, shall become law only if repassed by two-thirds of both the House and the Senate, provided that a minimum of 5% of the approving members in each chamber shall be from the minority party or parties.

- **Article 2, Section 2, new third paragraph**

When the President shall make treaties and appointments under this authority, the Senate shall fulfill their advice-and-consent role by holding a vote of the full Senate within 60 session days of the presentation of the treaty or announcement of an appointment, to withhold or grant consent for the treaty or appointment. If a vote is not taken within 60 days, the Senate members will permanently forfeit all pay for each day the vote is delayed. Forfeited pay will not be reinstated after a vote is held beyond the 60-day session period. No presidential nominations requiring advice and consent of the Senate shall be made within the 120 days preceding the date of the next presidential election.

- **Article 2, Section 2, insert new sentences to begin new fourth paragraph**

When the Senate is in session, the President may fill vacancies in Cabinet officers, Administration department executives, and other Administration appointees requiring advice and consent of the Senate, with appointees in a temporary acting role, without the advice and consent of the Senate, for a period not to exceed 60 days. During this 60-day period, the President shall nominate a formal appointee to be confirmed with the advice and consent of the Senate.

Amendment XXX—to Article 1, Section 8 of the Constitution

To detail the changes to provide greater transparency and accountability in the congressional budgeting, spending, and taxing processes; strengthening the independence of key executive departments and of the Inspectors General role for oversight of legislation implementation and ethical requirements; prohibiting congressional members from lobbying activities after serving; no bill exempting Congress from laws passed for citizens; providing oversight of congressional voting-district alignments.

Article 1, Section 8, insert new first paragraphs

To exercise the power to raise revenue, to lay and collect taxes, duties, imposts, and excises, to borrow money, and to propose programs involving the allocation of and spending of public funds, the Congress shall:

- Pass a balanced budget for each fiscal year no later than ten session days *before* the start of each fiscal-year budget cycle, except when a formal declaration of a state of war or national emergency has been voted for by both the House and Senate and signed by the President. Congressional members shall receive no daily compensation if they fail to meet this time requirement, until a balanced budget is signed by the President. The compensation of the members of Congress shall be forfeited permanently in this case, but the compensation of administrative staffs and suppliers shall be refunded when the balanced budget is signed.

- ○ New spending bills proposed by the Congress which were not accounted for in the approved fiscal-year balanced budget shall be offset with specific reductions in other spending or new sources of revenue to maintain a balanced budget during the fiscal year. Congress shall not increase the national debt and shall act to reduce existing debt in each fiscal-year budget cycle, except when a state of war or national emergency shall be voted for by Congress and signed by the President. In that case, the temporary increase in the national debt resulting from the temporary deficit shall be approved concurrently with the budget and deficit.

- ○ All bills that involve the allocation of and/or spending of public funds in each fiscal-year budget cycle shall include information defining the specific purpose for the bill; the benefit it is designed to provide; which group the benefit is intended to support; the expected outcome to be realized; and the goals or measures to be used to determine whether successful.

- ○ Funds collected via separate tax revenues for specific programs, such as Social Security, Medicare and Medicaid, shall not be used by the Congress for any other purpose, but shall be reserved for those programs only, except when a state of war or national emergency has been voted for by Congress and signed by the President.

- ○ In all cases when a state of war or national emergency that has been voted for by Congress and signed by the President to support allowing a budget deficit or directing the allocation of specific program funds for other purposes shall have expired, Congress shall pass a Deficit Resolution Bill defining a specific and appropriate time for returning the budget to balance and for returning the diverted funds to their original purpose and account.

- **Article 1, Section 8, insert new paragraph three (following the existing second and final paragraph):**

All Senators and Representatives who have completed any term of service in the Congress are prohibited in perpetuity from engaging in direct paid lobbying activity to any sitting member of Congress or any congressional staff member, or any appointed official, senior advisor, or staff member of the Administration.

- **Article 1, Section 8, insert new paragraphs to follow the existing last paragraph:**

Neither the House nor the Senate shall bring to the respective chambers any proposal for a vote or pass any bill that would by law exempt the members of Congress as individuals, or Congress itself as an organization, from the requirements of any laws enacted by Congress on citizens or organizations in the United States.

The Senate shall exercise an advice-and-consent role for the President's appointment of independent non-partisan Inspectors General in every Administration department and Congress. Candidates should not be former elected officials or officials in any political party. These Inspectors General shall have the authority to provide the major element of oversight for the appropriate actions to implement legislative programs and accountability for public spending and budgets, in terms of investigating the misuse of government funds, and to lead inspections when appropriate into possible offenses of ethical or moral violations, legal offenses, conflict-of-interest offenses or abuse of position, by elected representatives in Congress, the Administration departments responsible for implementing programs, and all key committee and staff members.

Charges of poor performance, loss of presidential confidence, or ethical or moral offenses by Inspectors General shall be brought before the Senate for investigation. The removal and/or replacement of Inspectors General following such investigation shall be initiated by the President with the advice and consent of the full Senate.

The Senate shall likewise exercise an advice-and-consent role for the removal of appointed and confirmed officials in the Justice Department and the Intelligence and National Security Agencies, the Secretary of the Treasury, the Director of the Internal Revenue Service, the members of the Joint Chiefs of Staff, and the senior military leaders of the United States Armed Forces, if initiated by the President. While serving at the pleasure of the President, these appointed officers shall execute their offices independently of the President and executive branch. Charges of poor performance, loss of presidential confidence, or ethical or moral offenses by these officials shall be brought before the Senate for investigation. The removal and/or replacement of these officials following such investigation shall be initiated by the President with the advice and consent of the full Senate.

Amendment XXXI—to Article 2, Section 1, Article 3, Section 1, and Amendments 12 and 20 of the Constitution

Revising the processes for allocating and certifying Electoral College votes; clarifying the limitations of the Emoluments Clause on the President and Vice President; providing for term limits for Supreme Court justices and federal judges, with the provision to be renominated and confirmed for additional terms.

- **Article 2, Section 1, delete second paragraph and insert new second paragraph**

Each state shall be allocated a number of Electoral College votes equal to the number of Senators and Representatives to which the state may be entitled in the Congress.

- **Article 2, Section 1, delete third paragraph and insert new third and fourth paragraph; repeal Amendment 12**

In an election for President and Vice President, each state shall allocate its Electoral College votes for the President and Vice President candidates on the ballot in the same proportion as the popular votes of the citizens of each state are recorded. State election officials shall complete and announce the popular vote-count results in each precinct, county, and the state overall, the proportion of the state's total popular vote won by each candidate, and the proportional allocation of the state's Electoral College votes to each candidate, as soon as possible after the election. The final popular and Electoral College vote totals shall be reviewed and certified by the Secretary of State and Governor in each state, no later than six weeks after the election, on the same date in mid-December in each state, as determined by Congress before the election. All recounts and challenges to the state's election results shall be completed within this six-week period. The state legislatures may challenge the initial election results during this period, but once results are certified by the Secretary of State and the Governor, they shall have no authority to challenge or otherwise alter or affect the certification and reporting of the results to Congress.

A certificate of the state's popular vote totals and the proportion won by each candidate, and the Electoral College votes awarded to each candidate, will be completed by the

Secretary of State and Governor in each state and presented in Congress, no later than nine weeks after the election, on the same date in early January in each state, as determined by Congress before the election. The Congress shall meet on that date to receive the certificate of the results from each state, to open the certificates and count the Electoral College votes from each state, but shall have no authority to challenge, change or reject the votes from any state, if properly certified by the state's officials as required herein. When the certificates of the votes from all states have been opened and counted, the candidates with the largest number of Electoral College votes shall be declared the new President and Vice President. In the event that there are two candidates who receive the same number of Electoral College votes, the candidates with the highest total of the national popular votes shall be declared the new President and Vice President.

- **Amendment 20, new Section 3 to replace existing Section 3 and Section 4**

If, at the time fixed for the beginning of the term of the President, the President Elect shall have died, the Vice President Elect shall become President. The Vice President Elect shall appoint an Acting Vice President who is constitutionally eligible to serve in the office of President, who shall be confirmed by a majority vote of both Houses of Congress. A new election for Vice President shall be held within six months of the appointment of the Acting Vice President.

- **Article 2, Section 1, insert new final sentence added to the end of the fourth paragraph**

No person who is constitutionally ineligible to serve in the office of President shall be eligible to serve in the office of Vice President.

- **Article 2, Section 1, insert new sentence added to the end of the fifth paragraph**

Neither shall the President or the Vice President receive any compensation directly from business assets or personal property owned by them during their period in office. Any such compensation shall be received by a third-party objective trustee of a blind trust as provided in Article 4, Section 4 of the Constitution as defined in the new Amendment XXXII of the Constitution.

- **Article 3, Section 1, replace second sentence in the first paragraph, add new second paragraph**

The justices of the Supreme Court and judges of the inferior federal courts shall hold their offices during good behavior for a term of ten years and, at the end of each ten-year term, shall be eligible for renomination and reappointment for an additional term of ten years. The justices of the Supreme Court and all federal judges shall be nominated by the President with the advice and consent of the Senate. All nominees for any Supreme Court justice or federal judgeship position shall have a demonstrated record of non-partisan, unbiased judicial experience in lower court positions.

The Supreme Court justices and federal judges shall, at stated times, receive for their services a compensation, which shall not be diminished during their continuance in office. The compensation levels shall be determined as follows: of the Chief Justice of the Supreme Court, equal to the Speaker of the House; of the Associate Justices of the Supreme Court, equal to members of Congress; of all federal judges, an appropriate level below that of the Associate Justices of the Supreme Court as set by Congress.

Amendment XXXII—insert new Article 4

Section 1

Congress shall pass Federal Election Finance Laws to set specific limits on the amount of money, gifts, or any items of value that an individual citizen may donate, collectively, to all federal candidates, parties, political action committees or issue advocacy groups in each calendar year, and authorize the Federal Election Commission to enforce such laws.

Each candidate, party, political action committee or issue advocacy group that receives and accepts such donations shall keep a record of each individual donor, organization, company, or group, and the amount and date of the donation. These records shall be filed quarterly with the Federal Election Commission, and these records shall be made available to the public upon request.

Within the Federal Election Finance Laws, Congress shall define penalties for violation of these laws, to include but not be limited to the forfeiture of the elected office for any candidate or elected official exceeding the donation limits from individuals, companies, organizations or groups by more than 10% in aggregate for a completed election.

The Federal Election Commission shall be empowered by law to implement the provisions of the Federal Election Finance Laws.

Section 2

Congress shall pass Federal Election Truth in Messaging Laws to establish a non-partisan, independent, unbiased Federal Election Message Oversight Board, with the authority to conduct proactive reviews of all campaign-related messages for or about candidates, created by any individual, party, political action committee, issue advocacy group, company, organization or group, distributed to the public via any media channel or vehicle, and to enforce the standard of being truthful in content.

The standard for truthful content of all campaign-related messages for or about candidates, parties or issues, shall require that the message content be substantiated at the time they are made by verifiable facts, data or other evidence. The responsibility for providing verified factual support for campaign-related messaging content is the speaker, the writer, the originator and/or the distributor of the message via any social media platform or media channel.

The Federal Election Message Oversight Board, upon review of messages found to contain false, unsubstantiated or misleading content that the speaker, writer, originator or distributor cannot adequately support, shall require changes to or the withdrawal of such messaging from public distribution until the standard for truthful content shall be established. All decisions and actions of the Federal Election Message Oversight Board shall be made public when completed, and shall disclose the reasons for the review, the supporting factual information, if any, submitted by the speaker, writer, originator or distributor of the message, the actions required by the Board, and the response, if any, by the speaker, writer, originator or distributor of the message.

The decisions of the Federal Election Message Oversight Board with regard to truthful content shall be reviewable by a federal court if challenged by the message speaker, writer, originator or distributor, but the revision or withdrawal requirement will be enforced until a federal court may otherwise decide.

The members of the Federal Election Message Oversight Board shall consist of five (5) citizens who are not serving and have never served as elected or appointed officials or political party officials at the federal or state level, who come from different regions of the country, with an equal number of members from each major political party and the balance from independent, non-party affiliated members, and who shall volunteer for consideration to serve. They shall be appointed by the members of the Federal Election Commission to serve a single term of six (6) years. They may be removed for reasons of performance of their role or violation of conflict-of-interest laws by a majority of the Federal Election Commission.

Section 3

Congress shall pass Federal Equitable Registration and Election and Voting Integrity Laws to establish a non-partisan, independent, unbiased Federal Election Oversight Board. This Board shall have the authority to conduct reviews of the equitable access of citizens to voter registration and voting processes, the integrity of voting processes, and the fairness of congressional voting-district alignments, in each state.

In exercising this authority, the Federal Election Oversight Board shall review the impact of each state's voter registration and voting laws and regulations, to ensure the equality in access to these processes among citizens with demographic or geographic differences in the states. The reviews and any judgments shall be based on data indicating the existence of an unfair disparity in the ease and convenience of access to voter registration and/or voting processes for citizens in any demographic or geographic group.

If the Board's reviews find any data-based evidence of disparities in the equality of access to the state's registration or voting processes, the Board shall require changes to the state's voter registration and/or voter access laws or regulations to correct the disparities. The review, data findings and the changes required completed by the Board shall be reported publicly when completed and communicated to each state.

In addition, the Board shall have the authority to review congressional voting-district alignments drawn by the states to ensure these alignments do not reflect a bias for one party, or a bias based on racial, ethnic, religious or other demographic elements. The reviews and any judgments shall be based on data indicating the existence of an unfair and/ or partisan bias in the alignments of the state's congressional voting districts versus the overall data of voting preferences and/or overall demographics in the state.

If the Federal Election Oversight Board finds any data-based evidence of any unfair bias in the alignment of congressional voting districts in any state, the Board shall require the state to redraw the congressional voting-district alignments. The evidence of unfair bias and the Board's suggestion for action to rectify the bias shall be provided to the state concurrently with the requirement to redraw the congressional voting-district alignments, and shall be reported publicly when communicated to each state.

Board requirements for changes to congressional voting-district alignments and to state voter registration or voter access laws or regulations must be communicated to the states at least one (1) year prior to an election, after which voter registration and access laws or regulations should not be altered.

The decisions of the Federal Election Oversight Board requiring changes to any state's congressional voting-district alignments or to any state's voter registration or voter access laws or regulations shall be reviewable by federal court if challenged by any state.

The members of the Federal Election Oversight Board shall consist of five (5) citizens who are not serving and have never served as elected or appointed officials or political party officials at the federal or state level, who come from different regions of the country, with an equal number of members from each political party, and who shall volunteer for consideration to serve. They shall be appointed by the members of the Federal Election Commission to serve a single term of six (6) years. They may be removed for reasons of performance of their role or violation of conflict-of-interest laws by a majority of the Federal Election Commission.

Section 4

All elected and politically appointed senior members of the executive, congressional and judicial branches shall comply with the following actions to avoid conflicts of interest:

Upon filing as a candidate for federal office, including President, Vice President and all members of Congress, or upon nomination for a senior position in the Administration, the candidate or nominee shall publicly release the most recent ten years of federal tax returns in addition to other personal financial disclosure requirements in existing law.

If elected or successfully confirmed to an appointed office in the Administration, the elected or confirmed official shall place all financial assets, including equities, commercial real estate and ownership of commercial business entities, into a blind trust administered by an objective third-party trustee, prior to taking the oath of office, for the period of their service. They shall have no direct communication from the trustee, either directly or indirectly with the trustee during their period of service. Each trustee managing the blind trust of an elected or confirmed official shall report the assets, income and transfers to and from the trust each year.

Supreme Court justices and federal judges shall provide public disclosures annually of all personal financial activities, including income, assets and transactions, and attendance at all events sponsored by political parties, issue advocacy groups and non-profit groups, companies and organizations.

Violation of this section of the Constitution or the Ethical Behavior Laws established by Congress by any officials shall be investigated and prosecuted by existing federal law enforcement practices. When the violation involves the President, the impeachment process shall follow the investigation, prosecution and trial requirements of Article 1, Section 3.

Amendment XXXIII — insert new Article 5

Congress shall establish a program of national service and require that all citizens complete two (2) years of national service between the ages of 18 and 30 in a full-time National Service Program role.

Section 1

Congress shall pass the National Program Service Law to establish the National Service Board to oversee the implementation of the National Service Program Law. The Board shall oversee the National Service Programs in each state, to coordinate the implementation of the law in each state.

The law shall define the initial service roles that qualify for the National Service Program, which shall include but shall not be limited to any military branch of service; any police, firefighting or first-responder role; any medical, teaching or social welfare department service role in under-served communities; any non-profit organization supporting under-served communities; any public or mental health service role; or other similar role defined by Congress.

Section 2

The National Service Board shall consist of five (5) citizens with relevant public, military, teaching in under-served areas, or community service roles, to be nominated by the President and confirmed by the Senate. The specific number and terms of Board members shall be defined by Congress in the enabling legislation.

The National Service Board, in coordination with the National Service Boards in each state, shall have the authority to determine specific service roles in each state to meet the requirements of the national service requirement, which may vary by state. The state boards shall review all requests for an exemption to the National Service Program requirement for citizens with a physical, mental, emotional or other disability which would prevent a citizen from meeting the requirements to serve in any available National Service Program role, and provide a waiver of the service requirement when appropriate.

Section 3

Service of two years must be completed no later than the citizen's thirtieth birthday. Service can begin upon completion of high school or be delayed for the completion of college, professional skills certification, graduate school, or any legal or medical certification. But service shall voluntarily begin no earlier than the citizen's eighteenth birthday and no later than the citizen's twenty-eighth birthday. If a service role has not been selected and begun by the citizen's twenty-eighth birthday, the National Service Board shall assign the citizen to a National Service Program role.

For naturalized citizens who complete the naturalization process on or before their twenty-first birthday, they shall voluntarily begin service no later than the citizen's twenty-eighth birthday or they shall be assigned to a national service role by the National Service Board.

Schedule of Enactment Following Approval of the Bill of Public Service and Accountability

Upon ratification of the Bill of Public Service and Accountability by the thirty-eighth state, the existing Articles IV, V, VI and VII of the Constitution shall be renumbered as Articles VI, VII, VIII and IX. Where new Sections within Articles have been added, subsequent Sections shall be renumbered accordingly.

- **Provisions of Amendment XXVIII (28)**
  All provisions shall become effective beginning with the first federal election and new Congress following the ratification of the Bill of Public Service and Accountability by the thirty-eighth state.

- **Provisions of Amendment XXIX (29)**
  All provisions shall become effective with the beginning of the first new fiscal-year budget cycle following the ratification of the Bill of Public Service and Accountability by the thirty-eighth state.

- **Provisions of Amendment XXX (30)**
  All provisions shall become effective with the beginning of the first new fiscal-year budget cycle following the ratification of the Bill of Public Service and Accountability by the thirty-eighth state.

- **Provisions of Amendment XXXI (31)**
  All provisions shall become effective with the beginning of the first federal election campaign year following the ratification of the Bill of Public Service and Accountability by the thirty-eighth state.

- **Provisions of Amendment XXXII (32)**

All provisions shall become effective with the beginning of the first federal election campaign year following the ratification of the Bill of Public Service and Accountability by the thirty-eighth state.

- **Provisions of Amendment XXXIII (33)**

All provisions shall become effective with the beginning of the first new Congress following the ratification of the Bill of Public Service and Accountability by the thirty-eighth state.

Part 2: Relationship to Other Government Improvement Initiatives

There are several independent efforts underway to address some of the same issues that we have raised and discussed in this book. However, none of these other efforts starts from the beliefs that (1) the rules for how Congress operates are made by the very people who benefit personally from them, instead of being written as Citizen Rules with the benefit of the country overall as the focus of the rules; and (2) the influences of career self-interest, partisan interest and donor interest must *all* be minimized in order for real change to occur and for the principles of our representative democratic republic to be restored in how our elected officials govern. I believe that a piecemeal effort to the changes we need will not be effective in addressing the three underlying causes of the divisiveness and dysfunction we have seen in Congress. The Bill of Public Service and Accountability includes multiple changes that work together and are required to effectively minimize the three underlying causes of the current level of divisiveness, and the omission of any of these changes will lessen the impact we seek. This is the basis for the comprehensive changes proposed in this book.

1. End (overturn) Citizens United

End Citizens United is sponsored by a political action committee, America's Promise, that is focused on giving Congress the power to limit the explosion of money in politics since the Citizens United Supreme Court decision. They are supporting a bipartisan bill introduced in the House on January 3, 2019, proposing an Amendment to the Constitution with the following language:

Proposing an amendment to the Constitution of the United States relating to contributions and expenditures intended to affect elections.

ARTICLE—

SECTION 1. To advance democratic self-government and political equality, and to protect the integrity of government and the electoral process, Congress and the States may regulate and set reasonable limits on the raising and spending of money by candidates and others to influence elections.

SECTION 2. Congress and the States shall have power to implement and enforce this article by appropriate legislation, and may distinguish between natural persons and corporations or other artificial entities created by law, including by prohibiting such entities from spending money to influence elections.

SECTION 3. Nothing in this article shall be construed to grant Congress or the States the power to abridge the freedom of the press.

This amendment is fairly consistent with the sections of Amendment XXXII in the Bill of Public Service and

Accountability, but fails to include the elements requiring truthful messaging in political campaigns, or those providing for an end to racial and partisan gerrymandering.

2. Balanced Budget Amendment

There have been many initiatives started with regard to the requirement for Congress to balance the federal budget. Most of the public-led initiatives were to raise signatures on petitions to Congress to enact a Balanced Budget Amendment. There have also been some public-led calls for a "limited" constitutional convention to "solely and exclusively" draft a Balanced Budget Amendment. There have been many efforts from within Congress itself, either to seek a Balanced Budget Amendment or to pass a resolution requiring either a balanced budget or a procedural limit on raising the federal debt ceiling.

The most recent effort was introduced in the House on January 8, 2019. The draft of that resolution is as follows:

Proposed Constitutional Amendment
This joint resolution proposes a constitutional amendment prohibiting total outlays for a fiscal year from exceeding total receipts for that fiscal year unless Congress authorizes the excess by a three-fifths roll call vote of each chamber. The prohibition excludes outlays for repayment of debt principal and receipts derived from borrowing.

The amendment requires roll call votes of (1) three-fifths of each chamber of Congress to increase the public debt limit, and (2) a majority of each chamber for legislation increasing revenue. It also requires the President to submit a balanced budget to Congress annually.

Congress is authorized to waive these requirements when a declaration of war is in effect or if the United States is engaged in a military conflict which causes an imminent and serious military threat to national security.

So in practice, this Amendment provides the "appearance" of a balanced budget requirement that can be simply eliminated by a three-fifths vote of both Houses of Congress. It is pretty obvious this is no requirement at all, as in practice it would simply be overridden regularly with no consequences. It also continues the dysfunctional process of having a debt limit authorization that is separate from the process of agreeing to spending and taxing income that actually determines whether and by how much the existing debt level would increase.

Under the requirements of Amendment XXX in the Bill of Public Service and Accountability, the requirement to start with a balanced budget at the beginning of the fiscal year and to change taxes and spending programs to wind up with a balanced budget at the end of the fiscal year cannot be overridden by a vote of Congress, only by the formal declaration of war or national emergency by both Houses of Congress and the President. In addition, spending on programs requires that a specific goal be set for the program, including the benefit to be achieved, the group to be supported or helped, and the measures of success to be realized from the program.

And finally, Amendment XXX requires that the debt ceiling would be established concurrently when the budget was approved. This would eliminate the very dysfunctional process of having Congress vote separately on spending and tax bills that result in a deficit that requires increasing the national debt, and then have a separate debate (otherwise known as a dysfunctional partisan fight that puts the financial security of the country at risk) over raising the debt ceiling to accommodate the deficit resulting from the spending and tax bills they passed separately. Too often this has resulted in shutting down the government for lack of agreement.

As a result, the proposed Amendment XXX will ensure not only a balanced budget, but also greater transparency and accountability in the congressional budgeting, spending and taxing processes. And the Amendment will ensure greater effectiveness and less dysfunction in the process, eliminating the chance that Congress could shut down the government over the failure to agree on a budget.

3. Repeal of the Electoral College

There is a national effort underway to repeal or bypass the Electoral College. This movement has gained momentum among Democrat activists, after the Democrat candidate for President won the national popular vote but lost the Electoral College vote, with states allocating their Electoral College votes on the basis of which candidate won the majority of the popular vote in their state, in two of the last five presidential elections.

While attempting to address the problem with the winner-takes-all approach to allocating Electoral College votes, this partisan approach would invalidate the purpose intended in the Constitution, to ensure that large-populated states did not overwhelm smaller states in the election of President.

Under the US Constitution currently, each state can decide how it awards its electoral votes. As a result, some states with Democrat legislative majorities have begun changing how they award their electoral votes, from the basis of awarding all Electoral College votes in the state to the candidate who wins the majority of the popular vote, to the winner of the nationwide popular vote. If enough states require their electoral votes to be allocated to the winner of the nationwide popular vote (instead of to the candidate who won the majority of the popular vote in that state), it would fix the partisan problems of the Electoral College without needing to amend the Constitution.

This "National Popular Vote" compact wouldn't take effect until enough states joined in, but we're closer to that than you might think—15 states and the District of Columbia have already signed on, totaling 196 electoral votes of the needed

270. Since the Democrats won the majority of the popular votes in only 20 states (and the District of Columbia) in 2016 but won the national popular vote by over 3 million votes, due to large Democrat vote majorities in several large states, the energy around this change seems to be focused in the Democrat states. And it is unlikely that any of the 31 states who largely have Republican majorities in the legislature will ever follow this example.

The change proposed in Amendment XXXI is not based on a partisan objective, but on the principle of better representing the original intent of the Electoral College in the Constitution. But the winner-takes-all approach to allocating Electoral College votes leads to ignoring the minority. When the candidate winning 51% of the state's popular votes wins 100% of the Electoral College votes, the principles of a representative democratic republic would seem to be compromised.

So the action proposed in Amendment XXXI would require all states to allocate electoral votes on a proportional basis related to the share of the state's popular vote won by each candidate. As a result, candidates would not choose to campaign only in states where they can win a majority of the popular vote, as they would have an incentive to also campaign in those states where they would win only a minority of the popular vote— but additional votes nonetheless. Hopefully this would help minimize one key aspect of the partisanship in the presidential election process.

Epilogue

This book was originally written in 2019–2020, completed while on my last vacation in Florida before the COVID-19 pandemic. Then we all witnessed a series of new concerning actions from Congress and the Administration during 2020, driven by continued divisiveness and the influences of career self-interest, partisanship and the winner-takes-all desire for power and control. These actions culminated in the dangerous actions of the President and many elected officials in Congress after the 2020 election, and the processes of not one but two impeachment trials. Neither of these trials followed the language of the Constitution for the "trying" of an impeachment charge in the Senate, as many Senators from both parties publicly failed to fulfill their oath to do "impartial justice." In addition, actions following the election involved unprecedented challenges to the core of our democracy: truthful speech, and free, fair and unbiased election processes. As a result, I felt the need to add some additional elements to the "Citizen Rules" that would help protect the country from similar or worse actions in the future.

Since the draft manuscript was accepted for publishing by Changemakers Books in February of 2021, the work has shifted to completing the publishing process and preparing to market and distribute the book, and to the actions required to build public awareness and interest in the book. As mentioned in the book, proceeds from book sales to the author will be used to provide funds to support the steps planned to implement the "Citizen Rules" and the six Amendments as detailed in the book.

Shedding the influences of career self-interest, partisan interests and the interests of major donors that have seeped into our politics and our governing processes to a damaging extent over the past four decades will certainly require the involvement of tens of millions of citizens and the eventual approval of most state legislatures. These influences did not rise quickly to the level we experience today, and we will not extract them from our system of government quickly either. But hopefully this book will at least contribute to beginning that effort.

No single author or book alone can implement the changes we need. But as Margaret Meade stated so inspiringly, "Never doubt that a small group of thoughtful people could change the world. Indeed, it's the only thing that ever has."

Ready to be part of a "small group of thoughtful people"?

Cited References

Abraham Lincoln Online, HYPERLINK "http://www.abrahamlincolnonline.org" www.abrahamlincolnonline.org

Advisor Perspectives, www.dshort.com

Author's calculations averaging data from US Office of Management and Budget data

Bureau of Economic Analysis data compiled by Statista.com

Concepts and Methods of the US National Income and Product Accounts, Bureau of Economic Analysis

Covey, Stephen R., *The Seven Basic Habits of Highly Effective People* (Fireside Books, Simon & Schuster, 1989)

George Washington's Farewell Address, The Avalon Project, Yale Law School

John F. Kennedy quotes, HYPERLINK "http://www.goodreads.com" www.goodreads.com

Joint Committee of Taxation, Summary of Conference Agreement, JCX-54-03, May 22, 2003

IRS Revised Tax Rate Schedules, 2003–2018, IRS.gov

Key Facts: How Corporations Are Spending Their Trump Tax Cuts, HYPERLINK "http://www.americansfortaxfairness.org" www.americansfortaxfairness.org

Levin, Mark R., *The Liberty Amendments* (New York: Threshold Editions, 2014)

McCullough, David., John Adam's Letters, *John Adams* (New York: Touchstone, 2001)

Medal of Honor Heritage Center, HYPERLINK "http://www.mohhc.org" www.mohhc.org

Pechman, Joseph A., *Federal Tax Policy* (Washington, DC: The Brookings Institution, 1987)

Procter & Gamble, www.pg.com

Reuters, HYPERLINK "http://www.reuters.com/investigates/special-report/usa-buybacks-cannibalized" www.reuters.com/

investigates/special-report/usa-buybacks-cannibalized

Steverle, C. Eugene, The Urban Institute

United States Constitution and Amendments

United States Declaration of Independence

US GovernmentSpending.com

US Office of Management and Budget

CHANGEMAKERS
BOOKS

TRANSFORMATION

Transform your life, transform your world - Changemakers
Books publishes for individuals committed to transforming their
lives and transforming the world. Our readers seek to become
positive, powerful agents of change. Changemakers Books
inform, inspire, and provide practical wisdom and skills to
empower us to write the next chapter of humanity's future.
If you have enjoyed this book, why not tell other readers by
posting a review on your preferred book site.

Recent bestsellers from Changemakers Books are:

Integration
The Power of Being Co-Active in Work and Life
Ann Betz, Karen Kimsey-House
Integration examines how we came to be polarized in our dealing with self and other, and what we can do to move from an either/or state to a more effective and fulfilling way of being.
Paperback: 978-1-78279-865-1 ebook: 978-1-78279-866-8

Bleating Hearts
The Hidden World of Animal Suffering
Mark Hawthorne
An investigation of how animals are exploited for entertainment, apparel, research, military weapons, sport, art, religion, food, and more.
Paperback: 978-1-78099-851-0 ebook: 978-1-78099-850-3

Lead Yourself First!
Indispensable Lessons in Business and in Life
Michelle Ray
Are you ready to become the leader of your own life? Apply simple, powerful strategies to take charge of yourself, your career, your destiny.
Paperback: 978-1-78279-703-6 ebook: 978-1-78279-702-9

Burnout to Brilliance
Strategies for Sustainable Success
Jayne Morris
Routinely running on reserves? This book helps you transform your life from burnout to brilliance with strategies for sustainable success.
Paperback: 978-1-78279-439-4 ebook: 978-1-78279-438-7

Goddess Calling
Inspirational Messages & Meditations of Sacred Feminine
Liberation Thealogy
Rev. Dr. Karen Tate
A book of messages and meditations using Goddess archetypes
and mythologies, aimed at educating and inspiring those with
the desire to incorporate a feminine face of God into their
spirituality.
Paperback: 978-1-78279-442-4 ebook: 978-1-78279-441-7

The Master Communicator's Handbook
Teresa Erickson, Tim Ward
Discover how to have the most communicative impact in this
guide by professional communicators with over 30 years of
experience advising leaders of global organizations.
Paperback: 978-1-78535-153-2 ebook: 978-1-78535-154-9

Meditation in the Wild
Buddhism's Origin in the Heart of Nature
Charles S. Fisher Ph.D.
A history of Raw Nature as the Buddha's first teacher, inspiring
some followers to retreat there in search of truth.
Paperback: 978-1-78099-692-9 ebook: 978-1-78099-691-2

Ripening Time
Inside Stories for Aging with Grace
Sherry Ruth Anderson
Ripening Time gives us an indispensable guidebook for growing
into the deep places of wisdom as we age.
Paperback: 978-1-78099-963-0 ebook: 978-1-78099-962-3

Striking at the Roots
A Practical Guide to Animal Activism
Mark Hawthorne
A manual for successful animal activism from an author with
first-hand experience speaking out on behalf of animals.
Paperback: 978-1-84694-091-0 ebook: 978-1-84694-653-0

Readers of ebooks can buy or view any of these bestsellers by
clicking on the live link in the title. Most titles are published
in paperback and as an ebook. Paperbacks are available in
traditional bookshops. Both print and ebook formats are available
online.

Find more titles and sign up to our readers' newsletter at
http://www.johnhuntpublishing.com/transformation
Follow us on Facebook at
https://www.facebook.com/Changemakersbooks